Talk To Me

Thank you for supporting Crosscut!

10/11/16

Talk To Me

Changing the Narrative on Race, Religion, & Education

by

Qasim Rashid

Affiliation Disclaimer

The author has written and published this book in his personal capacity. This book does not represent the official or unofficial views of any organization with which the author is affiliated. All errors, mistakes, and omissions are the author's and the author's alone and should not be attributed to any other person, entity, or organization.

To Ayesha, Hassan, Hashim, and Hannah Noor, whom I love more than words can express.

We have made you into tribes and sub-tribes that you may recognize one another.

— THE HOLY QUR'AN 49:14

Acknowledgments

Above all, it is by the sheer Grace of Almighty God that this book was possible. I thank Him for removing all difficulties, and praise Him for His strength, His protection, and His knowledge. I'm grateful for the prayers and support of His Holiness the Khalifa of Islam, Mirza Masroor Ahmad, head of the worldwide Ahmadiyya Muslim Community.

One of the driving motivations behind Talk To Me is to provide an additional platform to voices ignored by main stream media, politicians, and the press. Accordingly, to write about racism, misogyny, religious discrimination, and education reform, I sought the authorship of friends, colleagues, thought leaders, and scholars who have studied, experienced, and work actively to overcome these societal ills. These thought leaders have graciously authored about twenty-five percent of the chapters in Talk To Me. To them I express my deepest gratitude, appreciation, and respect:

Salaam Bhatti, Rabia Chaudry, Dr. Kashif N. Chaudhry, Muhammed Ahmad Chaudhry, Nusrat Jehan Chaudhry, Dr. Craig Considine, Pastor Leo Cunningham, Karen Leslie Hernandez, Brandon Jaycox, Kile B. Jones, Robert Salaam, Lisa Thweatt, Lee Weissman, and Billy Wood.

In addition, Salman Sajid and Salaam Bhatti provided exemplary help on professional editing, formatting, marketing, and organization.

Likewise, I'm grateful to the immense support I received from my Kickstarter Backers. Nearly 350 amazing individuals backed this effort and provided the support needed to make this book a reality. I've recognized them by name at the end of this book.

My wife, Ayesha, and children Hassan, Hashim, and Hannah Noor all impacted this book in their own way. As with my previous projects, writing this book required a heavy investment on their part. I am grateful for their time, support, love, and laughter. My parents and siblings likewise graciously provided their prayers and insights.

Finally, I am grateful to you, the reader. Your time is precious. From the bottom of my heart, thank you for investing it in this book.

Here's to our continued journey together to change the narrative on race, religion, and education. Thank you and God bless.

Qasim Rashid, Esq.
Washington, D.C.
May 17, 2016

Talk To Me: Changing the Narrative on Race, Religion, & Education
by Qasim Rashid, Esq.

Twitter: MuslimIQ
Facebook: AuthorQasimRashid
Instagram: AuthorQasimRashid
Website: www.qasimrashid.com
Email: q.rashid@richmond.edu

Cover Design: Salman Sajid

Editor: Kirkus Reviews

ISBN: 978-0-9893977-4-2

Contents

Introduction

"If ignorance is bliss, then knock the smile off my face."

—RAGE AGAINST THE MACHINE

"I frigging hate that guy."

"Hey, watch your mouth." We heard a familiar voice call out behind us.

"I said frigging, not the other F-word." My friends and I turned around to see Muhaimin walking up to us.

"That's not the word I was talking about."

"What? Hate? I do. That guy's a moron. Kept repeating the same thing over and over in his speech. So annoying. I hate it when people do that."

Muhaimin kneeled down on one knee to get eye level. He was twenty and a six-foot-three giant. I was eleven and tiny. It was 1993 and we had just finished attending an interfaith conference dubbed Religious Founders Day. The idea behind the event is that each faith sends a representative to speak on an issue universal to all—e.g., how to combat racism, how to overcome poverty, how to find God. Each representative presents his or her faith's solution by referencing that faith's respective Scripture.

The second-to-last speaker today was a Sikh speaker who heavily quoted Guru Nanak. Guru Nanak, for those not familiar with the Sikh

1

faith, founded Sikhism and is the first of the Sikh gurus. He was an exemplary person of nobility and dignity. I highly recommend studying his life if you haven't already. As I walked into that Religious Founders Day event, I knew none of this. I know it to this day, however, for two reasons. First, my parents dragged me to the interfaith event when I was eleven to listen to a Christian priest, Jewish rabbi, Buddhist monk, Muslim imam, and Sikh granthi talk about their respective faiths.

And second, because the Sikh granthi repeated Guru Nanak's teaching that "all religions lead us to a universal God" at least a dozen times in his speech. And now—over two decades later—I remember that quote. Thus, when I expressed my annoyance and frustration by saying "I frigging hate that guy," Muhaimin overheard and scolded me.

"But Brother Muhaimin, it's annoying," I insisted.

"He doesn't need to say the same thing a million times to get his point across. He thinks we're dumb or something."

Muhaimin never spoke quietly. When he spoke everyone listened, because he spoke with conviction and passion. He was articulate, confident, and compassionate. Though he was hard-hitting and direct, he also loved. His demeanor could never be confused for arrogance or anger. People heeded what he said because, simply put, he led by example.

"Let me ask you something, Qasim. Did you listen to all the speeches?"

"Yeah."

"What did the priest say about Christianity?"

"Umm, something about Jesus."

"What about Jesus? Give me something specific."

I shook my head; I couldn't recall.

"OK, what about the rabbi; what'd the rabbi say?"

"I think something about Moses."

"Are you saying that because you recall something the rabbi said about Moses or are you saying that because you know Moses is a prominent Jewish prophet so you're guessing that chances are he said something about Moses?"

I was busted. "OK, what's your point?"

"What about the Buddhist monk? Anything?"

I again shook my head, no.

"OK, OK, what about your father. He spoke last, as the Muslim imam, right? What did your own father say in his speech that ended not ten minutes ago, that you can recall and tell me right now?"

I stared at Muhaimin with a blank look. He turned his ear and put his hand up.

"I can't hear your Qasim, speak up. Give me something to work with here, come on."

"I...I can't recall anything specific."

"Hmm, I thought so. And now tell me again what that one thing was that the Sikh speaker kept saying over and over again that annoyed you so much?"

I looked down and mumbled, "All religions lead us to a unimmblmblmbl." I trailed off.

"I'm sorry; say that again—what was that?"

"All religions lead us to a universal God!"

"Ahh, now that's profound! Looks like he got his point across, didn't he?"

"Yes, sir." I moped.

"And looks like everyone else who didn't repeat themselves didn't get their point across, now, did they? So by your logic, are you calling yourself stupid for not getting their points?"

I didn't answer, for obvious reasons.

"Do you see how he communicated, my young brother? He took his most important point and he repeated it, over, and over, and over, and over again, so that even someone only pretending to pay attention, like yourself, couldn't possibly miss it."

I laughed, as did my circle of friends. Muhaimin was right; we were slacking. He continued.

"The Sikh brother wanted to make sure that if you walked away with even one thing, only one thing from this entire conference, it would be…" Muhaimin pointed at me with both fingers "…say it loud brother!"

"All Religions Lead Us to a Universal God."

"Yes! That's what I'm talkin' about!"

I sighed. "OK, fine, I get the point, sorry for calling him a moron. Can I go now?" I turned to leave without waiting for a response—partly because I was embarrassed about my gaffe but partly because I knew Muhaimin wasn't done with me yet and I hoped he would let it go. But no such luck.

"No, no, hold up, brother."

"What now?"

"Why did you say you hate him?"

I shrugged. "Why is that such a big deal?"

Muhaimin sighed.

Let me pause.

As I reflected on how to begin this book, this childhood incident repeatedly came to my mind for many reasons—two of which I'll mention right now. First, in many ways, I learned a simple but important communication tool, one that's served me well. And second, I became what I'll call "hate conscious," a term I'll explain shortly.

I can't really dramatize this. I wasn't some wild, rebellious kid on the brink of committing some horrible atrocity. But the point is, I didn't need to be. And I didn't have a chance to be, because of what Muhaimin saw in me as a preteen child. Muhaimin helped me shift my trajectory ever so slightly. And that shift is what has helped me appreciate what I have, what we have as humanity—and how much further we have to go.

It's one reason I concluded my first book, *The Wrong Kind of Muslim*, with "The ~~End~~ Beginning." We're just getting started, and in many ways, *#TalkToMe* picks up where *The Wrong Kind of Muslim* left off.

In *The Wrong Kind of Muslim* I asked readers to join the true jihad, the intellectual jihad of the pen against oppression of conscience. I wrote, "We cannot live our lives in fear and ignorance of the other, in fear of what we do not understand. No human being should be feared—we are all equals. Our struggle must not be confined to a certain time or place. Rather, it must transcend religion, nationality, gender, and race to truly have the global impact necessary to conquer the sword...let your voice be heard. Tell your story. Go and fight intolerance with tolerance, apathy with education, and fear with compassion...and by all means let nothing on earth stop you from what is *most* important—win the hearts."

#TalkToMe advances that conversation to the next level by cutting through the rust that prevents human beings from recognizing one another. *#TalkToMe* champions a jihad that involves communicating with people of different races, of different faiths, with leadership, with your children, and communicating a progressive and educated narrative of humanity that is all too often left by the wayside.

#TalkToMe is about what I believe are *some of* the most critical—yet most ignored—conversations of our time. Conversations so critical that in ignoring them, we are fostering an increasingly intolerant world.

We are failing our communication responsibilities to one another. And these failed communication obligations help further the violence, distrust, apathy, ignorance, and hatred that threaten us all. But I don't just mean any kind of communication. I mean meaningful and moral conversations.

Let's slow down a second.

How many times have you opened your e-mail in-box at work (or home) and groaned? There's your cousin Jim who sends you every forwarded chain letter imaginable. You tell him nicely to stop but he just doesn't get it. Your boss Tom who has emailed you the same thing seven times, the last six of which asked if you got the first one? And that's before you even get to delete spam.

More e-mails are sent and received today—over 100 billion a day—than at any point in history. That number is expected to surpass 130 billion a day in just a few years. Twitter manages over 500 million tweets daily, while Facebook is approaching a staggering 1.5 billion users. We find equally staggering data points on YouTube videos watched, text messages sent, WhatsApp chats set up, Viber, Telegram, or the thousands of other means of communication currently in existence or emerging with popularity. But all this data proves only one thing—quantity has little to do with quality.

I think the great Nobel laureate George Bernard Shaw said it best: "The single biggest issue in communication is the illusion that it has taken place."

Or if you're like me, you appreciate Homer Simpson's wisdom. In a classic '90s episode of *The Simpsons*, he gives advice to a friend going through a divorce: "The problem is communication, too much communication." By accident or otherwise, Homer explains the main point I'm making here. Problems aren't solved merely with more communication—we need *meaningful* conversations.

And with meaningful conversations comes the obligation of moral conversations. Well, what does this mean? Morality is a hot-button word. Any time someone preaches morality an alarm goes off and we put our guard up. If you find yourself putting your guard up, I ask you to hang on just one second before you close the gate and lock the door.

This is not a call to censor speech deemed offensive or blasphemous, whatever that means. This is a reminder that meaningful conversations can only exist if we elevate our morality in our speech. Look at it this way. How can we build bridges of understanding while deliberately insulting one another, because, you know, "free speech says we can"?

While I believe in secular governance, one flaw of absolute secularism is that it can't really legislate morality. In other words, we can't force people to behave according to our personal definition of morality. Why? Well, everyone has a different definition of morality and it isn't fair for me to force you to think or behave as I do—and vice versa. This is why freedom of conscience must remain free. In the grand scheme of things it is better to have a free exchange of ideas and let the best idea win out on its own merit, rather than try to force people to believe or speak as you believe or speak.

Thus, when it comes to morality in speech, it is only achieved when elicited without coercion or punishment. Forcing people to behave morally defeats the point of calling it morality. A person must choose to elevate his or her speech beyond offensiveness and vulgarity—beyond deliberately insulting others for the sake of insulting. And this is what I'm asking you to choose to do. No human-crafted law can dictate, much less enforce, such a standard. A conversation can only be meaningful when we hold ourselves accountable to morality higher than the basic legal requirement.

After the horrific *Charlie Hebdo* terrorist attack, I expressed some of the above in an op-ed on January 9, 2015, in *USA Today*:

> And this is why it is critical to make a distinction between protecting free speech and promoting moral and wise speech. Free speech purists raise the "nothing is sacred" mantra. To an extent I agree—no idea is above criticism. But as human beings, we would benefit by asking what utility exists in insulting for the sheer sake of insulting? Does it help build bridges of understanding with an opposing point of view? Does it help build compassion from an antagonistic enemy? Does it foster maturity among our youth as

they grow up? Insulting for the sheer sake of it does none of those things, but each of those things are vital to a progressive and peaceful society.[1]

So when I ask you to talk to me and to meaningfully engage, I'm not talking about the bare minimum respect the law says we have to show. I speak of a moral standard—one that elevates our speech with compassion, wisdom, and goodly exhortation.

Now remember, this course of action is a personal decision and not born of governmental enforcement. While the law doesn't force us to talk to those different than us, the moral standard places this higher burden on us. Therefore, and importantly, this standard of moral speech is often difficult to maintain. How do you not offend someone if you are a person of color and the person you are interacting with is racist? How do you not offend a believer who thinks atheists "eat babies"—and you happen to be an atheist? Obviously a million what-if scenarios exist.

The answer is in your intent.

A big difference exists between drawing deliberately demeaning and demonizing cartoons of a revered religious figure with intent to deeply offend another person, and offending another person because the person you're talking to is racist. The former is within our control to do or not do, and the moral standard of speech I propose asks us to forgo such insults, elevate our speech, and find ways to talk to one another with wisdom.

As for the latter, while the opposing party may be offended because he or she is racist, that, ironically, creates the critical need to approach

---

[1] Rashid, Qasim, USA Today: "Islam backs free speech," available at http://www.usatoday.com/story/opinion/2015/01/09/free-speech-islam-charlie-hebdo-column/21458257/ (last visited on January 18, 2015).

with compassion, patience, and goodly exhortation. That is where the aforementioned goal of "win the hearts" becomes infinitely more relevant. And as I said a moment ago, that situation illustrates why this moral standard is often significantly more difficult to embrace.

Communication without meaning and morality is like ocean water—you may have an infinite supply, but it can be the death of you.

#TalkToMe is not an academic book; it offers personal and intimate experiences. The stories in this book are real stories. They're practical examples from the lives of my friends, your neighbors, and our children—ordinary human beings doing extraordinary things. They're stories of how everyday people are conquering racism, xenophobia, and ignorance with meaningful conversations and moral speech. Some stories you'll find humorous, some frightening, and some particularly memorable. All are meaningful and provide a material contribution to ensuring that when communication takes place, it isn't a mere illusion.

As I've written before, words can accomplish in minutes what wars cannot in millennia. Likewise, I again remind my readers to reflect that nations and peoples do not go to war because they were too civil with one another or because they maintained too much open and honest dialogue. War begins when communication ceases. Fear begins where education ends.

But enough theory. I had a college professor who taught a ridiculously tough public speaking class. Any time a student jabbered on more than necessary he'd yell out, "I don't want to hear your oral diarrhea!" Yeah, it was embarrassing and hopefully you're not thinking that right now. But if you are, we're just about to get to the fun part.

Which brings me back to my conversation with Muhaimin some twenty-five years ago, when I became "hate conscious." I stood there wondering why Muhaimin thought it was such a big deal that I'd said the H-word. He was about to tell me.

"Qasim, I could see you saying you're annoyed because you didn't understand his effective communication tactic, but 'hate' is such a strong word. Brother, do you even know what that word means?"

I shrugged again. "I dunno. I mean I guess I know what it means. Just means I think he's dumb."

"Qasim, listen to me carefully. I want you to remove that word from your vocabulary."

"Why? What's the big deal? You're overreacting."

"I'm not. That word is absurd. It's anger. It's destruction." And then in patented Muhaimin argumentation style he added, "I'll give you three reasons why. First, what's our community's motto?"

"Umm, there is no God but Allah and Muhammad is His Messenger."

"No, that's our Islamic declaration of faith. I'm talking about our motto for how we treat humanity."

"Oh, that's love for all, hatred for..."

"Yes, yes, hatred for...?"

"...none."

"For NONE. You understand what that means? Hatred for none? We hate no one, no one on earth."

"Yeah but—"

"Let me finish. Two, do you know what hate has accomplished for humanity? What good it has done?"

"No."

"Name me something good hate has done for humanity. Go on, take your time."

"I don't know. I can't think of anything."

"That's the point. Hate does nothing good for humanity. It never has and it never will. So why use it at all?"

I remained silent. He continued.

10

"Third, and this is critical—hate is the root of all that is wrong on earth. Not only can hate never benefit humanity, it actively destroys humanity and everything we hold near and dear. Everything. Hate is why racism exists. Hate is why violence happens. Hate is why people do bad things."

"But we hate the people who do bad things," I insisted.

"No, we don't and we shouldn't hate them. Why? Hate drove them to do bad things, so ask yourself, how can hate possibly bring them out of that? We hate the murder, the racism, the theft—but we can't hate the people if we expect to pull them out of that hate. Hating the person will only make that person feel angrier, more alone, more unwanted. Hate will only drive people deeper into doing bad things; it won't ever make them stop."

"What will?"

"Dr. King said hate can't drive out hate, only love can do that. You see, brother, hate is a very strong word and it spreads negativity everywhere you go. Remove it from your speech. You don't need that word, you don't need those feelings of hate, you're better than that. Remove hate."

I sighed. "OK, I will."

"Remove the word 'hate' from your vocabulary."

"Yeah, yeah, I will, I promise."

"Remove the word 'hate' from your vocabulary."

"Yes, I said I would, OK."

"Remove the word 'hate' from your vocabulary."

"Why are you repeat...oh, OK, I get the point." I smiled. Muhaimin smiled back.

"Now you can go." With that, Muhaimin stood up and went on his way.

It's funny how things stick with you. Muhaimin knocked the smile off my face in a much needed way. To this day I feel guilty using the H-word for any reason, even when it's for something I really don't like, like mosquito bites. That's what hate consciousness does—it teaches you to recognize that hate doesn't solve anything. It forces you to instead think positively. And it inspires a solution-focused worldview. I like to think I've embraced Muhaimin's wisdom. I catch myself smiling when my son describes something he really dislikes by saying, "Dad, I don't love it, but I do love...," and then he tells me where his heart is.

Meaningful conversations ultimately stem from talks with the people we're around the most—our families. And here is probably the toughest part: In a world where it is easier to simply blame everyone else, such dialogue requires introspective thinking and introspective action.

Understand this principle: Meaningful conversations are not about words—they're about action. They push us out of our comfort zones and traverse new waters and landscapes. They oblige us to learn about those different than us *from* those different than us. And when these conversations are conducted effectively, the results are revolutionary.

When people engage in meaningful conversations, it enables, for example, Kile and Kashif—respectively, an atheist and a believer—to unite on the common platform of universal freedom of conscience. It permits Billy—a former self-described racist—to rise above the racism and support people not based on the "color of their skin, but by the content of their character," as Dr. King famously said. It enables a young man to courageously sacrifice his life without thinking twice, so that two others of a different religion can live a full life in peace. It empowers parents to expose their children to a different worldview so their children can learn to respect that worldview, even if they don't necessarily accept that worldview. As the old saying goes, a lot of problems would disappear if we talked to one another instead of about one another.

But we have a long way to go. Right now our country is in the midst of its most divisive period, arguably, since the Civil War. More hate groups and domestic extremist groups emerged in 2015 than in any year in American history. Hate crimes against Muslims or anyone who "looks" Muslim are skyrocketing. As a result, Sikh and Hindu Americans face increasing discrimination and violence, only for their appearance. Violence against women is epidemic. Black Americans are out of breath, literally, trying to convince the world that Black Lives Matter. Meanwhile government violence against innocent civilians is at a level higher than in any developed democracy on earth.

But this is not a doom-and-gloom book. It is about the inspiring individuals in our communities, families, and homes rising above this ignorance, violence, and hate. So let's go and get on our own way. This book is about my journey with people of all races and beliefs—a trek to find a way better than violence, better than terrorism, better than hate. It isn't an easy trek, but I hope you have as much fun reading this book as I have had writing it. I hope you find it a worthwhile contribution to who you are as a person.

Most of all, I hope you find it meaningful to have taken the time to #TalkToMe.

Chapter 1

The Jewish Kid

"Was he not a human being?"

—PROPHET MUHAMMAD'S
response when informed that the funeral procession he stood for
out of respect was that of a Jewish person.

That's what everyone started calling Joseph. One late fall afternoon just a few weeks before winter break, our fourth grade teacher introduced a new student to our class. I, too, was new in one way, having just transferred from a different elementary school at the start of the year due to district changes. But I had the benefit of the previous four months. Joseph did not.

With her hands on his shoulders, standing in front of everyone she announced, "Everyone, say hello to Joseph. He's new to our school so please take time to make him feel welcome and at home."

"Helllloo Joseph," we all responded in unison.

"Uh, hi." Joseph nervously answered.

"Joseph you can go sit at that empty desk over there. It belongs to another student who is ill today but we'll find you a permanent seat tomorrow."

Joseph nodded and quietly made his way to his temporary station. With that our day's lesson began and most of us temporarily forgot about him. In just a few hours, however, the recess bell rang—during which point everyone suddenly wanted to get to know the new kid.

I observed as several children surrounded Joseph on the playground to talk to him and find out more about him. It was a ritual every new kid went through, including myself just a few months prior. Nothing attracts a crowd like a crowd, so it wasn't long before nearly half the class circled Joseph to listen to what he had to say. At first the questions were what you'd expect.

"Where did you move here from?"

"Pennsylvania."

"Why did you guys move here?"

"My dad got a new job in Chicago."

"What does your dad do?"

"He's some kind of businessman. I don't really know."

"Do you have any cool toys at your house?"

"Ummm, I guess. I have a Nintendo."

"What games?"

"I don't know, a lot I guess."

"What games did you ask to get for Christmas?"

Suddenly Joseph paused. "Um, Christmas? We don't celebrate Christmas."

This idea seemed foreign and a few kids gasped. One particularly loud-mouthed child, Jason, spoke up.

"What? What do you mean you don't celebrate Christmas?!" I remained quiet. My family also didn't celebrate Christmas. My heart practically leaped with joy to know there was another kid like me in my class. Though now I also wanted to know why he didn't celebrate Christmas.

"We just don't. We're not Christian. We're Jewish."

Jason scoffed as if Joseph had revealed he was an alien. "No way. You're Jewish!?" He followed up with a loud laugh, prompting laughter from several other kids as well. For some reason I didn't quite understand, that question killed the conversation. No one wanted to know anything more about Joseph, and the students dispersed as quickly as they'd convened.

I overheard someone say, "Why the heck did we have to get a Jewish kid?"

I stood at a distance but still close enough to see the look of hurt on Joseph's face. I thought I should to go speak with him, but I didn't. I just stood and watched, unsure what to do. The scary way other students dispersed after Joseph revealed he was Jewish—that fear was powerful enough to keep me from engaging with him. Maybe there was something wrong about being Jewish that I didn't know about? I was already a minority myself as one of the only Muslims and Pakistanis in the entire school. Would I be casting myself further out by "getting caught" speaking with the Jewish kid?

This is what went through my nine-year-old mind. It bothered me to see the pain on Joseph's face. It bothered me more that I was afraid of talking to him. And it bothered me that I didn't know how others would react. Joseph sat by himself the rest of recess. He spoke only when spoken to by the teacher the rest of the day. Otherwise, he kept to himself and kept his head down. Who could blame him? I can only imagine what conversation he had with his parents when he got home. Or maybe he didn't.

That evening I got off my school bus and marched up our long, winding driveway in contemplation of what I'd witnessed. It still didn't make much sense to me. The only bullying I was used to seeing was of me, at recess and on the school bus. It was surreal to see someone else shunned.

At dinner that evening my father knew something was wrong from the simple fact that he hadn't once had to scold me to stop talking and eat my dinner. Instead I ate quietly and quickly. Finally he spoke up. "Qasim, what's wrong?"

I looked up and thought for a moment about brushing it off. After hesitating, I finally forced myself to advance the conversation. "Something happened at school today and I'm confused by it."

"What?"

Rather than provide details, context, or even a semblance of what I'd seen, I simply blurted out what was bothering me. "Is it OK to be friends with a Jewish kid?"

My father nearly dropped his glass of water. "What!? What kind of question is that? Who asked you that?"

"Today we had a new kid in class, Joseph. And all the kids were talking to him but as soon as they found out he was Jewish they stopped talking to him and just laughed at him. And I don't know why they did. But it didn't feel right and I didn't know what to do."

"Did you go talk to him then?"

"No, I didn't want the other kids to make fun of me too so I stayed away."

My father put down his utensils and looked at me with full attention. "Son, listen to me very carefully. Tomorrow you are going to go to school and you are going to go talk to Joseph. I don't care what any other kid says to you. You will go and be friends with Joseph."

"But what if he doesn't want to be friends with me?"

"I assure you he's not going to say that. You just do what I'm telling you to do."

"But what if the other kids laugh at me?"

"Let them. Let them laugh at both you if they want. I don't want you laughing at anyone."

"Then why did the other kids laugh at him?"

"I don't have an answer to that, son. But don't you ever come to me and ask if you shouldn't be friends with someone because of their religion. You be friends with good people; I don't care what religion they belong to. Do you understand?"

I nodded and felt relief that I had my father's support.

The next morning I began looking for Joseph the second I stepped off the school bus. I bumped into him as we both entered the front doors and stopped to get his attention. Unsure how to initiate the conversation, I said the first thing that came to mind.

"Want to play together at recess today?"

Joseph opened his mouth, as if shocked I'd asked the question. He closed it without speaking, then nodded and smiled.

"My name is Qasim Rashid. *Q-a-s-i-m*. There's no *u* after the *q*." I felt obliged to convey that bit of information to everyone I told my name to. Still do, almost thirty years later.

"That's a strange way of spelling. I like it," he said. "I'm Joseph."

"Yeah, I know. I'll see you in class, OK?"

Joseph nodded again and we parted ways. The simplicity of childhood is beautiful. Without pretension, the Muslim kid and Jewish kid in class made a friendship that just one day prior might've seemed obscure. And sure enough, during the coming months we were laughed at. But in the grand scheme of things, it no longer mattered—at least, not as much. We now had each other to rely on. Before long, the children like Jason became the minority, while the majority of our classmates eventually lost interest or moved on. I don't know if they necessarily learned their lesson or not. I do know, however, that for the rest of that year, the Jewish kid and the Muslim kid never had a recess without a friend to play with. That summer Joseph's family moved again. In a pre-Internet age, keeping in touch wasn't as easy.

But I reflect on why that friendship was possible at all. Two realities could have emerged when I spoke to my father that evening. Either reality would have altered my worldview for years or decades to come, or perhaps permanently. My father could have commended me for staying away from Joseph and urged me to not befriend him on account of him being Jewish. He could have told me to follow the lead of the majority, to play it safe and stay away from conflict. Or he could have given a lukewarm response, not lambasting Joseph but not asking me to support him either. He could have convinced me of the lie that such things shouldn't affect me, and let apathy rule my behavior.

The point is whatever my father would have said to his nine-year-old impressionable son would have been tattooed to that son's mind in a life-altering manner. But with all the possibilities before him my father chose the path that followed one simple rule: Look for the humanity in people. He empowered me to have self-confidence by respecting the faith of others. He didn't ask me to lecture the other students or tell them off the next day. Rather, he lovingly scolded me for even questioning whether it was OK to befriend a classmate who happened to be Jewish. He took personal accountability (and probably personal offense) that the question entered my mind in the first place. Indeed, it wasn't just what he said that affected me, but the conviction with which he said it.

As a result, he empowered me to worry not about what others thought of me, but about how I treat others. Most of all, he gave me the confidence to know that when such issues arose, I could turn to my father with confidence. This ensured an ongoing line of communication through thick and thin. A line of communication that paid immense dividends in ways I couldn't imagine at the time.

Perhaps the most obvious lesson was that not everyone believes the same thing. Not everyone worships the same way or has the same ideas. It got me to thinking: with so much diversity out there, why should I believe something just because I happened to be born into it?

Chapter 2

Tell Me What to Believe

"The cure for ignorance, is to question."

—PROPHET MUHAMMAD

Have you ever doubted your faith? It's OK if you have, or if you do.

It's a question I'm often asked today. And as I continued my journey as a child it crossed my mind with some degree of regularity. The short answer is yes, I have doubted my faith. Doubt isn't a bad thing. Knowledge comes from doubt. Progress comes from questioning.

Those who have read *The Wrong Kind of Muslim* are familiar with this story. I relate it here in brief for two reasons. First, because it is so relevant to the discussion at hand. And second, because as fate would have it, as I entered parenthood I soon found myself in a role reversal of sorts. In particular, it further speaks to that balance of empowering our children while ensuring they respect others.

The original incident happened in 1997. I was fifteen and enjoying my first job—ever. My supervisor Tom, then unbeknownst to me, was a die-hard evangelical Christian. One afternoon Tom took the time to systematically tear my religious beliefs to shreds. Or tear up what I at least thought I believed. Having stumped me and leaving me unable to respond, he flat-out asked me to convert to Christianity. I balked, insisting I could prove him wrong.

And by "I could prove him wrong" I meant "my dad can prove you wrong." There was only one problem. My father refused to help me. He would not step in to help me win a religious argument. "I'll tell you how to behave and force you to behave with morals and integrity if I have to, because how you behave means how you treat other people—and I'll see to it that it's with respect," he explained. "But you're not a small child who needs to be told what to believe. I won't force you to believe in any religion just because I believe it. You're not a robot to be programmed. You're a person with a mind of your own. You'll be judged on your own.

"So when it comes to religion, it's between you and God," he said. "If you want to find truth, go find it. But if you want to spend your life just proving other teachings wrong, then what you believe isn't a belief, it's being a blind follower. And you don't need me for that. In fact, you don't need anyone for that. You just need the desire to remain ignorant. Because those who believe blindly believe ignorantly. And that's a dangerous way to live."

His advice was just that—go figure it out on my own. And as much as I pried and prodded him to just help me "prove Tom wrong," he pushed back that much more. While he was adamant that I treat Joseph with the respect every human being deserves, he refused to compel any belief on me just because he believed it. The ensuing nearly two-decade journey has taught me two crucial life lessons.

First, I've discovered that we all have much more in common than in disagreement. Those commonalities can be a basis for friendship and strength. They are a basis for us to conquer ignorance and apathy. They are a basis for peace.

Second, I've discovered that despite our substantive differences in dogma, no excuse exists for religious hatred, oppression, or fear of one another. We need not gloss over our differences. Instead, we must recognize and celebrate them—as that is how we truly value people for who they are.

This is a frightening journey, especially for teenagers who often have hardly begun to figure out their personal identity. I should speak for myself—I had hardly begun to figure out my identity. Perhaps my father telling me what to believe would have spared me some grief as a teen, but it would have limited my ceiling for pluralism for decades to come. Meanwhile, as I soon found out, the growing pains are real, and they can leave a trail of confusion and frustration.

For the first time, I was about to encounter explicit anti-Muslim ignorance directed at me from adult.

Chapter 3

The Principal's Office

"I have never let my schooling interfere with my education."

—MARK TWAIN

"Qasim, go to the principal's office."

"What? Why? What'd I do?"

"You know what you did. Now go."

"I honestly don't. I have no idea."

"You know the rules: in your desk when the bell rings. You weren't in your desk."

"Oh, come on. I was at my desk and literally in the process of sitting down when the bell rang."

"In the process of sitting is not the same thing as sitting. You knew the rule. You broke the rule. Off to the principal's office you go."

"This is the stupidest thing I've ever heard. My butt was in the seat when the bell stopped ringing. There're kids that walk in after class all the time. How is my butt not being firmly in the seat when the bell starts ringing a violation?"

"I'm not here to argue about other students. I'm not here to argue about your butt's position. I'm not going to argue with you at all. Go to the principal's office. Now!"

I shook my head. This command was totally unfair. I was not a troublemaker in high school. Honestly. In fact, I got along great with most of my teachers. But Mrs. Daley and I just didn't seem to see eye to eye. Now, in full disclosure, it was no secret that I didn't like her class. Senior composition, or senior comp as we called it, seemed to me an epic waste of time. It's not that I didn't like English—in fact, my first three years in high school I enjoyed English immensely and had good rapport with my teachers. I was also in a creative writing class that same semester and connected well with the instructor. This senior comp class, however, was designed to teach us "effective, persuasive, and scholarly writing." I found the teacher neither effective nor persuasive and didn't then care much for scholarly writing. It wasn't my ideal class. "Besides," I thought to myself, "it wasn't like I'll ever have to use writing in the future anyway."

Mrs. Daley waited for me to get up and get going. "Now!" She insisted again. My classmates let out the oooooOOOOoooo sound everyone does when someone gets in trouble. I picked up my bag, removed my butt from its rightful seat, and slowly trudged out of the classroom.

"Give 'em hell, Q!" A friend called out from behind me. Without turning around I gave a thumbs up, good for a few laughs.

Mrs. Daley scribbled some words on a hall pass and followed me out. "Go straight to the principal's office and give this to the admin at the front desk." I read the note on the hall pass. "Insubordination and disrespecting the teacher."

My jaw dropped.

"What? Insubordination? I thought you said I didn't have my butt down in time? And how did I disrespect you?"

26

"You broke the rule, that's insubordination. You refused to go to the principal's office right away and called me stupid. That's disrespecting the teacher in front of the class."

"I said your rule was stupid! I didn't call you stupid! There's a difference!"

"Not to me there's not."

"I was only asking why I was being sent to the principal's office. That's a perfectly fair question."

"I'm not arguing with you about this."

"Great, so now even asking questions for clarity is disrespectful to the teacher? God forbid we ask questions in school." I waved my hands in the air for dramatic effect. "The last thing we want is for kids to ask questions. Sooo disrespectful of me."

"Oh, why do I even bother with you? Go now!" With that she turned around and went back to her classroom, closing the door behind her.

She left flustered and red and was probably angrier on the inside than she let on. I realized that at this point I probably was being disrespectful, though at the time I didn't want to believe it.

With no other logical choice I headed down the hall in the direction of the principal's office. Down three flights of stairs, past the library, and down another hall, I finally arrived. I opened the door and was greeted by the admin.

"What can I do for you, young man?"

"I, um, I got sent to the principal's office. Here." I reluctantly handed her the note Mrs. Daley gave me.

She glanced over the note and looked up with a smile. "All right, well, just have a seat over there for a few minutes and we'll be right with you, OK?"

I thought her smile was kind of unnecessary but I figured she was just trying to make me feel better about being somewhere I didn't want to be.

The principal's office was across the hall from the cafeteria. I could smell cafeteria food and felt my stomach rumble. Contrary to most high school stereotypes, we actually had great cafeteria food—especially these amazing chocolate chip cookies. I didn't have long to ponder before I heard a voice ask me to follow him.

"All right, Qaseem, follow me."

I looked up and saw—not the school principal, but my high school guidance counselor. He wasn't someone I'd met before, as the first three years my counselor had been someone else. She and I had gotten along great. I remember thinking and regretting that this—being in trouble—was my first substantive interaction with my new guidance counselor.

I looked up, "Um, OK. And it's Qasim, like Ka – Sim, not Qaseem."

"Right...just follow me to my office."

I got up and marched behind him down a narrow hall. He held the door to his office open and asked me to take a seat in front of his desk. He flipped up the doorstop and let the door slowly close. His office wasn't the neatest but I'd certainly seen worse. After we both sat down he reviewed Mrs. Daley's note again and looked up at me.

"So how are you doing, Qaseem?"

"Um, Qasim. I'm doing fine, Mr. Norman."

"Right, Kaasim. Sorry about that Kaasim. So I just had a chat with Mrs. Daley. Want to tell me what happened?"

"Yeah, sure, but I thought I was supposed to be meeting with the principal?"

"Well, you don't actually meet with the principal when they send you to the principal's office. Haven't you been sent here before?"

"No."

"Never? Not in your nearly four years here?"

"Not once."

"Hmmm, interesting."

I thought to myself it was odd he found it hard to believe I'd never been disciplined like this before. He continued.

"So when you get sent to the principal's office you meet with your guidance counselor. That's what we're here for."

"Oh. Well, they should call it that then." I knew I was being facetious.

"Call it what?"

"Call it meeting with your guidance counselor."

"I suppose...so anyway, want to tell me what happened in Mrs. Daley's class today?"

"Yeah, I mean, there's not much to tell. I was sitting down as the bell rang and she sent me here."

"That's it?"

"Yeah, that's it."

"You didn't call her stupid or argue with her in front of the class."

"No, I did not call her stupid." I insisted once more. "I said her rule was stupid and that it didn't make sense to me. So I asked her to explain it and she refused to."

"Well, some might say calling the rule stupid is calling her stupid."

"I disagree, but apparently that doesn't matter much here."

"Lose the attitude. Did you know her rule is that you have to be in your seat when the bell rings?"

"Yes, I knew but—"

"Well...if you knew the rule, then why didn't you just follow it? Why make a big deal out of this?"

"Mr. Norman, I was literally sitting down as the bell rang."

"But you weren't...all the way down."

"Jesus Christ, no, I was not 'all the way' down. My butt was probably upwards of four or five inches off my seat."

"I said lose the attitude, Kaseem."

"It's Qasim. I'm not giving you attitude. I was literally inches away from sitting in my seat. And frankly I've seen other students walk in later—well after the bell rang—and she hasn't sent them to the principal's...guidance counselor's office, whatever. I only asked her to explain why I was being sent and she wouldn't 'argue' with me about it. She just said I was being insubordinate and disrespectful and sent me here."

Mr. Norman wasn't looking at me while I spoke. He kept scribbling on his notepad and gave me one of those insincere nod and *hmms* every few seconds. I finished talking. The office was awkwardly silent for a few seconds while he continued to scribble. He paused for a second and looked over his notes. After a few more seconds he put his notepad down and looked up, finally looking right at me.

"Kaseem, I think I know what's going on here."

I stayed quiet, having given up all hope that he would ever pronounce my name right. But I soon learned that was the least of my worries.

"Do you know what's going on here, Kaseem?"

"I get the feeling you're going to tell me."

"Well isn't it obvious to you?"

"Uhhh, no, not really. I mean the only thing that's obvious is I'm in trouble and I still don't quite understand why."

"Do you think your behavior is responsible for this?"

"Fine, I wasn't 'entirely' in the seat when the bell rang. And I shouldn't have said it's a stupid rule, though it is; I should not have said it out loud. I'm not the one making a big deal out of this. So, I just don't see why it's that big a deal that I have to go through all this for something really minor."

"That's because it seems you're missing the bigger picture."

"Which is?"

You could have given me a million chances to guess what was going to come out of Mr. Norman's mouth next. As God is my witness it would not have been enough chances. Never in a thousand years would I have guessed it. And as I reflect on it I feel not only embarrassment and humiliation, but also infuriation. I see one of the earliest examples in my life of what bad leaders do.

He looked at me dead in the eye, almost like he was piercing right through me. "Well, let me put it this way. You're a Muzlum right?"

In 1999 I was at a stage in my life when my religious identity wasn't fully realized. I was still reeling from that experience with my father a few years prior when he refused to help me "beat" an evangelical Christian in a religious argument. I was a Muslim by name and, to be fair, I prayed regularly. But I was nowhere near at a comfort level with my faith. I didn't know why I believed what I thought I believed. As a high school senior I was in a period of investigation, contemplation, pontification, and significant confusion.

And now, adding to that confusion was my high school guidance counselor who suddenly asked me if I was a "Muzlum" in the middle of a conversation about Mrs. Daley's attendance rule. His question caught me off guard. It was something not just out of left field but out beyond the parking lot. "What could possibly have motivated this question?" I thought to myself. After watching me spend a few moments figuring out just what was asked of me Mr. Norman spoke up once more.

"You are a Muzlum; right, Kaseem?"

"I...yeah, I guess, I mean. So what?"

"Well, don't you think that explains why you've been treating Mrs. Daley with such disrespect?"

"What the hell are you talking about?" I raised my voice more than I'd intended.

"Watch your tone, young man."

"I, sorry, but what in the world? What—I don't see the connection."

"Mrs. Daley tells me you have a history of insubordination in her class."

"I told you this is the first time I've ever been sent to your office. What *history* is she talking about?"

"Well I'll just go out and say it. It seems pretty clear you're disrespecting Mrs. Daley because she's a woman and you're a Muzlim."

My jaw dropped for the second time that day. I was dumbfounded and after what felt like a punch in the gut I finally blurted out, "Where on earth are you getting this from!? What in the world are you talking about? Did she say that!?"

My mind wasn't upset or offended because I still didn't understand what was going on or what I was experiencing. I was in a state of utter confusion. Mr. Norman could have told me aliens were abducting zoo animals and that's why I was in trouble and it would have made about as much sense to me. And this is where I wished my father had just told me what to believe. Things would've been so much easier for me right now. The burning frustration and confusion was intolerable. I didn't yet appreciate that this struggle, this true jihad, was among the most priceless gifts ever given to me.

But for now I was confused and angry.

"No, she didn't, but it's no secret that Muzlums don't think highly of women and that Izlam looks down upon women. Do you think it's fair to say that because you were taught as a child to disrespect women you have difficulty showing respect to Mrs. Daley?"

Another punch to the gut. I didn't intend for my voice to shake but it did.

"No, no, that's not fair to say at all. How the hell do you know what I was taught as a child? That doesn't even make any sense. Have other female teachers complained about me?"

Mr. Norman took a deep breath. "Well, no."

"Any students?"

He paused again. "No, not that I'm aware of."

"Anyone at all besides Mrs. Daley?"

"I don't think so."

"Then where is this Islam thing coming into this?"

At the time I didn't fully comprehend what Mr. Norman was stating. I didn't realize the massively ignorant and stereotypical judgment he was imposing upon me. I didn't realize what terrible leadership he was demonstrating. I just figured he was a teacher and he knew what he was doing. Sure, I had a big mouth, but even with that big mouth the thought of accusing him of discrimination was beyond me. There was a fear of authority in my mind, and I was living that fear in real time.

Perhaps I'm being naïve, but I don't believe he was intentionally malicious, bigoted, or Islamophobic. I didn't sense hatred or contempt from him. Still, his approach was without a doubt discriminatory, full of ignorance. And as I reflect, I still feel humiliation and fury. Humiliation that a judgment was made about me that had no semblance of justice, logic, or compassion. And fury that a teacher could say something so ignorant to a student, not know any better himself, and have no accountability afterward. I pushed on, pleading my case.

"How is it fair to make this claim that I disrespect her because of Islam when no one but you has said this? Do you think maybe she just doesn't like me?"

Undeterred, Mr. Norman continued dismissively. "Well, that's certainly one theory. I'll think about it. I'll talk to Mrs. Daley and I'll see to it that this issue is resolved. You be sure to be in class on time and don't call her stupid."

I thought about objecting again but stayed quiet, still in a state of confusion.

"And you'll only have to serve an hour-long detention."

"What? Why do I have to serve any detention at all?"

"I'm not arguing with you about this, Kaseem," as he finished scribbling his notes.

I just shook my head. "Yeah, I'm not surprised. And for the last time, it's Qasim."

Mr. Norman paused from scribbling and looked up at me again with a stern look. "You're dismissed."

I got up and walked out of his office, down the narrow hallway, and out of the principal's office. The episode was more frustrating and confusing than I could have anticipated when I sat down a microsecond too late that morning.

The aroma of freshly baked cookies called my name. This time I complied without delay, and without argument.

I've reflected on this incident often. What could I have done differently here? It's easy to excuse myself as a 17-year-old kid. Maybe I could have spoken to my old guidance counselor. Maybe a trusted teacher—of whom I had several at my high school. Maybe I could have really gone to the principal's office and conveyed what transpired in my meeting with Mr. Norman.

But I didn't do any of those things. I didn't know I was able to. And who knows how many other Muslim students experienced something similar? Who knows if Muslims were the only minority about whom Mr. Norman was wholly ignorant?

The lesson from this encounter, for me, is that despite their best intentions, teachers may not always properly recognize diversity. After all, today only 20 percent of teachers are of color, while just over 50 percent of students are of color. We need to work on improving this disparity to encourage training and hiring of teachers who reflect and respect the diversity that is our student body.

Educators, particularly administrators and counselors, need ongoing education on dealing with student diversity. They may not realize what they've heard is far from reality. Mind you, my encounter occurred two years before 9/11, well before the Iraq War, and decades before anyone heard of the barbarities Daesh and Boko Haram have unleashed on women. But ignorance found a way.

Nothing can undo what I underwent the better part of two decades ago. But that experience was a pivotal life lesson. As the old saying goes, life is the most difficult teacher because it gives the test first and the lesson second. I'm confident I'm not the only Muslim student to face an incident like this. A recent survey unearthed that nearly 50 percent of Muslim students in California report being bullied for their faith.

To help improve communication, raise awareness in teachers, and change this narrative, I regularly speak at elementary schools, middle schools, high schools, and teachers' conferences and to government organizations on how to talk about Islam to young children, teenagers, and civilians. I do it in part to ensure minority students today don't have to suffer what happened to me as a student. I also do it because teachers are intelligent, compassionate people. And they are not only willing but also eager to learn.

That's one of the many great things about most teachers—they know better than anyone what they don't know, and they are among the world's most dedicated individuals when it comes to learning more.

The goal here isn't to beat anyone down. The goal is meaningful communication and elimination of ignorance. I will continue to do what I can to educate educators, help write curriculums, and make myself available.

As for Mrs. Daley's class, I managed to keep my butt in its seat on time through the rest of the year. I titled my final paper, "The last paper I'll ever have to submit in this class ever again, after which I will no longer have to be answerable to anyone here ever again...ever." To which Mrs. Daley replied when she handed it back, "You make it sound like you were wronged."

At least this time she didn't send me to the principal's office.

Chapter 4

Trust Me, I'm a Cop

"Racism is a moral catastrophe, most graphically seen in the prison industrial complex and targeted police surveillance in black and brown ghettos rendered invisible in public discourse."

– CORNELL WEST

I feared Mr. Norman's authority so I didn't speak up. I often wonder if my fear of Mr. Norman's authority was due to a separate experience with another person of authority just a year or so prior.

You see, I believe in respecting authority. But authority isn't always perfect, as demonstrated by America's high statistical ranking among developed countries for police violence against civilians. What do you do when an officer points a gun at your head? If your initial thought is, "Well, you probably did something to deserve it," then slow down, breathe, and stop jumping to conclusions.

Instead, ask yourself, have you experienced the reality of driving while brown?

The second police officer pulled up, withdrew his gun, and pointed it directly at my head from about fifteen feet away. I cursed myself for getting out of my car in the first place. I was a mere sixteen years of age, only five months into my driving experience, and in way over my head.

This was my first time being pulled over. It was December 1998. Like most Chicago winters, this year's brought plenty of snow. It had piled up at least two feet high with drifts even higher. The day was cold and gloomy. It was about 7:00 a.m. and evidently too early for the snowplows to be out cleaning anything that wasn't a major highway. I drove my brother to work.

"Just stay calm, young man; this'll all be figured out soon enough." The police officer's words didn't do much to calm my nerves. "You'll have to trust me on this one; I'm a police officer."

The officer, a white man, perhaps mid-to-late thirties or early forties, stood in a confident manner and spoke in a confident tone. He was just doing his job.

"Does he have to point that thing at me?" as I motioned to the gunner cop, who was also white. Before the officer answered, I added, "And are you going to bother telling me why you pulled me over in the first place?"

My brother could tell I was getting agitated and urged me to stay calm.

"Stay calm?!" I shot him a dirty look and whispered, "This prick's got a friggin' gun pointed at my head. What the hell do you want me to do?"

The cop in front of me spoke up. "All right, just give me your driver's license and I'll make sure you're on your way in just a few minutes."

"Officer, with all due respect," I said in a not-so-respectful manner, "so far you've pulled me over, made me get out of the car into the freezing cold, and have demanded my license without giving me any indication of why you're pulling me over. You're not getting my license until I know what's going on."

I was in way over my head. I remembered Mr. Sumka's driver's education class from earlier in the year. "Now this is an important lesson. An officer always has to tell you why he's pulling you over. Otherwise, you have no legal obligation to give him your license."

"Well Mr. Sumka," I thought to myself, "you never told us what to do when the psycho cop pulls out his gun."

Following Mr. Sumka's advice, I had been arguing with the officer. Perhaps not the brightest move, but that didn't seem to matter much then. For a good fifteen minutes we'd been arguing: me trying to get him to tell me why he pulled me over, and him insisting it was for my own good. That's when the gunner cop had pulled up. Now, the officer in front of me just waited. He knew it was just a matter of time. He had every advantage. He was dressed for the cold, and I wasn't. I was late for work, and he was at work. I had a gun pointed at my head, and he didn't. Lesson learned. Person with gun pointed at his head never has the upper hand.

After another minute of futile resistance, I gave in.

"Fine, take it, but this is really ridiculous." I took out my license and handed it to him. Only a newly licensed sixteen-year-old knows the pain of handing over your license to a cop for the first time. It's like a punch in the gut and a knee to the face at the same time. It was my driver's license, my freedom license, my manhood license, and now the cop had it. Even though I knew handing over the license meant sitting in my car away from a gun pointed at my head, part of me regretted giving in.

"All right, now you just sit tight and I'll be back in a minute."

I turned to go back inside my car. But the officer had other plans.

"Whoa, whoa, now wait a minute. I'm gonna need you to just stand right there, son. I'll be right back, OK?" The officer gave me that fake concerned look cops give when in reality they couldn't care less whether you agree or not. He motioned for me to stay standing outside, motionless, away from my warm heat-filled car.

"Wait, what? Now I gotta continue to freeze my butt off out here?" By now I was at my wits' end. "All right, you know what? Do whatever the hell it is you gotta do; I'm done." I crossed my arms and stood there, trying to pretend the cold didn't bother me.

The police officer smirked and walked back to his cruiser. "Will just be a minute, son," I heard him call out.

I scoffed at him calling me son. Meanwhile his compadre stood still, hidden behind his own car door like a coward, peering over the barrel of his pistol, still aimed right for me.

I'd never had a gun pulled on me, not before that day. Neither by a gangbanger—and there are plenty of those in Chicago—nor by a police officer, who only seemed to show up when I was driving. It wouldn't be until years later that it would happen again; ironically, with another cop in another country altogether. But for those who have been so unfortunate, when a cop pulls a gun on you it messes with your head. You begin to wonder what you may have done. You begin to recount your steps, recount who you hung out with and when. Sometimes you begin to imagine things. I tried to show a tough shell to the officer, but inside I was scared out of my mind. It wouldn't have taken much for me to crack and admit to something, anything, if it meant getting that gun pointed in a direction that didn't involve a bullet traveling through my brain. And that thought continued to go through my mind. A simple slip of his finger and I'd be a 6 o'clock news headline.

Inside I was frantic.

A minute turned into two minutes, which turned into four. Ten minutes went by. Then another ten minutes. I checked the time again. It was already past 8:00 a.m. I was late for work. I was freezing. The cop didn't care.

What seemed like another hour passed and the cop finally opened his door and finally stepped out. He lumbered toward me in a stoic manner, carefully choosing his steps. He approached me and, to my surprise, handed me my license. And then, just as stoically as he walked up, he turned around and walked back without saying a word. And as he walked back the gunner cop put away his pistol, got back in his car, and pulled away. Without turning around, he yelled back, "All right, have a nice day, son; be more careful next time."

I stood, in confusion, in shock, and in anger. "Hold on a second!!" I yelled. "What the hell do you mean be more careful next time??" I demanded. "Be more careful about what? Are you seriously walking away without telling me why you pulled me over?"

The cop paused. "It's not important; you can be on your way now."

"Yes, Officer, it is important, I need to know what I've done wrong," I said. My brother called out to me to forget about it and get back in the car. I refused. "Officer, what's the deal? Why the hell did you pull me over?"

He stopped and I walked up to him to face him, probably closer than I'd intended. His eyes darted back and forth. He couldn't think of a reason. His previous confidence had vanished, as had my previous insecurity. Finally he blurted out, "You...and your car, you...matched the description of a bank robbery last night; we had to be sure you weren't the robber." He may as well have added just as insincerely, "Yeah, that's it, that's what happened." With that, the officer quickly walked to his car and pulled away before I could respond or comprehend what he just said.

I was stunned. I didn't know whether to laugh or scream in anger. I stood there for a second until my brother called out to me. I slowly walked back to my car and sat down inside, frozen but hot with anger.

"What happened?" my brother asked. "What'd he say?"

I was still speechless, unsure what had just happened.

"He said...that I matched a bank robber from last night, and they had to make sure it wasn't me."

My brother just stared at me with a blank look on his face.

"That's what I got for trusting him," I added.

Then my mind began to race. What if I ran out of fear of authority? Would I have been shot at? Would you be reading this book today? For a sixteen-year-old kid whose first interaction with an officer included a loaded gun pointed at my head, what reason is did I have to trust any officer in the future?

The statistics back up this reality. Officers pull over people of color at nearly twice the rate they pull over white people. The subconsciously biased person responds to these facts by claiming, "If people of color have nothing to hide, then they shouldn't mind being pulled over."

The commonsense person looks at these facts and realizes that this systemic, unjust approach must change before genuine trust can be developed between people of color and police. I believe police officers are good human beings with a genuine desire to serve their communities.

But as long as black children are shot and killed by police 21 times as often as white children, and as long as American police officers continue to lead the developed world by a wide chasm in murdering civilians, actions speak louder than words. All signs point to systemic racism, and until we extinguish that racism with justice, we cannot expect peace.

So how do we remedy the decaying relationship between people of color and police? Well, it begins with acknowledging the current status quo. Few white people profess open racism, and the vast majority believe they are not only not racist, but also well educated on race issues. But as Dr. King observed, "The majority of white Americans consider themselves sincerely committed to justice for the Negro. They believe that American society is essentially hospitable to fair play and to steady growth toward a middle-class utopia embodying racial harmony. But unfortunately this is a fantasy of self-deception and comfortable vanity."

Dr. King described a state of affairs half a century ago that still isn't recognized today. You see, the remedy is not simply not being racist. We must be antiracist—we must actively work to end racism. In a world where systemic racism still exists and even thrives, the ultimate burden of responsibility rests on what we tell our children about how to treat others.

Everyone is bound to make mistakes—that's part of the human experience. That officer who profiled me and pulled a gun on me made a mistake. My high school guidance counselor made a mistake. Yes, nothing can undo those mistakes. But what's most devastating is when people perpetuate those mistakes by refusing to learn from them. Such perpetuation is how systemic racism, anti-Semitism, and Islamophobia becomes ingrained in society.

I knew one thing—I wanted to learn from my mistakes. As I continued my development in my teen years I reached out to my friends of different faiths and different races. I took my father's advice to "figure it out" to heart, and did as best as I could to follow that path. Stumbling through the process, I tried to cut corners to hurry it up already. But as anyone with life experience knows, there's no such thing as a shortcut to knowledge and understanding. You can't Google an entire religion or race and expect to magically know what you're talking about.

After all, the racially motivated terrorist who committed the 2015 Charleston attack murdering nine innocent people because they were black admits his "knowledge" came from Google scholarship. The same is true of the Islamophobic terrorist in Norway who gunned down 77 people in 2011. Indeed, the American Islamophobes he cites as his inspiration are themselves Google scholars without a shred of education on Islam. By contrast, truly understanding those different from you requires actual education, built on time, patience, justice, and compassion.

And with my attempts to cut corners, it wasn't long until I hurt someone I cared about. Granted, the damage wasn't intentional, but just because a wound wasn't intended doesn't mean it isn't painful. The struggle continued. And as I rushed to try and understand why I believed what I believed and how to communicate with others in a respectful manner, I soon had to face the consequences of my own impatient recklessness.

Chapter 5

When Necessary, Use Words

"I have always thought the actions of men the best interpreters of their thoughts."

—JOHN LOCKE

We found ourselves playing a game of pickup basketball in the high school gym. It was probably 1999.

"All right, if I make this shot you gotta come to my mosque this week."

"Ain't no way you're gonna hit that," Lamorne replied.

"I hear you talking smack but I don't hear you taking the bet."

"Fine, deal, take the shot."

"Alex, you're the witness." I launched a prayer of a shot from near midcourt. The ball floated through the air and hung for a split second, before majestically swooshing through the net with a crisp crunch.

"Aw, hell no. How in the..."

"Ha! No excuses, bro. You lose. Alex, witness!"

"Witness!" Alex yelled out.

I continued my teasing of Lamorne. "You should just give up now and convert to Islam. God wants you to. Otherwise I wouldn't've made that shot."

"Whatever, man. Fine, if I make this hook shot from behind the three-point line you gotta come to my church next week."

I laughed with a reaction similar to Lamorne's before my half-court shot.

"No chance you'll make it, dude."

"Oh, now who's talking smack but not taking the bet?"

"Ha ha, fine, fine, go for it."

Lamorne stepped behind the three-point line and threw up just about the most awkward hook shot I've ever seen. My jaw dropped as the ball spun through the air in a perfect arc and crunched through the net just as my shot had a moment prior.

"Where's your God now, Qasim!" Lamorne laughed with delight as I stood there shaking my head, laughing that I just got beat at my own game.

Lamorne was a Christian. I was a Muslim, probably. We were both teenagers in high school. In other words, both of us were sure we'd figured the world out and had nothing left to learn. I, he, and Alex had been discussing and debating religion for some months now. I don't know what Lamorne's intentions were, but mine were fully entrenched in my mind—get Lamorne to convert.

And the irony was I couldn't even yet say with confidence that I'd found my peace with Islam. I was trying to convert him to something my adolescent mind didn't understand. There was nothing religious about my approach—it was teenage ego through and through. But in those know-it-all days of youth, my double standard didn't bother me much. More accurately, it didn't yet bother me enough to do anything about it.

A few days later, I picked up Alex, Lamorne, and Lamorne's brother Devon in my rust-encrusted 1990 Toyota Corolla. The hood wouldn't stay down so I had to tape it down with duct tape. The door handles were broken and the only people who knew how to actually open the doors were my closest friends. The clutch was on its last legs and the air-conditioner didn't exactly work. Still, it was my car that I paid for with a summer's income from working at a car wash, and I was proud of it.

We piled in and headed to al-Sadiq mosque on the south side of Chicago at Forty-Fifth and State. Al-Sadiq is Chicago's oldest mosque and one of the oldest in America, established way back in 1922. This evening we were holding our weekly open house.

"So what are we gonna be doing tonight?" Lamorne asked as we pulled into the mosque parking lot.

"Nothing big: simply have a dialogue, have conversation, and break bread together. Really, it's low impact. More just to have an open discussion."

Lamorne nodded.

We walked in just as the formal session was about to begin and found our seats. As advertised, it consisted of a simple lecture and a short prayer. We soon broke for fellowship and talk. I left Lamorne and Alex for just a few minutes. Devon went with me to greet some friends. Five minutes later we returned to find Alex and Lamorne both cornered by one of the more zealous members of our congregation—let's call him Ed. Ed meant well, but his actions spoke louder. Prayer book open and arguing Scripture with a fiery passion, Ed spoke a mile a minute, raising his voice and demanding Lamorne and Alex answer.

Each time one of them would open his mouth to respond, Ed would cut him off and throw more Scripture at them. Lamorne wasn't the type to say he couldn't handle it, and neither was Alex. But their body language was clear—neither wanted to be there. My conscience told me this was wrong, this isn't how guests should be treated, but my ego won the fight. I sat and watched as Ed continued his onslaught unrestrained, gloating to myself that now Alex and Lamorne would *have* to concede defeat. Defeat of what, I wasn't even sure. But it was defeat and that's what mattered. Devon remained quiet.

Before long, and fortunately, it was time to go. Lamorne and Alex pulled themselves free of Ed's clutches—God knows I was no help—and we marched back to my car. Packed inside and driving down Interstate 290 back to the suburbs, I turned to Alex, Lamorne, and Devon and said brightly, "So what'd you guys think?"

"Dude, that was not cool," Alex replied. "That was bull crap." This was saying a lot, because Alex is pretty much impossible to anger.

"What do you mean bull crap? You're just sour because you lost an argument, aren't you?"

"Lost an argument!?" replied Lamorne. "Qasim, that wasn't an argument, that was an ambush. You said we'd come to the mosque for food and fellowship. That bull crap was not food and fellowship. That was a goddamned ambush. What the hell, man?! Not cool at all."

Devon remained quiet and just shook his head, but his view was clear. I'd messed up big time.

I wanted to respond but, looking at Lamorne and Alex, I remained quiet. I recognized the look on their faces. It wasn't the look of someone who lost an argument. It was the look of a friend betrayed—someone told one thing, and given another. I'd promised them one experience and given them something wholly different. As the drive wore on I began to realize something that stung at my soul. I'd burned my own friends exactly how my supervisor Tom burned me years prior. The look on their faces was the same look I had on my face when my faith was ridiculed. With Tom, I was humiliated, my ambusher gloated, and I stood silent. And now I'd done that to Lamorne and Alex.

At first I wanted to blame Ed. After all, he's the one who actually did the ambushing. But frankly, that would've been the easy way out. They were my guests, my responsibility, and this was my failure. I was furious at my own hypocrisy, and worse yet, I couldn't even get myself to admit I was wrong to my friends. We rode in silence the rest of the way back to suburbs. I dropped off Lamorne and Devon, and then Alex, and then headed back to my place.

And then it truly hit me.

I gulped with the realization that I had to go to church with Lamorne next week. Now, I'd been to churches before, several times—but never Lamorne's church. I had no idea what to expect and now was even less sure. After how I'd let Ed treat Lamorne at my mosque, I feared the worst. What if his minster tried to debate me? What if he shut me down and ambushed me the way Ed ambushed Lamorne? What if he called me out publicly? I was not looking forward to this trip. I was in over my head and way out of my comfort zone.

Our home phone rang Sunday morning around nine. It was Lamorne.

"Hey, I'll be going to church with my family. The service starts at 10:00 a.m. I'll meet you by the front door around 9:45, OK?"

"OK," I quietly said.

"You're still coming, right? You're not backing out, are you?"

"No, no I...I'll be there. 9:45, front door."

"And you know where the church is right?"

"Yeah, I know: off Naperville Road, I drive by it all the time."

"All right, see you soon." He hung up.

I showered, dressed, and dragged myself out to my car. All the while I increasingly regretted making the basketball bet with Lamorne. His church wasn't far from my place—maybe a fifteen-minute drive. I arrived and parked behind the church, slowly making my way to the front door. As I walked in I saw Lamorne standing off to the side, exactly where he said he would be. Devon was with him, quiet as usual.

Lamorne smiled and shook my hand. I mustered a smile back.

"Come on, let's grab a seat, Qasim."

I followed the two brothers and we found spots near the front. I sat between Lamorne and Devon. The church was beautiful and the pews filled up fast. Lamorne's minister came onstage and began the sermon with a prayer. I sat and listened quietly, just waiting for the moment when he would call me out and ambush me, the heathen that I was. I knew it was coming. It was only a matter of time.

A few minutes passed. Then a few more. My anxiety turned to cautious optimism and I slowly let my guard down. Before I knew it, and much to my surprise, I was enjoying the sermon. I leaned over to Lamorne. "Is this your usual minister that you talk about?"

"Yeah, why?"

"No reason, just, I'm enjoying his sermon."

Lamorne nodded. "Yeah, Brother Rich Little, he's good. Wanna meet him?"

"No, no I don't think—"

"Yeah, we'll meet him."

"Shhh you two!" Devon scolded.

The sermon soon ended and I felt Lamorne's tap on my shoulder. "Come on, let me go introduce you to him."

I took a deep breath. "This is it," I thought to myself. "It's payback time." I couldn't say no. Not a chance. I nodded and followed Lamorne out of our pews and up the aisle to the stage. We approached the small circle of people who had surrounded Lamorne's minister before us and waited our turn. My cautious optimism vanished and mind raced, frantically thinking of what to say in response to the minister's imminent verbal assault. My mind drew a blank and now it was too late—we were up to bat.

"Hi, Minister, this is my friend Qasim I told you about." Lamorne motioned toward me as I stepped forward. "I invited him to your sermon today and he said he enjoyed it. I just wanted to introduce him to you."

The minister looked up at me and I forced a sheepish smile.

"Yes, Qasim, my brother!" He gave a grin a mile wide and extended his hand. I grasped it and we shook. "Rich Little at your service. How are you! So good of you to come. Lamorne mentioned that you would be attending today. I'm so glad you could make it."

"Really?" Was my confused response.

"Why, of course. It's always good to have guests here. I want you to know you're always welcome here any time you want, OK? No need for formalities or formal invitations. Come here and enjoy yourself."

"Uh, um, sure, thanks, Minister, I appreciate that. I really enjoyed your sermon today."

"Well good, good, that brings a smile to my heart, Qasim. I'm glad to hear it." He then turned to Lamorne. "Thanks for bringing him, son. I'd love to chat but I have to prepare for the next session. We'll catch up soon, OK?"

"Yes, Minister," Lamorne said.

Minister Little turned to me. "Qasim, hope to see you again soon, OK?"

I smiled yes, and he headed down the aisle in the other direction. Lamorne turned to me. "Well, that's pretty much it. There's some food in the back if you want to grab a snack. Otherwise, that's basically our service."

We both got quiet for a minute. Devon was already quiet. I breathed a massive sigh of relief that my fears of being ambushed were unfounded. This is probably where I should have apologized for being such a jerk earlier in the week. I wish I could say I did, but that particular hallmark moment didn't happen.

"Lamorne, this...this was good. Thanks, man."

"Yeah, don't mention it."

I nodded and took my leave. Lamorne and I shook hands and we parted ways. I headed back out to my car and drove back home, reflecting.

Sometimes I wonder if anyone's made more mistakes than I have when it came to learning how to conduct interfaith dialogue. Likewise, I wonder if anyone has been more fortunate than I with the friends and gracious souls I've come across. My experience at Lamorne's church helped revitalize two important communication lessons I'd previously ignored—inadvertently or otherwise.

First, it isn't my place to worry about other people's relationships with God, just as no one else has any right to compel my relationship. No one can appreciate this principle without first being honest with himself about who he is and what he believes. Those most adamant about pushing their beliefs on others are often those most insecure in their own beliefs. They compel their beliefs on others to compensate for the weakness of their own faith.

I had gloated as Ed ambushed Lamorne and Alex not because I agreed with Ed, but because I saw Lamorne and Alex "couldn't" respond. That boosted my egoistic wish to feel that my beliefs therefore "must" be right. That teenage know-it-all wasn't honest about what he believed, so he couldn't appreciate why it was so destructive to impose a belief on others.

I recognized a need to double down in my personal studies, reflections, and research. I realized the need to communicate with myself in a transparent manner—one that required I step out of my comfort zone to engage with new ideas. No one wins by lying to others, and those who lie to others typically start by lying to themselves. I falsely told myself I was confident in my beliefs, when in reality I'd simply reverted to a comfort zone my own father had forced me out of in the past. Ed's treatment of Lamorne was a catalyst that pushed me out of that zone once again. That's why I feared attending Lamorne's church—it was out of my comfort zone. But having heard that sermon and met his minister and *not* been ambushed, I realized once more that my own comfort zone—not a different point of view—was the culprit preventing me from being honest with myself.

It was around this time that I learned of a beautiful quote commonly attributed to St. Francis of Assisi: "Preach the Gospels wherever you go. And when necessary, use words." Interfaith dialogue is less about words and more about how you treat others and serve humanity—those of your faith and especially those not of your faith. Religion aside, a person's true value is determined by how he or she treats people. If you want to know whether someone is a good person, see how that person treats waiters and waitresses, janitors, doormen, the pizza delivery guy. See how people treat those who have no power to benefit them. I had no substantive power to benefit Minister Little. And whether or not Lamorne had conveyed to him how he was treated at my mosque, Minster Little treated me with immense respect and courtesy at his church. In my conversation with him he beautifully preached the Gospels—and did so without quoting a single word of Scripture.

The good news is Lamorne, Alex, and I are still friends some 15 years later. Lamorne (Morris) is a successful television and film actor. You probably know him as Winston on *The New Girl*. And Alex is an accomplished financial analyst. I love the fact that they're the same goofy kids with weak basketball skills I knew back then. And while we now live thousands of miles apart, we still talk regularly. Devon too, and he still seems to get his point across without having to say much.

Seems like he had it right all along.

Chapter 6

Communicating with a Brat

"The mediocre teacher tells. The good teacher explains. The superior teacher demonstrates. The great teacher inspires."

—WILLIAM ARTHUR WARD

As you step out of your comfort zone, inevitably at some point or another you will get burned. This is fact. What's also a fact, however, is that the harm done by staying inside your bubble is far greater than the harm done by stepping out into new waters. Every so often you'll come across someone who can only be described as a brat. And believe it or not, there's an effective way to communicate with such people. I know, because I was once said brat, and Muhammed Ahmad Chaudhry found a way to meaningfully communicate with me when few others could.

I didn't know Muhammed Ahmad Chaudhry very well in 2004, but I knew three things. One, that he was a nonprofit education CEO of SVEF in Silicon Valley. Two, that he was the vice president of Muslim Youth USA, visiting town for some national conference. Three, that I was stuck on airport duty to pick him up one Chicago summer afternoon.

Every Chicagoan knows our city has two seasons—winter and construction. And right now we were in full swing of construction season. Having to drive from the suburbs all the way to O'Hare and back to pick up some big shot CEO I hardly knew, on an afternoon when I'd rather be doing most anything else, wasn't at the top of my to-do list.

Still, I'd volunteered to help with the conference, and while I would've preferred something a little more glamorous, I did as I was told. As a member of Muslim Youth USA myself, I'd heard our national board constantly preach servant leadership and service to humanity. Yet I felt it was contradictory that here I was—not a leader, but stuck serving a "leader," like a chauffeur. It really bothered me that while our leadership got escorted around like celebrities, we nonleaders were expected to drop everything and jump to work without complaint.

I mean, was it criminal to simply hire a cab?

My present responsibility seemed just another mind-numbing duty in a long list of inefficient, irrelevant, and hypocritical ways to do things. I drove to the airport that afternoon repeating these complaints and frustrations in my mind, over and over again—among others. It's funny how when we have one trying experience with a person or organization, we suddenly remember the million other things that apparently went wrong or are wrong with the situation in question. Such was my mental condition on that drive. The incessant gridlocked and stop-and-go traffic only added to my frustration.

I finally arrived at O'Hare quite annoyed at Muhammed. My phone buzzed, the screen showing a number I didn't recognize. It assumed it was Muhammed. It was.

"Hello. As-salaam alaikum?"

"Salaam; is this Brother Qasim?"

"Yes, is this Muhammed?"

"This is Muhammed. Are you here? I'm standing in front of the United gate."

He sounded especially chipper, which added to my annoyance, considering my sour mood. As I pulled up I saw a fit gentleman with graying hair wearing jeans and a polo shirt. Typical California hippie CEO, I thought to myself. "Yeah, I think I see you. I'm in the silver Subaru."

I slowed down and pulled over, still inwardly grumbling about how this was such a waste of my time. Right then I had an epiphany. It suddenly occurred to me that this was my chance to voice my complaint, or rather, complaints. After all, I was going to be stuck for the next hour and a half in a car with the vice president of Muslim Youth USA. What better time than now to air my grievances? And who better to hear them? I'd heard Muhammed talk the talk about servant leadership, about his work with kids at SVEF—now was my time to see if he could walk the walk.

I got out of the car and popped the trunk. Before even placing his bags in the trunk Muhammed walked up and gave me a hug. A full two-armed bear hug. Caught a little off guard, I hugged back awkwardly.

"It's so good to see you, Qasim. How are you?" He smiled.

"I'm, uh, fine. Here, let me get your bags." I forced a smile.

"No, no, I got it."

Muhammed put his own bags in the trunk and headed to the passenger side door. I sat back in the driver's seat and we pulled away from the curb. Before I could get a word out, Muhammed spoke again.

"Thanks for taking time out to get me. I know Chicago traffic can be impossible, especially with all the construction you guys have going on every summer."

"I, yeah, don't mention it. No problem." Privately, I wondered if he'd somehow read my mind. He continued.

"No, really. It is so nice to be picked up by a friend than having to take a cab. For my day job I have to suffer through cab rides all the time.

It's so nice to have a brother pick you up and let you relax, especially after a long flight. Plus, those cabs are expensive."

Now I was getting annoyed that he was shooting down my complaints before I even had a chance to make them. I smiled politely and nodded.

"So I don't think we've had a chance to talk much, Qasim. Tell me about yourself. What do you do with your free time?"

Finally, my chance to retaliate! I didn't waste any time. "Well I don't have much free time nowadays. I work full time and I'm finishing my undergrad—taking a full load of classes, actually." And then I went for the jugular and didn't mince words. "And to be honest, I was actually kind of wondering about your thoughts on why we waste so much time in Muslim Youth USA?"

"What do you mean?"

"Well, like this, for example. It just doesn't make much sense to spend three hours picking up one person when frankly a cab ride *would* save a lot of time."

Admittedly, I felt guilty, having said "No problem" just 30 seconds earlier when he thanked me for picking him up, yet now complaining about it. But it felt good to vent.

Muhammed didn't respond, but nodded. I took it as an opening to keep talking.

"So you're vice president of Muslim Youth USA, right?"

He nodded again.

"Good, because I've been holding this in awhile. Why do we have to—" and the rest was a blur.

I spent the next hour letting him have it. Every grievance, every issue, every complaint, every whine you could think of, I had already thought of, and I made sure Muhammed knew it. All the frustration building up on my drive to O'Hare now found its release. I remember trying not to raise my voice but I'm sure I probably failed at that. I remember trying to sound respectful but I'm sure I failed at that as well. I remember finally not caring and removing the filter on my mouth to air everything conceivable—and after sitting through a cramped flight all the way from California, poor Muhammed was on the other end of it.

We were still about a half-hour's drive from our destination when I finally stopped to take a breath. Muhammed hadn't said much more than a word or two the entire trip. He didn't seem angry or offended; instead, he nodded in agreement with much of, if not everything, I said. It felt good to tell him off. My ego elated and confidence soaring, I finally concluded, "So, Muhammed, these are some serious issues that I really find problematic. Hypocritical, really. I think you agree. And they need some serious resolution, and fast."

With that I rested my case. "Checkmate," I thought to myself. "Let's see him resolve these issues now. So easy to sit on his perch and dictate what to do. Let's see him come down from his ivory tower and resolve these problems. Down here in the trenches where it matters."

Muhammed stayed quiet for another minute as we pulled up to a tollbooth. Before I could pull out my wallet he handed me a $5 bill and motioned to me to use it to pay the toll. I complied, while still waiting for his answers to my laundry list of grievances.

I was convinced, he couldn't answer. And while a small part of me felt guilty for being so blunt, my ego still prevailed. And frankly, ego aside, wasn't this what he signed up for with his constant preaching of servant leadership? "Let's see him serve now," I gloated to myself again.

We pulled away from the tollbooth. Traffic had finally opened up and it felt good to slam the gas pedal to the floor. My turbocharged engine catapulted us forward. As we accelerated to speed Muhammed finally turned to me. "Qasim, you're right. These really are serious issues. Your complaints are valid."

I was caught off guard that he conceded so quickly. I expected a rebuttal, a response, a reply, a rebuke—something! Something I could latch on to as an example of his "holier-than-thou" attitude. Instead, he said, "I agree; we need resolutions, and we need them fast."

I stayed quiet still but nodded, wondering why he was giving in so quickly. I kept waiting for the "but you're wrong because" statement. He continued down a different path instead. "It seems you understand these issues pretty well. So help me out here: what do *you* think we should do?"

If life had a pause button, I would've hit it right then and there, because that was absolutely the last thing I'd expected Muhammed to say. Instead I blurted out almost angrily, "What!?"

"I said I agree. And I'm asking for your help on what we should do to resolve these issues you've listed."

"Wait—what? Why are you asking me?"

"Well, why wouldn't I? I'm not here to dictate or force something on you. I want to know what you think. I need your help. What are some solutions to these problems you've listed?"

I looked at Muhammed, confused. Remembering that we were on the highway, I glanced back at the highway, then back at Muhammed.

"What's your solution, Qasim?" He asked again.

I opened my mouth to speak but couldn't think of anything to say. He wasn't supposed to ask me that. He was supposed to argue with me or tell me I'm wrong. He was supposed to tell me to have more faith in my leadership, or to have more trust in God, or to be more obedient. He was supposed to tell me to just shut up and drive. I brought a gun to a word fight and he responded with an olive branch and a side of cake.

How do you fight an olive branch with a side of cake!?

Finally I sputtered out, "I...I don't know. I don't, I hadn't really thought of that. I guess I thought it was your job to figure it out."

Muhammed remained calm as he had the entire drive. "Well, it wouldn't be much for servant leadership if I did all the thinking for you, now, would it? Wouldn't it be better if I listened to your ideas and solutions instead?"

Now it was my turn to remain quiet, though not entirely by choice. While moments earlier I was riding high with infinite confidence, I suddenly felt humiliated. And not because of Muhammed—but because I recognized that I'd unknowingly humiliated myself. Muhammed saw my confusion and continued. "I'll make you a deal. I want you to write down everything you've said and email me your complaints. And with your complaints I want you to propose your solution. The sky's the limit. Let me worry about logistics. My job isn't to tell you what to do. You tell me what to do. My job is to listen to your needs and solutions and do what I can to ensure they're met."

I didn't look at Muhammed this time and just stared forward.

Muhammed waited another few moments to let me digest what he'd just conveyed. "That sound fair, Qasim?"

I could only nod slowly. Mike Tyson said it best: "Everyone has a plan until they get punched in the face." I felt like I'd just been punched in the face. And the worst part, it was with my own fist. It's a good thing we were almost at our destination.

I reflect on that conversation with Muhammed often. Muhammed's communication during that car ride wasn't effective just because of what he said, but mostly because of what he didn't. It would have been easy for Muhammed to dismiss me as some punk kid, a brat who likes to complain and nothing more—because, frankly, that's exactly what I was. But instead he swallowed his ego and let me vent, let me speak, and made himself listen. He empowered me to be who I was and enabled me to speak without inhibition or intimidation. He ensured communication took place in a manner that ensured clarity and accountability. He made himself accountable to listen, which in turn made me accountable to convey a solution. He put the ball back in my court and empowered me to take the shot.

Since 2004 I've learned a great deal about Muhammed, but nothing more important than what I learned in those final thirty minutes until we reached our destination. As those minutes dragged by in silence I sat and reflected that I now knew a fourth and fifth thing about Muhammed.

Don't come to him with a complaint unless I have a solution ready, and damn could he walk the walk of servant leadership.

Chapter 7

9/11 Changed Everything

"The Constitution is never tested during times of tranquility; it is during times of tension, turmoil, tragedy, trauma, and terrorism that it is sorely tested."

—U.S. CONGRESSMAN MIKE HONDA

9/11 changed everything.

Mac's lesson about coming to a problem with a solution was suddenly that much more important. Kids graduating high school or even college today barely remember 9/11, if at all. But 9/11 changed everything. Many have written on the sheer horror of that day so I don't intend to regurgitate what many already have. But in the context of my by-then four-year-long journey to step out of my comfort zone, just as I'd begun to finally find some sense of identity and understanding of who I was, my entire world was thrown into a tailspin.

I was a 19-year-old college student with long hair and a shaggy beard that infamous Tuesday morning. We huddled around a TV in the lobby at work, and we watched live as the second plane hit. I thought of my brother Tayyib, a US marine, who was then stationed in Germany. Confused, we returned to our workstations, but no one worked. We stayed affixed to the then remedial Internet news feeds, but mostly tried to catch glimpses of the television.

Suddenly I overheard, "I say we round up these damn towelheads and ship them the hell out of our country." I didn't look up to see who it was. But it didn't matter. The coming days threw my psyche into disarray. My grades plummeted and I became withdrawn. My college cross-country coach noticed the change and called me into his office about a week after the attack.

"Qasim, you're not yourself."

I nodded but stayed silent.

"You can trust me. What's going on."

To date, the only real death I'd encountered was that of my grandma when I was four, a cousin when I was ten, and an uncle when I was sixteen. I was fortunate to have all my immediate family and to not yet witness or experience terrorism or fatal violence. But now I couldn't get the images of 9/11 out of my mind. The pictures of people, innocent people, literally jumping to their deaths to escape the flames inside the twin towers. The ongoing footage of a war scene that emerged like a flash of lightning. The death and destruction was overwhelming. Even though I knew no one who'd died, let alone had a family member or friend who died, the sheer loss of humanity tore at my soul. Sitting there in front of the coach, I broke down in tears.

But the trauma alone wasn't what had changed my demeanor. Indeed, I believe every American felt that same pain, anger, and aggravation. The other dimension to my pain in those days was the reaction of many of those whom I considered trusted friends. Several people I considered friends now consciously avoided me. I heard the snide remarks in the periphery, asking if I could be trusted, whether I should be trusted. They thought I didn't notice, and maybe I wished I hadn't. But it was all too real. And the distress was something very few could understand—at least that's the reality I felt.

My nation was hijacked, my identity was hijacked, and my faith was being called onto the mat. I realize however, that this was another testament to my father's push to make me figure out what I believe on my own. He made me build my identity on my own. When you build something on your own, you understand how it works and why it works. Rather than inheriting an identity that wasn't mine, I was building my own, and this massive blow to the base of who I was would prove—in due time—to strengthen my character, my resolve, and my understanding.

But for now...for now it burned. I was way out of my comfort zone and it burned. Those defining weeks, months, and years permanently changed my life's trajectory. The event helped spawn my desire to understand why people commit terrorism, why people fear one another, and what needs to happen to overcome that fear. My life experiences to date were limited, but flashed images of racism, Islamophobia, anti-Semitism, death, good and bad leadership, and the impact of parenting all became factors.

I was fortunate, however, as my mosque became a beacon of confidence. "This is terrorism and nothing justifies this terrorism," was the consistent message I heard. The moments after an act of terror are critical. Had my mosque preached a message of intolerance, who knows where I would be today?

Consider that in the weeks after the 2015 terrorist attack in Charleston on the historic black Emanuel African Methodist Episcopal Church, seven more black churches in the South were set on fire and destroyed. Racism motivated the attack in Charleston, and a continued message of racism preached in churches perpetuated the attacks on the black churches that followed. This is a topic we'll cover in detail shortly.

The message of tolerance in my mosque afforded me the clarity to continue my struggle and journey. I sought for a religious identity as well as a secular identity. Finding that identity was a stepping-stone to what would eventually lead me to write *The Wrong Kind of Muslim* and certainly this book. To understand where I was going, I first needed to understand where I came from. I understood that history when I researched and wrote *The Wrong Kind of Muslim*. I also needed to understand where my country—America—came from. It's not just cliché to acknowledge that those who do not learn the lessons of history are doomed to repeat them. It is fact.

And post-9/11 as I dug into American history, what I found was both awe inspiring and horrifying. America has a brilliant history, but also some horrific dark chapters that no one likes to talk about. At least, no one talked to me about these things growing up.

I began to realize that 9/11 didn't just change my future, but it also changed my past.

Chapter 8

The Only Good Muslim Is a Muslim Who Kills Other Muslims

"We can't afford to be killing one another."

—NELSON MANDELA

Once upon a time in a magical land far, far away, wise men wrote on a parchment they called the Constitution. And part of that Constitution guaranteed universal religious freedom for all people. That magical land was named America. I call it magical because while on paper this sounds utopian, and while it should be commended for many reasons, we must also have the courage to call out the errors of our founders and forebears. Unfortunately, that hasn't happened enough, and the more I delved into our own nation's history the more this painful reality came to the forefront. It is this blindness to or unawareness of our own history that fuel many of the problems we see today regarding racism, Islamophobia, and anti-Semitism.

There are painful, benighted chapters we simply don't talk and educate ourselves enough about. America's founders made noble declarations of religious freedom and equality, all the while waging war on and destroying millions of Native Americans. They did so while enslaving tens of millions of Africans and using Manifest Destiny as the justification.

Unfortunately, too few Americans are aware of the struggle America has gone through to get to where we are. Too few today remember the persecution that Mormons, Jews, and Catholics faced in American history. For example, on Oct. 27, 1838, Missouri Governor Lilburn W. Boggs issued an official order: "The Mormons must be treated as enemies, and must be exterminated or driven from the state if necessary for the public peace." Boggs believed American Mormons were not real Americans, but dangerous enemies. He believed murdering them was the right decision, to maintain the peace.

Three days later, seventeen Mormon men and boys were killed. Incidentally, historians generally agree that the militiamen who murdered these Mormons could not possibly have known about Governor Boggs's order. This fact only shows the destructive culture that develops when a government ignores its founding principles and endorses religious persecution, especially against a minority.

But Mormons weren't the only victims.

Ever hear of the Know-Nothing Party? They were a nineteenth-century anti-Catholic political organization. It might sound crazy to some, but anti-Catholic sentiment once elected dozens of members to Congress. On mayoral Election Day Aug. 6, 1855, the Know-Nothing Party rioted against Catholic immigrants in Louisville, Kentucky. When the dust settled, twenty-two martyred Catholics were laid to rest.

The Know-Nothings believed American Catholics were infiltrating America for a secret Vatican takeover. Sound familiar?

Jews have not fared well in American history either.

In fact, recognizing prevailing anti-Semitism and emphathizing with oppressed peoples, American Jews played a significant role in supporting the civil rights movement of the sixties. A century prior, on Dec. 17, 1862, General Ulysses S. Grant issued Order No. 11, which read, "The Jews, as a class...are hereby expelled from Tennessee within twenty-four hours..." As morbid of a comparison as it might be, General Grant promoted virtually the same stereotypes against Jews that Adolf Hitler would use some seventy years later. Grant believed that American Jews violated trade agreements and that they did so in order to amass wealth and harm the army. Thus, Constitution be damned, Grant demanded the Jews be expelled.

Expelled Jews, murdered Mormons, and massacred Catholics—and all in addition to the centuries-long slaughter, enslavement and displacement of Africans and Native Americans. And consider the horrifying reality that all these events took place despite the First Amendment—our Constitution's most powerful fail-safe to ensure religious freedom. The justification came via the excuse of ensuring security against the threat each American minority allegedly posed. In reality, these atrocities resulted because Americans chose ignorant fear over educated dialogue.

Fear is indeed a powerful change agent, and the twenty-first century has introduced a new target to promote fearmongering and win political votes. Every tactic used today is nothing new—all are simply a regurgitation of age-old tactics used to demonize Mormons, Catholics, and Jews.

Today, a core group of politicians continue to call Islam and America "incompatible."[2] To date, some thirty states have passed, or attempted to

---

[2] Rick Santorum: Sharia 'is evil': Politico

http://www.politico.com/news/stories/0311/51166.html (last visited on Dec. 6, 2011).

pass, some sort of anti-Sharia laws. Elected government officials have proposed discharging all Muslims serving in the military from service.[3] Others have proposed that Islam is not a religion, but a fascist ideology.[4] Tennessee state Rep. Rick Womick, for example, wants to "expel all Muslims from the military" because, allegedly, "they are commanded to kill us." Donald Trump's call to ban Muslim immigration and issue special ID cards revives Hitler's Nazi ideology.

Even while in office former Florida state representative and notoriously ignorant Islamophobe Allen West propagandized, "We are in a war against a political, theocratic, authoritarian ideology and it is called Islam!" At a February 2011 anti-Islam rally, an Orange County politician wanted her marine son to send "these terrorist [Muslims] to an early meeting in paradise." We'll revisit this anti-Islam rally. In January 2011 Newt Gingrich demanded all Muslims publicly repudiate Sharia altogether and without exception—especially if they want to run for public office. In 2015 and 2016, Ben Carson and Trump promoted the same hostility. Senator McCarthy would be proud. Even terrorists like Anders Breivik cited American anti-Muslim bigots as the motivation for his rampage that killed seventy-seven Norwegians.

According to Pew Research Center, roughly 60 percent of Americans, or some 200 million, have never met a Muslim. This ignorance has a real-life impact. One afternoon not long after Congressional hearings on "Muslim radicalization" I received an email from, let's call him Kevin, stating, "Your interpretation of the Quran seems to be very different than [that of] the imams across the world."

---

[3] Tennessee State Rick Womick (R) interview on the Steve Gill Show, http://www.youtube.com/watch?feature=player_embedded&v=xRMq2nWat0o (last visited on Dec. 7, 2011).

[4] Id.

I think he meant it as a compliment.

"But, you do have the obligation to spread your religion in common with the terrorists."

I was unaware of this obligation; glad he reminded me.

"The only difference is that you do it in sheep's clothing. What these Muslim radicalization hearings are doing is in defense of American values. Still curious, why did you come to the 'Great Satin.'"

I think he meant Satan, although I'm not a big fan of the fabric either.

Already, Kevin was engaging in the classic discriminatory tactic used throughout American history—grounded in the misguided belief that constitutional principles are not compromised if the actions are taken while claiming defense of national values.

"The only people who are fooled by Muslims like you so-called 'moderate' Muslims," he added, "are the left loon progressives who are blinded by political correctness. But you have a lot of work to do Rashid because they are a very small part of our population, and freedom-loving people, you know, the ones that our soldiers will put their lives on the line for, are waking up."

Now, none of the above was particularly remarkable, as I've received countless emails of the sort. So rather than get into a lengthy discussion (famous last words), I responded to Kevin by cutting to the chase:

"My brother served eight years in the Marine Corps as well, protecting both [my and your] freedoms, as a Muslim who believes in every bit of Islam."

Kevin replied quickly. "Really, did he kill Muslims overseas?"

"Does killing make someone a better American? Or is eight years in the Marine Corps still not enough proof of being a 'good American'?"

I wanted to see if he was actually advocating killing Muslims as a loyalty oath.

"All you seem to do is answer questions with questions. Did your brother stay out of combat because of his religious beliefs? Or did he kill Muslims in defense of this country? If he did, then yes, he is a good American, if he didn't then he did not belong in the US Marines."

"So then the only good American Muslim marine is one who kills other Muslims?

"Forget it Rashid, you are obviously a spin doctor..."

Alas, he refused to answer my question directly, but I think I got my answer. Remarkably, here was an American citizen who would not trust Muslims in America unless they literally killed other Muslims.

And Muslims are the ones to be feared?

Maybe it matters, maybe it doesn't, but Kevin mentioned his affiliation was with Christianity—though he was anything but Christlike. My brother Tayyib, an American citizen and a Muslim, was willing to sacrifice his life as a US marine for people like Kevin. Yet, according to Kevin, Tayyib wasn't marine enough and did not belong in the armed forces. Now, granted, Tayyib is not a decorated war hero; he doesn't have any purple hearts, and he didn't carry his wounded friend two miles through live combat uphill. He did, however, put his country first—before himself, before his family, and before his future.

Fear and ignorance are powerful change agents. But here's the silver lining in our history, should we choose to learn from it. Twelve years after issuing Order Eleven, President Ulysses S. Grant became the first sitting President to attend a synagogue, where he openly acknowledged his prior reprehensible actions. Indeed, Grant concluded, "Leave the matter of religion to the family altar, the church, and the private school, supported entirely by private contributions. Keep the church and state forever separate."

Mormons waited 137 years, but in 1976 Missouri Governor Christopher S. Bond finally rescinded Governor Boggs's anti-Mormon order. And Louisville, Kentucky, a city that had been known as the site of the nation's most deadly anti-immigrant riots, elected a German-born mayor just a decade later. Today, before Justice Scalia's death, six Supreme Court justices were Catholic, the remaining three Jewish; Joe Biden is the nation's first Catholic vice president; and fifteen members of Congress are Mormon, including former Senate majority leader Harry Reid.

Religious pluralism is in our culture and must remain so if we are to stay committed to our founding principles. That is, if we choose to stay committed to those principles and block out the calls to engage in discrimination.

In fact, after Donald Trump suggested special ID cards for Muslims, Tayyib tweeted an image of his Marine Corps ID from his @MuslimMarine twitter account with the text, "Hey @realDonaldTrump, I'm an American Muslim and I already carry a special ID badge. Where's yours? #SemperFi #USMC." The tweet went mega viral with nearly forty thousand retweets, reaching millions of people, and dozens of news agencies reported on it. As a result, thousands of people emailed Tayyib expressing their solidarity with him as an American Muslim. Thousands broke down walls of fear and spoke to a Muslim for perhaps the first time. It was just a small example of the power of meaningful communication.

But before we can write a chapter about how we as Americans overcame Islamophobia, we must realize how serious an issue it has become for American Muslims—and therefore for America.

Amazingly enough, America's Sikh and non-Muslim Indian communities have also faced increasing anti-Muslim backlash for looking "Muslim enough." After Osama bin Laden was killed in May 2011, two men in Northern California assaulted an Indian-American, claiming he was a "jihadist" who was angry that "Osama had been killed." Even looking Muslim in America is quickly becoming less a life choice and more a life sentence. More than one thousand anti-Sikh assaults have occurred in America since 9/11.

Islam is not a threat to America, nor is America a threat to Islam. But if we cannot even engage in meaningful dialogue about the situation with one another, what hope does our country have of avoiding the deplorable religious discrimination mistakes of yesterday? Without meaningful communication, we execute our own futures at the guillotine of intolerance.

As I said, 9/11 changed everything for many people. And in trying to repair the damage done, I've learned that interfaith relations intimately intertwine with race relations. Keep that in mind as I shift in the next chapter to a story written by my friend Robert. Indeed, 9/11 changed everything, especially for a young black marine who once led Bible study in the White House.

Chapter 9

Longing for the Return of My Rose-Colored Glasses

by Robert Salaam

"You may encounter many defeats. But you must not be defeated."

—MAYA ANGELOU

I was a devout Christian for many years.

I'd been baptized. Once I understood the significance of baptism, I recommitted myself by being baptized again in my late teens. My grandfather raised me during my formative years. He was a pastor and minister for more than fifty years and had his doctorate in theology. I was not a CINO, or "Christian in name only."

The church and the business of God had been my passion, my life. I often referred to religion as my hobby in the sense that people took their hobbies seriously, and I took religion seriously. I went to church several times a week and Bible study was a daily routine. This routine included many hours of daily debate and study with my grandfather. In high school I sought out and excelled in classes on the Old Testament and New Testament. I thrived with the opportunity to read, study, and comment line by line for a grade.

This passion stayed with me when I left to serve in the United States Marine Corps. In boot camp I was the lay leader for my platoon and was the designated "religious guy" when it came to Christendom. When we didn't have a chaplain at my duty station, I volunteered to help fill that role. I sent daily inspirational messages from the Bible and even led a Bible study. I wasn't perfect, but I was truly working toward emulating and following my grandfather. It was common knowledge in my family and our circle that I would follow him as his successor in the church.

One ordinary Tuesday morning, I heard on the radio the most unbelievable, shocking, and life-altering announcement I'd ever heard before, or since.

America was under attack.

I sat stunned while in the maintenance control room of my unit. There are no words, even after all this time, to fully convey my emotions that morning. I've tried many times to do so, even in several published media outlets. The results and impact of that day set me on a collision course with the very religion blamed for the atrocities of that day. As marines, we are taught to know our enemy. As a proud marine, I felt it was my duty to seek out and study the religion of Islam.

I rushed in, eager to disprove and point out the vileness of this religion, but God had other plans. Imagine my shock, not to mention that of my family, when in the coming days after 9/11, I pursued a path that eventually led me to accept Islam. What I realized was that my enemy was not Islam, but extremism and ignorance. In Islam, I found universal truth, brotherhood, and answers to questions I hadn't even asked. It was with this understanding of my newfound religion that I embarked on my journey of faith with rose-colored glasses, glasses that have since been cracked in some ways and shattered in others.

There's a belief among some Muslims that Islam is above racism and racial discrimination. Well, Islam may be, but Muslims are not. I've heard Muslims boast about Prophet Muhammad's words in his final sermon: "A black is no better than a white, nor a white better than a black. An Arab is no better than a non-Arab, nor is a non-Arab better than an Arab. You are all equal in the eyes of God except by piety and good works." I've heard imams boast about how Prophet Muhammad effectively ended slavery and how his companions consisted of Arabs, Africans, Persians, and Romans.

All true, and while Islam rises above racial discrimination, the sad reality is that this lesson is lost upon too many Muslims. The denial and the refusal to talk to those who are speaking out about racism in Muslim communities, only ensures racism continues to plague Muslim communities across America and frankly the world.

I came into Islam as most newly minted converts often do, eager to learn and excited about my new understanding. I remember it like it was yesterday. I heard the announcement that America was under attack, the shock as I realized I might be going to war, and the prayer asking God to give me clarity and understanding for the challenge ahead.

So there I was, several weeks after 9/11, free to leave the base to explore the world as a Muslim. I had my pristine rose-colored glasses in tow. However, one event placed the first of many cracks in my glasses. This incident and the resulting trauma not only skewed my vision of what it meant to be a Muslim in the real world, but also was my first test of my Islamic faith. Had I been a lesser man, I'd probably had left Islam that day and returned to my previous religion.

Doing what any new Muslim would do, I went to a local mosque. I had no idea what a mosque in America should look like, but there was a tiny hole in the wall not far from Marine Corps Base Quantico in Virginia. The Muslims used this small building for prayer services, as their purpose-built mosque was still under construction. I went there during a time when there was little to no worship activity. I hadn't figured out when prayers and things like that were supposed to happen yet. The first person I met was a guy in a robe and a skullcap. His commanding beard nearly touched his chest. Though in hindsight he could have been Southeast Asian, he looked like every stereotypical construct of an Arab that I was aware of at the time.

Needless to say, to my post-9/11 militaristic mind, he looked like the enemy. In all fairness, a young guy with an obvious marine's haircut and bearing probably looked suspicious to him as well.

Either way, I smiled and marched forward while butchering my "Assalaam alaikum" greeting. I had no idea whether it was my unfamiliarity with Arabic or my nervousness getting the best of me. Though I was scared to approach this guy and finally meet a real Muslim, I was even more excited because I wanted someone to whom I could confess my ignorance, fears, and hopes.

I wanted a fellow Muslim to know how lonely I was as the only Muslim I had ever known.

The Qur'anic passages telling me what I was doing was perfectly normal reigned supreme in my new Muslim mind. Even though I couldn't relate to any situation in my background where it would have made sense to seek religious fellowship with someone outside of my race, this experience was supposed to prove the unique brotherhood and equality inherent in Islam. There I was and there he was.

I reached out my hand to shake his. "Hi. I'm Robert."

He looked at my outstretched hand and then back to my face as if I were crazy for daring to speak to him. The look he gave me was of disgust. Maybe time has embellished the event in my mind, but I still feel the pain as if it was fresh. I clearly remember how I felt and his rebuff even with my sincerest hopes to the contrary. I felt unwanted, but more than that, unwelcome and undesirable for fellowship. It was as if I were beneath him.

At first, I thought I did something wrong. "Maybe we aren't supposed to shake hands in Islam?" I tried to rationalize in my mind. My rose-colored glasses were obscuring my vision, obscuring the obviousness of what was happening.

With his cold eyes and a hardened face turned to me, he asked bluntly, "What do you want?"

I pulled back my hand, which had hung exposed in the air, failing to be grasped. Steeling myself against even more heartache that I was certain was coming, I hoped for a change in demeanor or tone. A change I already knew deep down wasn't coming. Trying not to display my shock or anger, I was more stunned than anything. I attempted to get my words out with as little tremor in my voice as possible. It didn't work.

"Um, I'm Robert. I'm a new Muslim and need to learn more about Is...Islam. Can I learn here?" Asking such a simple question felt akin to a crucible. It didn't feel right. It wasn't supposed to be like this. My rose-colored glasses began to feel heavy.

The Muslim guy stared at me for what seemed like an eternity. I stood, awkward, feeling uncomfortable, angry, embarrassed, and confused.

Finally he spoke. "Come back later."

By "later" it felt that he meant never again. With that, he turned his back to me and headed inside. I heard a crack as the lens to my rose colored glasses snapped in two and fell to the ground. In that moment of clarity, I knew "later" would never come for me, at least not at this mosque. The harshness and brevity with which I was met ensured that I would never visit that mosque again.

I've kept that promise for more than fifteen years now.

Dejected and taken aback, I headed back to my car and eventually back to the barracks. I wondered what I did wrong. It took some time to convince myself that I was not at fault, but what troubled me more than anything was how the entire encounter played out. In my mind, I was supposed to be embraced as a fellow believer and there would be joy in the streets and peace on earth. Light would shine from heaven and somewhere an angel would get its wings.

Instead, I found myself over the next couple of days wondering, contemplating, and fearing I'd made a mistake in leaving my religion. One of the standout teachings of Islam was the promise of universal brotherhood. My very first interaction with another Muslim made that teaching seem nonexistent. He refused to even talk to me. With broken heart and broken glasses, I found myself believing the whole thing a sham, no better than the churches I'd grown up with.

I stewed with my hurt for several days and nights. And though some would have thrown out their Islam card, proverbially speaking of course, I'm glad I didn't.

Not only did I find that Islam is in fact a brotherhood and a sisterhood, but I also learned that although one brother had tarnished my initial outlook, no one is above falling short of their higher ideals. I wished I could say this was a one-time incident, but it was not. On the whole, however, I've experienced more brotherhood and sisterhood than not.

I feel for those with a similar story, those worried they won't be accepted because of their Western dress or nonstereotypical ethnicity. You're not alone and you don't need rose-colored glasses. All you need is a whole lot of prayer, a whole lot of study, and a whole lot of patience.

Never let the actions of others lead you toward disbelief, no matter how much they may hurt. I often think back on my journey to Islam, and this scenario plays prominently in my thoughts. I wonder why I didn't act on my urge to give up on Islam and return to the church. I wonder how many other new converts do just that because of similar or worse experiences: when they meet "born" or other Muslims who don't behave in the way a new convert expects.

Remember that belief is personal. Always has and always will be. Your faith is between you and your Lord. Do not allow the influences of the world, the flesh, and even fellow believers determine what should be an unshakable bond between you and God. I've heard many who have left Islam attribute their exit to the behavior of other believers. Some of the most prominent anti-Muslim and anti-Islam pundits and celebrities use this excuse: because this Muslim or those Muslims did x, that "proved" something about Islam that prompted them to leave and then advocate against the faith. Rarely if ever do they say it had anything to do with core beliefs—that they no longer believe in one God or that Muhammad is the messenger of God.

So whether newly minted Muslim or old-hand Muslim, steel yourself against the disappointments of and from the believers, because you will face plenty. I've been a devout Muslim for many years and my rose-colored glasses are broken. I never needed them. Peace, internal and external, that we attain when we overcome our fears can only come from experience and from talking to one another.

Chapter 10

Oppression of Conscience Is a Cancer We Can Cure

"If we don't believe in freedom of expression for people we despise, we don't believe in it at all."

—NOAM CHOMKSY

You can see why I admire Robert so much. His struggle is heartfelt and deep, and he marches on despite the obstacles before him. He's engaging in meaningful communication and using it to rise above the bigotry and intolerance around him. Racism among Muslims is a real issue, and those who pretend it doesn't exist are typically the ones most apt to exhibit racist tendencies. I admire Robert because he's willing to have these "taboo" conversations in an honest, respectful, and courageous manner. Having known him nearly a decade now, I marvel at how passionately and compassionately he responds to critics.

I started this book with a story about interfaith dialogue. It's been an intimate part of my life for as long as I can remember. And as our world becomes increasingly connected, we run into new ways of connecting with people of different faiths—even if we never meet them in real life.

But our advanced means of communication hasn't done enough to improve interfaith or interracial relations. A few years back someone sent me an angry message that included the following gem. "Your work is pathetic and useless because you don't see the world as it is. You insist on engaging in unwarranted extreme peacefulness."

"Unwarranted extreme peacefulness? I'll take it!" I replied in total sincerity and honesty.

I didn't get a reply.

As a trend, worldwide we find a frighteningly intolerant reality where religious oppression has become the status quo. It appears we may need more of that extreme peacefulness. According to Pew, nearly 70 percent of the world's population lives under some form of oppression of conscience—that's roughly 5.25 billion people. This means that if you can worship (or not worship) without oppression or compulsion, you're the minority on earth.

Moreover, in those nations where oppression of conscience is highest, so are terrorism, violence, ignorance, and corruption. Meaningful communication requires we break through the oppressive narratives with education and learn about one another from one another. Until we affirmatively take such a step, we cannot make a difference to improve the condition of those suffering.

We may not solve all the world's interfaith issues over one dinner table conversation, but that can't stop us from trying. For example, what might a person who lost his family on 9/11 have to say about interfaith dialogue—especially between Christians and Muslims?

The following chapter is by my friend and colleague Dr. Craig Considine. Craig is a Catholic Christian and a religious scholar, currently teaching at Rice University in Houston, Texas. He introduces us to a hero who emerged from the rubble of 9/11—David McCourt.

When I heard Craig's story, I knew it's one the world had to hear.

Chapter 11

A 9/11 Hero and a Not-Christian-Enough Christian

by Dr. Craig Considine

"When we meet real tragedy in life, we can react in two ways—either by losing hope and falling into self-destructive habits, or by using the challenge to find our inner strength."
—DALAI LAMA

We have all met someone in our lives we consider to be a kindred spirit. For some people, this person might be a father or mother, a brother or sister, a teacher or a coach. One of my kindred spirits was a complete stranger I met at a hotel thousands of miles away from my home.

The stranger was David McCourt, a hero who emerged from the 9/11 atrocity.

Throughout 2008 and 2009, I carried out sociological research on Muslim Americans. Along with several other young researchers, I traveled around the United States studying the post-9/11 experiences of Muslim Americans and how non-Muslims perceived Islam in America. On a winter evening in February 2009, our group attended an interfaith lecture on the relationship between Judaism, Christianity, and Islam. During the question-and-answer session, David stood up and offered his views on Islam and his perception of non-Muslims in America. His words were so insightful and moving that we asked to meet him the following morning for a more in-depth discussion on issues pertaining to US foreign policy and the so-called "Muslim world."

In the lobby of a Palm Beach hotel, I had the chance to listen to David as he shared his views about everything from Islamophobia to the "war on terror." David, a Christian, was curious as to why a small group of young Americans had such a passion for interacting with Muslims and understanding Islam.

He finally flat-out asked, "Craig, I am somewhat surprised to see you traveling around the country studying the experiences of Muslims. Are you Muslim?"

"I am not," I replied. "I am a Catholic who feels the need to build up relationships between Christians and Muslims." I went on: "Our world is in trouble. All of this hatred and religion-motivated violence is disheartening. I'm hoping that this research can help to share real stories about Muslims living in America. There's just so much misinformation about Muslims in the media."

"I agree," he said. "That is commendable work. You don't hear about people like yourself, Craig. Christians trying to understand 'the other,' especially Muslims."

"Well, I suppose it's a rare thing, especially these days with so much misunderstanding about Islam and hatred toward Muslims."

"Very true. So you're a Christian studying Islam?"

"That's right. I am training to become a scholar. My Christian faith certainly drives me to seek knowledge, and I try to use it in a productive manner. I love Jesus because he was a proponent of peace. Peace is what is missing in the world."

"Boy, that is certainly the truth. I think you and I are a lot alike, Craig." He paused to gather his thoughts. "One thing that I thought about a lot after 9/11 was Jesus's message to 'love your neighbor, as well as your enemy.' This passage nearly brings me to tears. It is such a powerful idea. If only Christians would believe in it and practice it more."

I sat silent and let him air his story. He continued: "I know exactly what you are saying and how you feel. I have a story to tell you about my experience with Muslims. I should tell you how I got here."

Over the next few hours I listened in awe as David told me about the massive impact that 9/11 had on his family and religious beliefs. His forty-six-year-old wife, Ruth McCourt, and their four-year-old daughter, Juliana, were aboard United Flight 175, which crashed into the World Trade Center towers in New York City.

I can't fathom how David must have felt to lose his family in the blink of an eye. In the lobby of the Palm Beach hotel, David talked to me about his incredible transformation.

"I was so depressed after 9/11. I lost my wife and daughter, the best two things in my life. I was filled with sadness, but also hate. I hated Islam because it was Muslims who killed my wife and daughter. I hit rock bottom. I nearly committed suicide. I could barely even get out of bed or lift my head. It was real depression."

I didn't know what to say, so I did what felt was right—I quietly listened to him talk to me.

"I saw a few doctors, and they told me that I just had to change my thinking, that I needed to start seeing my loss differently. But that was hard too. I felt like I was stuck, that I would never be able to get out of the depression and that dark mindset that I had developed."

I finally chimed in. "So then, how did you get from there to here? You seem to be...better now." I didn't want to be presumptuous, but he really did come across as confident and genuinely happy.

"I turned to God. It's that simple. I started to have faith that He had a better plan for me. That's how I overcame my sadness and anger. By believing in God and having faith in my relationship with Him. Medicine could not fix me; neither could the advice and comfort of those around me."

"That's remarkable, David. He helped you when you called out for His assistance."

"Yeah, that describes it well. I reconnected with my Creator and had a spiritual awakening. It was profound and difficult to explain in words."

"It sends chills up my spine. It's beautiful. Tell me more."

"Well, it was beautiful, and remarkable, if I can say so myself. I believe God was telling me to open my heart and mind to things that I previously perceived as threatening." David paused and then looked up. "Craig, you want to hear an interesting story?"

"I'm all ears."

"A few months after 9/11, I received a package in the mail from a Muslim American. He was a total stranger. This Muslim sent me a book on the peaceful example of Muhammad and how 'terrorists' like those of 9/11 were neglecting Muhammad's teachings and the true message of Islam. At first I wanted to throw it out. I almost did. But I gradually came to think that the book may have been a gift from God. So I started to read it. I was shocked at what I was reading. I never thought Islam was about peace."

I jumped in. "Something similar happened to me when I got to college! I knew nothing about Islam, but when I started reading about it, I was shocked as well. What was in the book you received?"

"Well, it was about Muhammad. It showed he was nothing like what the media says he is. Reading that book helped me to see him as an honorable person who was genuinely trying to do the right thing for his neighbors."

I smiled, reflecting over my own experience of talking to Muslims. David continued.

"The most important thing I learned was that Muhammad considered himself to be the carrier of previous Jewish and Christian teachings, and that he had great respect for Jews and Christians. That amazed me! You know, there's a powerful message there for today's broken world. I could go on about Muhammad, but I think you get my point."

"Yeah, I know what you mean. I've studied him as well and admire him for similar reasons."

"In retrospect, I moved away from having animosity toward Muslims and bitterness towards Islam to engaging with them and respecting their religion. After actually talking to Muslims I have compassion for Muslims."

David went on to explain that he believed God asked him to respond to 9/11 by building bridges of goodwill and peace, instead of sowing the seeds of divisiveness, between Muslims and non-Muslims. He went from treating Muslims as objects of fear, hatred, and distrust to seeing them as just and merciful people.

"David, your story lifts up my heart. It is amazing that you overcame the hardship and pain. For you to open up to the idea of building bridges is honorable. I get that you felt inspired by God, but what did that look like practically? How did you get started? What'd you do?"

"Well, I was fortunate to come across some really great people, and they helped me do a lot more than I ever could have on my own. I started something I call 'BRAVE Juliana.' It's an educational program that teaches nonviolence and conflict resolution to children in elementary schools. And then this nonprofit called Help USA encourages Americans to live safer, happier, and more productive lives—they also assisted me in creating the program. I wanted to honor my daughter Juliana by encouraging peaceful activism and interfaith dialogue among youth. What could be more helpful to overcome all of this religious bigotry?"

"That's just amazing, David." But he wasn't done yet.

"I also helped to create a 'peace garden' at Lyman Allyn Art Museum in New London, Connecticut. The garden honors both my wife, Ruth, and my daughter Juliana. I love this garden deeply because it is a metaphor for renewal and healing for those who have passed away."

Talking to David left me in awe, nearly speechless. "You are so courageous, a true hero!" I finally said. Several hours had passed since we first began talking. I didn't want to rob David of his entire day, so I asked one more important question. "David, what can I do to thank you for being such an inspiration?" The answer he gave me is one I wish to convey to everyone—especially those who might have some fear of or uncertainty about those of a different faith.

David looked me directly in the eye. I looked into the gentle eyes of a man who would forever be pained at the horrific loss of his wife and daughter. A man who at one point was on the verge of suicide. A man who was once filled with hatred for all Muslims and love for none. From that dark abyss emerged a David who gazed at me with conviction and said, "Spread love and peace. Reach out to others; talk to them. And especially reach out to those who are voiceless and maligned. Keep doing what you are doing, Craig. Seek knowledge, as this is the most useful tool for humanity."

In 2013, almost a dozen years after that fateful day in 2001, David died of cancer. He was a man of faith. He was a Christian. And he conquered bigotry and loved his neighbor Muslim as himself.

Now that's worth talking about.

Like Qasim, I experience the harsh consequences of stepping out of my comfort zone. Sometimes those consequences come from complete strangers, other times from people who mean the world to you. How you respond makes all the difference in the world.

I often reflect on David's example when I'm forced to "prove" my Christianity. Christmas Day is supposed to be an occasion of joy, happiness, peace, and love. That is how I see it as a Catholic. Jesus Christ wanted people to love one another, regardless if they were family members, friends, or enemies. Certainly, Christmas was not intended to be a day on which darkness reigns and hatred between Christians and Muslims is exacerbated.

Several years ago on Christmas Day, a family member and I sat in front of the television. An image came up on the screen that depicted Islam and Muslims as aggressive and violent.

He ranted, "These Muslims are nuts! You can't even go to a place like Egypt as a Christian. They will just kill you. Chop your head right off!"

"Right," I answered, grudgingly. "Yeah, it's definitely not a good thing what's happening to some Christians in the Middle East."

It was difficult for me to respond to his comments in a way that was educational and not condescending. I felt like telling him, "You've been brainwashed into thinking that Islam calls for the killing of non-Muslims. You hate Muslims because you have been programmed by the media to hate them." But I realized that people do not respond favorably to these kinds of remarks, which challenge their perceptions.

My family member continued with a question I didn't expect. "Craig, tell me more about the Qur'an. You study Islam."

"Well, the Virgin Mary is highly revered in Islam. Jesus Christ, whom Muslims consider to be a prophet, is mentioned more times in the Qur'an than the Prophet Muhammad."

Unconvinced about the facts that I was sharing, he gave me a curious look. "Really? But they are told to kill us. Is Muhammad their prophet? Isn't that his name? I heard bad things about him as well."

Interested in hearing more about how he came to learn about Islam and Prophet Muhammad, I asked him, "Where've you been reading this stuff? I've never heard these things."

"You know, I read the newspapers and I watch the television. You cannot deny that Muslims are crazy, Craig. Come on!"

I felt like telling him right then and there that his blindly believing the media is the problem. Instead of making him feel bad about his ignorance, I asked him a simple question. "Do you know any Muslims?"

"No; they smell."

I didn't retort in kind but asked instead, "Have you ever read the Qur'an?"

"No. Why would I ever read it?"

I sighed.

This interaction between my relative and me highlights the problems with how Islam and Muslims are often incorrectly portrayed and perceived in the United States and elsewhere around the world. One of my aims, in my work as a Catholic scholar, is to prevent people from developing misconceptions of others. Too many Christians and Muslims in the world think negatively of one another. As a researcher, I use knowledge and history in a way that can bridge the ever-increasing gap between followers of Christianity and Islam.

My experiences as a researcher of Islam have without a doubt been challenging. Some of my old friends have grown suspicious of my interest in studying the lives of Muslims. They think that I have become a Muslim and that this alleged conversion is a "weird" and "bad" thing. These old friends simply cannot understand why a non-Muslim would ever study a "foreign" religion. All they see is negative images and depictions of Islam in the media, so it is not surprising to see them think in this negative manner.

My relationships with these old friends have changed significantly over the years. Our discussions hardly ever veer into the realm of my research. When they do, these friends tend to frame Islam and Muslims in light of "terrorism" and "threats to America." It appears they have little interest in promoting peace; instead they see peace as impossible and dialogue between Christians and Muslims as useless.

Some of my old fraternity brothers have insulted me for my inter-faith efforts and political stances on US foreign policy regarding the "Muslim world." Some of these men are immersed in politics and governance in Washington, DC. On one occasion several years ago, I caught up with a brother who asked me point blank, "Craig, what do you really do?"

Surprised, I replied, "What do you mean what do I really do? I'm an aspiring researcher; you know that."

With a peculiar smile, he replied, "Ha, but that's not what others say about you. People have told me that you're working for the Muslim Brotherhood. They say that you're on some FBI list. It's like you're a secret Muslim or something. That true?"

It hurts to feel misunderstood, but it also hurts to feel that I was looked down upon for researching Islam and interacting with Muslims. These stereotypes and misperceptions bother me because I have come to know so many kindred spirits who happen to be Muslim. I often tell people that Islam has enriched my life because I have been able to forge friendships with Muslims who are just, generous, and peace-loving people. By befriending so many Muslims around the world, I have developed the utmost confidence in the idea of Christians and Muslims living side by side in peace and harmony. Christians and Muslims need not be regarded as sworn enemies, but rather allies in the fight against contemporary problems like excess materialism, hatred and bigotry, as well as selfishness and greed.

Since 2008, I have been lucky enough to travel around the United States and Europe to spend time in Muslim homes, schools, and mosques. The fieldwork that I have participated in and carried out has been enriching beyond my wildest imagination. Personally interacting with Muslims in their own environments has allowed me to see them for the loving and beautiful people they really are, rather than having media or some radical Muslim cleric define what Islam is and is not.

My research has also brought me into contact with Muslim scholars, imams, writers, activists, and artists, all of whom have touched my soul because of their humanitarian work and deep religious and moral convictions. Some of my best friends and the people I confide in most follow Islam. I often tell people with whom I interact that "Islam has brought me closer to God." I truly believe that. Islam has strengthened my belief in the Almighty and reminded me of the powerful bonds that Christians and Muslims share.

Over the years, I have often received more love and peaceful communications from Muslims than from my fellow Christians. Consider how self-appointed "experts" on Islam have responded to my interfaith work. On an ongoing basis, Islamophobes who claim they are Christian have called me a "Christian hypocrite" for praising Prophet Muhammad. Believe it or not, fellow Christians have sent me hate mail that calls on me to "defend freedom and defeat jihad." Because of the ability Islamophobes have to brainwash the masses, I've been publicly attacked. One administrator of an anti-Muslim website called me a "pseudo Catholic ****" for speaking positively about Islam. Apparently, love made me not Christian, or not Christian enough. I wonder what Jesus would've felt about that? While these attacks do not surprise me, they are certainly alarming.

I stand for peace and goodwill between Christians and Muslims, whereas Islamophobes fan the flames of hate and push for the extermination of Islam worldwide. The greatest challenge for those seeking knowledge and peace is to win the hearts and minds of people. We need to convince people worldwide that peace is possible. This can only be achieved through education and social interactions between different groups of people.

The attacks that Islamophobes have launched on my research and character have only emboldened me in my efforts to bridge the gap between Christians and Muslims. The persistent efforts of bigots to bring down my research and degrade my thoughts have taught me that the struggle for truth and peace is not for the weary or fainthearted; it takes courage to stand up to hate and discrimination.

Thankfully, I have learned from personal experience that Christians and Muslims can certainly coexist and even love one another. My friendships with Muslims and my relationship with various Islamic communities worldwide is a reflection of this fact. To back down to those who throw insults is to give in to abuse and evil. What the world really needs is more compassion and love!

That is a truth I learned firsthand when I met a hero of 9/11 named David McCourt.

Chapter 12

The Rally for Sanity

"My humanity is bound up in yours, for we can only be human together."

—ARCHBISHOP DESMOND TUTU

Craig is my Christian brother. I see firsthand the hatred and vitriol he gets from extremists claiming they are Christian. In reality, such hatred inspires Craig to work even harder for peace and compassion.

But many have argued to me that all too often, people are simply too "set in their ways" of hate to change. I don't buy it. Giving in to such a thought is to give in to hatred. Hatred can't stop us from trying. If we want to maintain our sanity in society, quitting simply isn't an option. And in that spirit, a remarkable woman named Sharon didn't quit. A woman with a failing heart, raised in a self-described far right intolerant mentality, and who had never met a Muslim—Sharon stepped out of her comfort zone and reached out to me.

I only wish I had the chance to tell her good-bye before it was too late.

I first met Sharon online. And that's when I last met her too.

In October 2010, I and about a half dozen other American Muslims joined Jon Stewart's Rally for Sanity. We custom-made "Muslims for Peace" T-shirts and passed out thousands of "Muslims for Peace" fliers at the rally.

It was an amazing opportunity to talk to countless people we never would have met otherwise. For months after, I received e-mails and messages from those who grabbed a flier and just wanted to say "thank you."

But one particular message, and one particular friendship, rises above them all. Shortly after the rally I received a message from a beautiful soul named Sharon.

"I know my twenty-year-old granddaughter would love to have one of these T-shirts!" she wrote. "What a WONDERFUL thing you're doing at the rally in DC. Wish I could afford one of those shirts! God be with you."

What could I do but reply, "I'll see if I can get you an extra one. Be in touch, OK?"

Almost instantly Sharon replied: "Such kindness...Been reading the posts on FB. Brought me to tears several times. My physical heart is failing me, but my spiritual heart beats strong for the cause of peace. There ARE people in the world who wage peace. Would that there were more of them!"

Comforted by the beautiful message, I replied, "It's people like you who keep our world together. Keep fighting the good fight, Sharon."

"There is no other option, Qasim."

We continued our dialogue. I had no idea who she was or the seriousness of her heart condition. I had no idea of her history.

One day Sharon made a confession. "I used to support Reverend Billy Graham's organization," she wrote. "But when Franklin Graham started his little crusade against Islam, I told them not to mail me any more stuff. I explained why I wanted to be dropped from their mailing list. So, of course, Franklin mailed me the book he wrote about the 'evils' of Islam. What a putz! I put the pages through the shredder."

I smiled a mile wide. "Sharon, thank you so much for standing up for what is right. May God bless you for doing so."

"It's my pleasure. I imagine you've met more than your share of Islamophobes. Y'know, some people have to have an enemy, Qasim, someone they can talk negatively about or look down on. They're some of the most miserable people around."

She had a point. And she continued.

"I grew up around people like that, was schooled in 'judgmentalism' and Biblical legalism. But one day in 1984, during a church service I had a kind of epiphany. Suddenly, the shackles of judgmentalism fell away, and I cried through the rest of the service. It was like someone lifted an unbearable weight off my back."

I reflected on Dr. Martin Luther King Jr.'s wise words: "I have decided to stick with love. Hate is too great a burden to bear."

"Since that day," Sharon then wrote, "I refuse to allow that back into my life. I must admit, I really don't have any close Baptist or Pentecostal friends. It's not because they're not also children of God, but because I don't think the oppression and constriction under which they live is compatible with Christ's message. He did *not* teach hate! He did not teach ostracism."

I was nearly in tears by the time I finished reading. I responded as best as I could. "Indeed, Jesus (peace be upon him) said, 'Judge not, lest ye be judged.' Many people, Muslims and Christians alike, forget that all too much today. I'm glad to hear that by God's grace you've moved well past that. It's inspiring to see."

Over the coming months and years Sharon and I developed a powerful friendship. She was a devout Christian, I was a practicing Muslim— yet we continued to talk to each other like long-lost friends.

One day when we were involved in a deep exchange about our understanding of God, Sharon wrote, "For some time now I've felt that the divisions between us are constructs of society and culture, and that truth lies in the beliefs we share—the supremacy of God, the brotherhood of humanity. Isaiah 1:18 says, 'Come, let us reason together'—in other words, 'let us settle our differences,' which fits with the second commandment to love our neighbor as ourselves. And Matthew 22 tells us that all the law and the prophets hang on those first two commandments: to love God with all our heart, soul, and mind, and again, to love our neighbors as ourselves. I don't know how much clearer it could be, Qasim!"

Sharon took a keen interest in my work, and I in our friendship. Shortly after terrorists brutally murdered three Ahmadi Muslims in broad daylight in Indonesia in 2011 she emailed me, "Qasim, my heart is so heavy over the events of the past few days in Indonesia—the ghastly, vicious mobs that killed Ahmadi Muslims and others who burned Christian churches. I cannot imagine how your faith community just keeps taking it. It is the antithesis of our God of love and peace. Godly people don't do things like this."

We talked about our families, our children, and our spouses. We talked about the journeys we'd been on to get to where we are. She lamented that she spent so many years of her youth in hatred of the other, in contempt of anyone not like her. I tried to comfort her, pointing out that she had now adopted a religion of love—the love that Christ and Muhammad both taught and exemplified.

She watched me closely on social media and whenever I'd receive a death threat she'd jump into action, reporting the person and chewing them out like a grandmother protecting her grandchild. When I launched my first book, *The Wrong Kind of Muslim*, she compassionately contributed five dollars, though I specifically asked her not to, as she lived on a fixed income.

She impacted people in ways she never knew, e-mailing me one day, "Qasim, I didn't realize until just now, when I read that you'd liked one of her posts, that my own daughter is also one of your friends. Kinda brought a tear to the ol' eye, Q. God bless and keep you."

Her watchful eye seemed to catch everything. The last message I received from her was a perfect reflection of the compassion with which she lived. On January 16, 2013, she emailed, "Qasim, I appreciate getting your Twitter updates, but this last time around, it seems some have no qualms about threatening you publicly—like the guy who said, 'I know where you live.' Moving your name up on my prayer list...worried about your safety. God bless and keep you, friend."

I was less upset about the death threat, or that the guy apparently knew where I lived, and more upset that it caused Sharon stress. I replied candidly, "Thank you, Sharon. People can threaten; it is God who protects."

"That's why I'm praying, Q. (cyber hug)."

Sharon died four weeks later due to heart failure. I never got a chance to say good-bye to my friend. I never got a chance to communicate with her one last time.

We had often talked about how her health prevented us from meeting—even though I traveled to California several times while she was alive. She joked, but more hoped in sincerity, that we would meet in the next life.

I'm looking forward to that day, when I get to talk to my friend once more.

Chapter 13

Muslims Want Your Blood

"And whoever saves a life, it is considered as if he saved an entire world."

—HOLY QUR'AN 5:33;
MISHNAH SANHEDRIN 4:5;
YERUSHALMI TALMUD 4:9

Meaningful communication requires action. Sharon took the time to act and reach out to me. When you act, as she did, you send a message more powerful than any mere declaration. When you act to serve all humanity, you create the conditions for true healing to begin. And when you act to save lives, you write the narrative to advance humanity in ways few other actions can.

By the time I arrived in law school in 2009 I felt firmly committed to interfaith relations, and felt the need to go beyond mere dialogue. I wanted to get into the realm of action. The highlight interfaith event of my law school time was a 9/11 blood drive—a drive made possible by a

Christian professor emphatically embracing the opportunity to sponsor the Muslim Law Student Association.

Previously we'd coordinated an interfaith Habitat for Humanity with the Christian Law Fellowship and the Jewish Law Students Association. I was fortunate to have great friends like Amy Weiss and Davy Crumplar, Jewish and Christian, respectively, who shared a similar passion for interfaith work. These were memorable events. Who can argue against Muslims, Christians, and Jews working together to clean and build homes for the less fortunate?

But it was in MLSA's second year of existence, 2011, during the 9/11 Muslims for Life blood drive, that the power of interfaith work and communication to benefit all humanity really hit home. That year the Ahmadiyya Muslim Community USA started the program to honor the victims of 9/11. The idea was that on 9/11, terrorists claiming to act in Islam's name shed the blood of innocent people to take lives. In response, American Muslims would lead an interfaith initiative to shed our own blood to save innocent lives. (As of the writing of this book, the interfaith initiative has collected well over thirty-five-thousand blood donations, saving over a hundred thousand lives).

So here we were at the launch of this inaugural blood drive, in the newly inaugurated Muslim Law Student Association, and I'd just finished donating blood. Fortunately, we already had over a hundred blood donations, saving up to three hundred lives—no small feat. A bit woozy, I stepped out of the Virginia Blood Services bus, looking for the nearest box of juice and bag of cookies. But before I could take a step, an elderly gentleman made eye contact with me from a short distance. He locked in his glare and briskly darted in my direction.

Realizing he was coming toward me, and with conviction, I stayed put with no idea of what to expect. Still glaring, he approached without speaking and grabbed my forearm—tightly. I remember thinking his grip was tighter than I'd expected.

Quietly he leaned in and asked, "Are you the young man responsible for this blood drive?"

I nodded.

"Do you know who I am?"

I shook my head.

"I am a Christian. Do you know how many Christians died on 9/11, young man?"

I didn't speak at first, but just took a deep breath. He continued to hold on to my arm tightly. Finally, I calmly responded, "I'm not sure, sir."

Without missing a beat, he continued. "Do you know how many Muslims died on 9/11?"

Again I remained quiet. I hadn't the slightest idea what his ultimate point was. Perhaps he wanted to express his grievance that more Christians died than Muslims? Perhaps he wanted me to simply acknowledge it? I've learned it is better to remain quiet when I don't know an answer, so I did just that. Meanwhile those standing around us became aware of the tense conversation between us and stopped what they were doing to observe.

"I don't know how many Muslims died that day, sir. I'm sorry."

"Do you know why I'm here today?"

Again, I had no answer and indicated as much. I wondered if this was going to be another one of those burn moments, having stepped way outside that bubble of protection. The tension was becoming tangible.

"I'm here because I heard about your blood drive. I'm here to tell you something, young man. And I hope everyone here knows this."

He spoke with conviction. He had raised his voice some. There was excitement in his words. I braced for impact. I didn't know what was going to emerge from his mouth next but we all stood silent, waiting. He tightened his grip on my arm and pulled it yet closer to him, turning my forearm palm face up, and continued.

He pointed to himself with his free hand, "I am a Christian." Then he pointed and poked at my chest, "You are a Muslim. And I'm here to tell you one thing I know for damn sure. That if I cut your arm, and if you cut my arm, we'll both bleed the same red blood."

I could sense a sigh of relief come over the crowd around me. The gentleman's eyes had welled up with tears.

"Humans died on 9/11. That's all I care about. And when I heard there was an opportunity to save lives in their honor, I knew I had to be here. And when I learned it was a young man of the Islamic faith who was leading the effort, I knew I had to meet him. That is what I came to tell you today, young man."

With that he pulled me in closer and hugged me tight. I hugged back. And for a moment I, and everyone who witnessed the exchange, found ourselves overcome with emotion. Maybe it was in reflection of the lives lost that day, maybe it was in reflection of the countless civilians lost in the wars after that day, or maybe it was just the realization that despite our differences and all the excuses to turn away, he instead took the time to come talk to me.

Because in the end...we all bleed the same blood.

Chapter 14

Earning the Privilege

"When you have children yourself, you begin to understand what you owe your parents."

—JAPANESE PROVERB

I am struck by how life creates opportunities for those who seek them.

I went to law school in part because I wanted to build my platform to advocate for pluralism, tolerance, and compassion. Now, some of you might wonder what any of that has to do with being a lawyer. Fair question, and we'll get to that, I promise. But, for the time being, I'll say that I marveled at the amazing minds and personalities I began to connect with simply by living a life outside my bubble, outside my comfort zone. It was around this time that I truly began to appreciate how much safer life is for humanity when we stay outside our bubbles. When we build those bridges and alliances with people of different races and different faiths, we find natural protections against being burned. We build a stronger shield against intolerance and bigotry.

It's at this point that life comes full circle and you come face to face with a scenario your parents warned you about your whole life—you have children of your own. Suddenly you're put in the driver's seat and a car seat appears where you used to sit. You look around for the adult and come to the horrifying realization that...you're it. You're the adult.

And once you get over the shock, you realize that your children are really the ultimate test of whether what you believe is superficial or real. Promoting interfaith harmony and race relations is great in theory, but useless unless implemented through action in your own life and passed on to the next generation. Parents who keep their children from having to step outside their bubble do their children a massive disservice. Denying children that experience is downright unjust, and it's a violation of the privilege of parenthood. Parenthood is the privilege of teaching your children how to serve a future generation of humanity that you'll never get to benefit from.

Indeed, what is parenthood without the recognition that it is among the world's greatest privileges? And more important, how can we respect our children if we don't first respect the privilege of being a parent? Earning that privilege is among life's most satisfying endeavors—and also one of the most frightening ones.

For my wife, Ayesha, and me, that privilege began one fine day. And about three hours earlier on that otherwise normal day, we had no idea what we were in store for.

Ayesha and I awoke for predawn prayer and prayed together. I then hopped in the shower to get ready for work. I knew Ayesha had a regular checkup in a few hours but had previously asked a friend to take her for me. This week, however, my father was visiting from Toronto and was supposed to be her transportation. I'd been working like a madman, trying to save up for law school. I left every morning around 6:30 a.m. and usually didn't return until late, sometimes after 11:00 p.m. Weekends were no different. Today would be no different.

Up until that morning, everything seemed normal. Routine. Nothing out of the ordinary. I descended the stairs toward the front door to begin my ninety-minute commute from Bolingbrook, Illinois, to downtown Chicago. I grabbed and turned the doorknob, but didn't pull. Something came over me. I can't describe what exactly, but it made me pause. I looked back and saw Ayesha coming down the stairs holding the railing, cautious about each step.

I suddenly blurted out, "I'm going to call my director and tell him I'll be in after lunch. Let's go to the doctor's together today."

She smiled. She didn't say it but I could tell by her expression she was relieved. She was tired of me not being there. I felt guilty for not being there for her, for our soon-to-be newborn. She and I both knew why I was working the extra hours, though neither of us was happy about it. At least not during these precious and precarious weeks.

I sent my director a text and sat down for a normal breakfast for once. Normal felt so abnormal.

"How are you?" I asked.

"Much better." Ayesha smiled back.

A short while later, we were in my Saturn and on our way.

I turned to Ayesha to continue our first normal conversation during daylight hours in what seemed like months. "Do you think he's flipped again?"

Ayesha smiled once more. "I have no idea what to expect from this kid. If he's pulling these stunts now, God only knows what he'll be doing after he's born."

I chuckled. Ayesha was right. Our yet-unnamed son had flipped around at least three times now. Each week brought a new scenario of what doctors expected. The only constant was change.

We pulled up to the doctor's office and parked. I got out quickly and went to help Ayesha out of the car. She reminded me she didn't need my help and pushed my hand away. I insisted and she resisted. I insisted once more and finally she scolded me: "I'm fine!"

I wisely backed off.

We strolled through the parking lot and into the unassuming building. We called the elevator and rode up to the second floor and into the waiting room.

"The doctor will be just a minute; just sign in and have a seat for a few minutes," we were told. The lady at the front desk was someone new. I didn't recall seeing her the last few times I'd accompanied Ayesha, though now that seemed like eons ago. But she seemed nice enough. A few other sets of parents sat waiting for their appointments. A board mounted on the far wall dominated the room. It displayed dozens of pictures of proud parents holding their newborns. Bold and colorful letters spelled out "Our Kids" at the top.

I asked the receptionist, "Excuse me, are these kids that were born...er, birthed...did the doctors who work at this clinic deliver these kids?"

"Yes Mr. Rashid," the receptionist cheerily replied.

"You know, you could've just asked me," Ayesha teased. "I've only been coming here every week for the last—"

"Nine months?"

"No, last four months. It was only once a month before then. You should know that."

"Yeah, I should. Well, will they put our baby's picture up there afterward too?"

"I don't see why not."

"Um, Mrs. Rashid, you're up."

Ayesha and I looked up to see the receptionist beckon us to the door for our appointment. Ayesha replied, "Actually, Rashid isn't my last name; I kept my maiden name."

"Oh, so you two aren't...married?"

"We *are* married; I just kept my maiden name."

"Oh, then well, right this way please." The receptionist seemed uncomfortable at the thought of a married woman not changing her name.

As we walked down the hall and got out of earshot I turned to Ayesha. "Look at you causing trouble."

"What do you mean?"

"This is what you get for not changing your name." I smiled.

"You know what? I was about to, today; that was the plan. But now I think I'll just keep my maiden name forever."

"Ha, well, you've been coming here every week and they don't even know your name...and apparently that means you're not married now."

"Hey, she's new; it's her own fault. Who does she think she is?"

We arrived at the exam room and went inside.

"Apparently she's someone who has never met a woman who kept her maiden name," I said. "By the way, Rashid is a pretty awesome name if you ask me."

"Good, keep it. I'm happy with my father's name." Ayesha wasn't about to let me win this one.

"Fine, be that way," I responded with a tease.

"I will."

"Good."

"I know it's good."

"That's what I just said."

"I heard you."

"I know you did."

"All right then."

"Yes, it is all right."

"You don't have to remind me it's all right."

"I'm not reminding you, just saying I agree that it's all right."

"It sounded like you were reminding me it's all right."

"I said all right to show agreement, not reminding."

"The tone with which you said all right clearly indicated reminding."

"How else was I supposed to say all right? What is an acceptable tone of all right for you?"

113

"I don't like the tone with which you're asking me about proper tone."

"Well I really don't know any other way tone to—"

"Um, am I interrupting something?" Ayesha and I both looked up to see the doctor standing with a confused look on her face. Neither of us was sure how long she'd been standing there.

Ayesha smiled and blushed a bit. "No, Dr. Chen, it's fine. We were just joking and such."

"What's the good word, Dr. Chen? I don't think we've met. How are you?" I reached out to shake her extended hand. She gave me one of those three finger handshakes—the kind you give when you don't really feel like shaking someone's hand. Dr. Chen quickly freed herself from my clutches and turned to Ayesha.

"Well, Mrs. Rashid, let's have a look here. Can you sit up on the patient's table?" I shot Ayesha a quick smirk.

"Oh, I'm fine too, thanks for asking!" I said under my breath so only Ayesha could hear me.

Ayesha tried to hide her laughter while I grinned a dorky smile. She stepped up on the patient's table and nodded to Dr. Chen that she was ready.

"OK, we're just going to start with the usual—let's get a read on your heartbeat." After a few moments she added, "Well, Ayesha, your heart sounds great. Let's see how the little guy is doing." Dr. Chen put on her stethoscope on Ayesha's belly and began listening again.

"What if we find out we're having twins?" I whispered to Ayesha.

"Shh, we're not having twins. We're having a baby."

"But wouldn't twins be cool?"

"Mr. Rashid, can you please be silent for a moment."

Dr. Chen was looking down at her watch. I made a face at her, again so only Ayesha could see me. I got her to giggle. Dr. Chen looked up at her with one of those "I'm trying to work here" looks.

I shook my head. "No sense of humor," I thought to myself.

"Hmm...that's odd." Dr. Chen casually remarked.

I raised an eyebrow. Turns out, those aren't words you want to hear as a soon-to-be parent when the doctor is inspecting your unborn child.

"What's odd?"

"Well, it's probably nothing; let me get another stethoscope; I think this one stopped working." Dr. Chen left the room.

I turned to Ayesha. "What is her deal? Did she skip the class in med school where they teach you how not to be a jerk?"

Dr. Chen returned just as quickly as she'd left and without saying a word, went back to work listening to our baby's heartbeat. Another minute passed. She kept moving the stethoscope, even momentarily checking Ayesha's heartbeat again.

"OK, the stethoscope is working fine; that's good news."

"But?"

"I'm not sure how to say this so I'll just be blunt—please don't panic, but we can't find a heartbeat."

I shot a look of disbelief at Ayesha. Just as quickly my eyes darted back to Dr. Chen. "Pardon, what?"

"I, can't find a heartbeat, but please don't panic."

"Wait...what? What does that mean? Why can't you find a heartbeat?"

I could sense Ayesha's rising stress. I felt it in my gut as well.

"I'm not sure. It's not where it is supposed to be. I think we need to operate now. But really, please, don't panic, this—"

"Please stop saying that. I will panic if I want to. Why do you think it's OK to start a sentence—" I caught myself. "OK, just, why can't you find a heartbeat?" I demanded more than I asked. "Come on, talk to me."

"I don't know..."

115

The baby wasn't due for another ten days. It had already been a difficult pregnancy, but we'd had a great doctor. Things were starting to normalize. We were anticipating what any couple in our stage of life does.

Tragically, however, our regular obstetrician had suffered a stroke just a week prior. While she would make a full recovery, right now in the days before our first child was born we got stuck with a total stranger. We didn't much care for this new doctor. She was cold, abrupt, rushed, and had terrible bedside manner.

"Let me check again."

It seemed like an eternity passed. I bit my lip and took to prayer. Finally the doctor breathed a sigh of relief. "OK, OK, I have something, but...OK, don't panic but—"

"STOP SAYING THAT!" I spoke louder than I'd intended and startled both Ayesha and the doctor.

"Qasim, calm down." Ayesha looked at me, worried but stern.

I took a deep breath. "Look, Doc, I get it, but stop saying that, just...it's not helping. Just tell us what is going on."

She looked annoyed that I was getting annoyed. "I found the heartbeat but it's slightly low..."

Ayesha chimed in. "How low?"

"It's about thirty-five beats per minute."

"What is it supposed to be?" I spoke with urgency, feeling increasingly annoyed with how slowly she fed us information.

"It's supposed to be about 135 beats per minute."

"You call that slightly low!? What planet are you on!?" My annoyance was glaring now. I didn't care any longer. This doctor was just unreal. "Why? What's going on with him?"

She ignored my question. "We need to operate now. I'll meet you at the hospital in twenty minutes."

"Is he going to make it that long?! We didn't even bring anything from home."

"We don't have a choice—no going home. Go to the hospital, now."

In hindsight it sounded stupid that I even worried about going home. But again, this wasn't something we'd prepared for. This wasn't how we'd planned on welcoming our child into the world. Everything was wrong. I thought of my baby cousin who died during delivery a few years prior due to medical malpractice. My mind raced. I had no idea what to expect and suddenly every horrible possibility became a probability bordering on inevitability.

I drove Ayesha to the hospital while pretending everything was OK. Cracking bad joke after bad joke in a sad attempt to keep Ayesha distracted from the perilous situation we were in. Ayesha finally asked me to just shut up and drive, and I complied. I suddenly remembered to call home and tell my family that we were headed to the hospital. But honestly, how do you convey something so worrisome over the phone?

My dad picked up.

"Hey, Dad, I'm taking Ayesha to the hospital now. Baby's coming today. I'll try to swing by to pick you up in a bit."

"What do you mean the baby's coming today? What's wrong? What's happened?"

I swear my dad's a psychic.

"Nothing's wrong. Why would you think something's wrong?"

"Tell me what's going on son. The baby wasn't due until next week."

Ayesha chimed in. "What's he saying?"

"Uh, Dad hold on." I turned to Ayesha. "Nothing; he's just asking if you're OK."

"Ayesha's fine, Dad. Look, I gotta go; see you soon." I hung up before he could answer.

I still have the video of Ayesha and I walking into the hospital room. I'm still cracking terrible jokes and Ayesha is still shaking her head. But she was smiling. I'd gotten her to smile, though I know what her mind was focused on.

Ayesha's doctor had called the hospital and told them to expect us. When the nurse received us the first thing she did was check our baby's heartbeat.

"OK, good news, the heartbeat sounds strong. It's over one hundred beats per minute." Ten minutes later they checked again and thankfully the heartbeat was still strong. Whatever caused the temporary stress had passed...or so we thought.

"Do I have time to go home and get my family?"

"Well, now that the heartbeat is stable, we don't need emergency surgery. We'll likely operate in about four hours. Can you go and get back in that much time?"

I nodded. "Yes, I can be back within an hour."

"OK, let us get your wife fully set up and then you can go ahead."

"Great; sounds like a plan."

They hooked Ayesha to all the medical equipment an expecting mother is typically connected to and left. Ayesha and I sat, breathing a sigh of relief. We could see the monitor show our unborn son's heartbeat consistently around 125 to 135 beats per minute, exactly where it was supposed to be. Suddenly, and what almost seemed like a flicker, I saw it drop to thirty-five beats per minute, then spike back up.

"Ayesha did you see that?"

"What?"

"The heartbeat, did you see it drop?"

By the time Ayesha looked up it had gone back to normal.

"I think we're in the clear now, Qasim. Don't worry."

Still, I kept an eye on the monitor. Another minute passed at a normal rate, and then another. And just as suddenly the heartbeat once more dropped to the low thirties. I expected, hoped, prayed for it to pop back up but much to my horror, it stayed.

I ran out of the hospital room without saying a word to grab the first nurse I saw. It was someone different than the person who'd greeted us. "I need you now, please."

The nurse didn't bother asking why and followed me in. I pointed to the heart monitor and she audibly gasped—again, not the best bedside manner. She ran out and grabbed our assigned nurse, who came into our room in a hurry as the nurse I grabbed briefed her on the update.

Our nurse jumped into action. "I don't know how we missed this or what's going on, but we are on it. Mr. Rashid, please go stand over there." She pointed to an out-of-the-way corner and I obliged without delay. The nurse checked to ensure the machinery was working properly—it was. After a few tense moments, she sighed in relief. "OK, I've got the heartbeat again, and it's normal. We'll need to operate in two hours instead of the original four I told you.

I realized I needed to get my family now. In hindsight, maybe I should have stayed with Ayesha, but in these uncharted waters I had no idea what was right and what was wrong. All I knew is I needed my family there and went for it. After telling Ayesha I'd be right back I was out the door and down the highway, speeding like a maniac. It probably wasn't one of my smartest moves. Home was twenty minutes away; I made it in about fifteen. No sooner did I walk in the house than my cell phone rang. It was Ayesha calling from her hospital room in a panic.

"Qasim, something's happened. They can't find the heartbeat again. They're going to operate now. I need you back here now."

I grabbed my family, and twelve minutes later we were back in the hospital room. Along the way I'd briefed everyone on the situation. Ayesha had already been prepped for surgery and was headed to the operating room. I literally jumped into scrubs in seconds and stumbled in behind her.

Before I knew it I heard a child crying. I was stunned. After what felt like a trip to hell and back, after every horrible scenario had played out in my mind, after all the confusion, uncertainty, and fear—we were privileged with the gift of parenthood.

Hassan cried the most beautiful cry I've ever heard.

"Well, that explains it. The poor little guy couldn't breathe," Dr. Chen spoke out loud as she delivered Hassan. "All that flipping around and the umbilical cord was wrapped around his neck, twice!"

A nurse carried our newborn to the scale to get him weighed, measured, and cleaned up. He continued crying his eyes out. I put my hand on his chest and spoke to him as I had for so many months in the dark hours of the night. In mere moments his loud cry turned to a whimper and soon a calm sigh of comfort.

In some ways this chapter was a spark that started this book. And the spark that started this chapter stems back to the day Hassan was born. Once Mom and baby were secure in their hospital room and the rest of my family had arrived, the family went out to celebrate at a local Chicago establishment, Portillo's. (As an aside, if anyone tells you they're from Chicago but are not aware of Portillo's, they're not to be trusted.)

I drove beaming with pride, like any new father, and turned to my dad and smiled.

"You know, Abbu, I'm really still at a loss of words today. What an insane day."

"Yes, son, but thank God everything turned out OK."

"Yeah, and you know what really excites me? I mean, don't get me wrong, I'm going to savor every moment of Hassan's life. Every second."

"But?"

"But I really can't wait until he's old enough that I can talk to him, hold a conversation with him." I turned to him again. "Abbu, at what age can you really start to have those dialogues where you can reason with kids?"

As soon as I said it I bit my tongue, but my father pounced like a lion on its prey.

He smiled and calmly replied, "Reason with your kids? I'll let you know when it happens, son."

I let out a loud laugh and gave credit where it was due. "Well played, Grandpa, well played."

That conversation from early 2009 stuck with me, embedded like a splinter in my mind. And in the coming months and years as Hassan began to speak, I frantically recorded his words, thoughts, conversations, and dreams. Before I knew it I was holding regular conversations with him. Sometimes about simple things like crayons and sports, and other times about matters so deep they blow my mind.

Ayesha and I have worked to create a home where our kid can always come talk to us. Because the day children stop coming to their parents with their problems is the biggest sign something is severely wrong. That is a sign a parent isn't fulfilling the responsibilities that go with the privilege of parenthood.

One of the most amazing lessons of parenthood I ever received was from my dear friend Nusrat Jehan Chaudhry—who is the author of the next chapter. She's a mother, but not in the way you think. She's lost many children and saved countless more. But however you view her, she gets what it means to embrace the privilege of parenthood.

She understands better than most anyone I know what it means to live outside the bubble.

Chapter 15

A Parent by Any Other Name

by Nusrat Jehan Chaudhry

"Each child comes with the message that God is not yet discouraged of man."

—RABINDRANATH TAGORE

"Happy Mother's Day," blares the announcement over the intercom, delivered promptly at midnight by a festive coworker.

I listen quietly to the not-so-subtle reminder that Mother's Day, the most lucrative of Hallmark holidays, has arrived. Its followed by well wishes to coworkers and mothers present with their infants in the neo-natal intensive care unit (NICU). I whisper to myself, "Every day is Mother's Day in the NICU and in Islam" and carry on with my three-patient-care assignment. I try not to let out the tears that wish to flood from me because I miss not being with my own mother or because I don't get the chance to be one.

"Happy Mother's Day," I cheerfully say, both to every patient's mother in the NICU and to my coworkers. They instinctively reply with the same wish, then catch themselves as they recall I do not have children. I do my best to sidestep the error in their message. Trying to lighten the mood, I turn to the patients' mothers present at midnight and ask if they have plans for the day, yet inside I feel their angst, knowing that their plans had not included being in the NICU for Mother's Day.

I will never forget the first premature infant in my care, Eva.

Born at 26 weeks, Eva suffered from all the maladies a preterm infant her age undergoes. I was new to nursing and to the NICU. I was idealistic and hopeful and made the big mistake of promising her parents that she would survive. No one can predict outcome—no one. It was a rookie mistake, one I won't make again, but one I'd already made. One too late to take back.

"Nusrat, the only reason we are leaving is because you are here to look after Eva," Eva's parents said, adding they needed to get some sleep and heading off to bed.

These were powerful words of trust handed to a new graduate nurse. I felt confident that the night would go well, but Eva had other plans. By 5:00 a.m., Eva started struggling. By 7:00 a.m. we were administering CPR. Her lifeless body rested in my trembling hands. I was terrified.

I looked at the doctor frantically and blurted out, "We are giving epi."

The doctor nodded in agreement.

My already attached a syringe to her IV site and infused the epinephrine. We continued the lifesaving measures and I prayed frantically for God to bring back Eva. I pleaded with God, asking that He let her parents have her. That they trusted me and that I trust Him. And then, suddenly, I experienced for the first time what happens when someone comes back from the dead. Eva's body suddenly came alive while my

124 of

hands were upon her, and I shivered, experiencing the power of God and medicine combined.

From that moment on, I knew to pray for my infants while I was at work. For some, I sought the prayers of others, including the Khalifa, His Holiness Mirza Masroor Ahmad. I once sent a message to Pope John Paul via one of his close aides to pray for a primary care Catholic patient. I have been known to stop priests and nuns on the street to ask them to pray for a Christian baby in need of as many prayers as he or she can get. It's safe to say I believe wholeheartedly that prayer and medicine combined do a great deal of healing and give guidance to those who care for their patients. And it's safe to assume that rarely are parents opposed to NICU nurses who truly give each child their all.

The joy of pregnancy and having a baby rarely includes the plan of being in the NICU. NICU nurses know the agony mothers undergo and know the boundaries to respect as they step into a role usually reserved for mothers. It takes a special mother to endure the experience of the NICU, and in my experience mothers of the NICU are unique ladies. They have to place all their maternal instinct into the hands of a stranger. This is a selfless act, since they are forced to put aside their own intuition to trust the work of a skilled professional.

Anyone who thinks that is an easy task has never fully loved a child. Mothers naturally guard their infants, but every doctor will tell you a NICU nurse are famously known to never mess with a patient. The vigilance of NICU nurses may be the only medical example that comes close to describing motherhood. Mothers trust us and are grateful that their children are safe and loved.

Every year 10 to 15 percent of babies born in the United States come to the NICU for reasons including prematurity, birth defects, breathing and cardiac irregularities, and infections. This percentage amounts to roughly half a million children a year. Since one out of eight babies born in America is premature, our primary patient population are premature infants who have an average stay of one hundred days.

For twenty years now I've watched mothers at the bedsides of their delicate children. I still imagine how hard it must be to watch one's fragile child struggle with health issues and the torment the mothers must feel in not being able to do more for their baby. Early on in my career, I was dubbed the "patron saint of lost causes." I would gravitate toward patients who had limited time on earth. It wasn't intentional, but I felt such empathy for the child that I ultimately found my way to embracing the role of primary care nurse.

As a night shift nurse I find myself clustering my shifts so my average tends to be five twelve-hour night shifts in a row. My record to date is fifteen night shifts in a row. Most of my coworkers are perplexed as to what compels me to do this to myself. But when I tell them I was inspired by the love for a primary patient, they nod with understanding.

I tell them about my fifteen shifts with Zachary and all that happened in those two weeks.

These children belong to their parents, but when they are in the NICU they are with extended family—they are our babies. Zachary and I spent six months together. Some might say he was out of our hands from day one. When that day finally came, the day of his departure from life, I hesitated to leave that morning. He and I shared a fixed gaze upon each other as I walked away. When I came back twelve hours later, the nurses said he never slept during the day and seemed to waiting for someone.

After receiving the report from Shari, the day shift nurse, I went to his side and gently stroked his head and face and told him it was safe to go to sleep. I will never forget his big brown eyes closing. His mother asked to hold him shortly after I got to the unit. His vital signs still remained stable so I felt there was still time. As soon as I lifted him up in my arms I felt his soul leave. I trembled inside as I felt the twenty-one

126

grams of the weight of his soul leave. I hastened to place him in his mother's arms...and he instantly departed. There was no hiding my tears. Yet they were silent tears, since the focus was now on his mother and her comfort.

Vivian, the neonatal nurse practitioner, and I stood by Zachary's mother and held her as she wept. Then she left quickly, leaving me the challenge of beginning his postmortem care. Just the thought of never again seeing his beautiful face and the prospect of preparing him for the morgue gnawed at me like a knife wound. I choked up, telling the transport orderly to please be gentle and careful as I handed Zachary over. I walked the halls, still stunned by his death, unsure what to do. A neonatal nurse practitioner, Tracy, saw me and hugged me.

"He waited for you, Nusrat."

She said this to me knowing that the loss of a child in the NICU resonates beyond the child's immediate family. The child's caretakers feel the burn, the burden, because we give our all in taking care of these babies as if they were our own children. In many ways they are.

Mia, Sara, Natalya, Muhammad, Stephen, Sulaiman, Carl, Vicki...and the list goes on, of those who touched our lives, even if for a few days. The memory of their lives never leaves me, because I am sure they took a piece of my heart with them. Often, parents who lost their infant stay in touch with us. Aside from them, we were the only ones who truly knew their baby. We provide solace for them in knowing their struggle, and we smile with them in remembering the good.

"Why don't you lose hope?" I'm often asked.

"Because I know that life goes on," I reply. "And before I know it, another life is born, for me to have another chance to give my very best. I can't give anything less than that. Our patients become our temporary babies, and they deserve the very best."

Losing children is never easy. Being a parent to so many, and seeing so many close their eyes for the last time, is never easy.

I stay in neonatal nursing because it's the two times I get to feel the hand of God—once when He gives life when a child is born and once when that life returns to Him at death. And sometimes, I get to feel God's hand in between those two occasions. This is the closest I get to be with God and I don't think anything could beat that feeling.

The NICU fulfills me spiritually and fills a void in ways that are hard to explain. My past challenges with fertility and desire to be a mother can at times find me in a difficult place when I'm surrounded by babies. But the NICU lifts me up and inspires me to perhaps a greater purpose. With my primary patients, I have had dreams warning me when my patient is falling ill or dying. I know such a connection can only happen when hearts truly connect. I have seen prayers answered instantly for my patients and have always treated each child as his or her mother's most prized possession—as my most prized child.

Some mothers endure the NICU for a year. Karen was one such mother. Karen lived in another state, yet by day three of James's life she was in a nearby apartment. A stay that was expected to last three months lasted eleven. In that time, I saw the courage of a mother who never lost hope that her son would survive and leave the NICU. James underwent three stomach surgeries, one cardiac surgery, one brain surgery, and a liver transplant, among other ordeals. At times when I yielded to doubt, Karen reaffirmed that our prayers and effort would be met with success. That James would survive. And together we prayed.

As an Ahmadi Muslim, I would recite prayers from the Holy Qur'an for James as well as those recited by Prophet Muhammad and Mirza Ghulam Ahmad, peace be upon them both. When I couldn't be at work, Karen would recite these prayers for him on my behalf, despite being Catholic. And when James chose to smile for no one else but me, Karen graciously said, "I am just glad he is smiling for someone." Karen's trust and willingness to let me love her son while she wasn't able to be present affirmed that each child is more than just a patient to the heart of a NICU nurse.

Karen is not alone in her courage. It seems to be part of the composition of a NICU mother. I have seen Mary take two subway trains and a bus in the middle of the cold winter night to see her infant and bring us homemade cupcakes on Christmas. I have seen Linda smile at me in the midst of tears as I spoke at her daughter's funeral. I have seen Barbara bravely take on the challenge of a child with special needs. NICU mothers are amazing, to say the least, and inspire me with their trust each time they selflessly say, "I can sleep tonight knowing you are there."

In my twenty years in this work, I have found that I can still make a difference in the life of a child not necessarily by being their mother, but by being their guardian and advocate during their time in the NICU. I've learned that the privilege of parenting isn't just biological—it is also emotional and spiritual.

I recall when my dear friend Suriyya lost her firstborn child. Salahuddin was just three days old. My friend had had her own battles with fertility and finally came close to motherhood, only to have it taken away from her.

As she agonized in her grief, I conveyed how much her son's life mattered to everyone he met. And that while he was away from her during his care in the NICU, he was well loved and everyone did all they could for him. In this exchange she succumbed to tears, yet later told me she found comfort in my experience, words, and faith. I didn't need to be a mother to know how to comfort her. I only needed to take the time to talk to her.

Mother's Day will always tug at my heart. Despite my sister-in-law, cousins, and close friends sharing their children with me, I still feel the void. My friend Lisa insists that my soul was meant to belong to the universe and shared with more than just the children I still wonder about not having had. My friend Marilyn and my Aunt Fatima always send me a card on Mother's Day to remind me that what I do is a different kind of parenting.

And while their kindness is very comforting, it was only this year that I finally realized something critical. I realized what Mother's Day could mean to me when my valued NICU friend Gayle reached out to me and gave me some words filled with typical Gayle wisdom.

"Nusrat, you help so many mothers appreciate this day, with all the babies you helped all these years...they may not be mothers if it wasn't for you."

I would like to think that in some small way this is true. This is my form of the privilege of being a parent, and I intend to continue embracing it with every person who talks to me.

And when we do talk, please feel free to wish me a Happy Mother's Day.

Chapter 16

The Uphill Battle

"I say to you quite frankly that the time for racial discrimination is over."

—PRESIDENT JIMMY CARTER

I marvel at Nusrat's work.

Her actions as a parent to hundreds, if not thousands, of infants is awe inspiring and humbling. It transcends a biological connection and ventures into an emotional and spiritual bond. Parenthood isn't exclusively relegated to having children of your own—it is a privilege to serve the next generation of youth.

And indeed it is critical to understand that such actions become particularly difficult when the deck is stacked against you and you find yourself constantly trudging uphill. How do you find the strength, patience, and courage to march forward when someone up top keeps throwing down boulders? How do you manage the uphill battle?

I recall the day we arrived in Richmond, Virginia, in the summer of 2009. Less than a mile from our new apartment, we stopped at a traffic light.

Astonished, Ayesha said, "Qasim, will you look at that."

I looked up and saw probably one of the most offensive bumper stickers I've ever seen. It showed a caricature of President Obama and said, "I'll keep the slavery, and you keep the CHANGE," with "change" lettered to resemble Obama's campaign slogans.

Unfortunately, this wasn't our first such experience in Richmond, nor in the United States in general. There was the time at LAX when TSA refused to let Ayesha sit or hand me our then-infant child for more than twenty minutes while they did a background check on her.

When I asked what they were so concerned about, the TSA rep callously said, "That thing on her head is making me nervous."

"You mean the scarf?"

"Whatever you call it, it's making me nervous."

Responding to such behavior is difficult. If you respond in anger you validate their preconceived notion that you're a threat. If you sit silent and do nothing you empower them to continue mistreating people through profiling based on prejudice and stereotypes. Meanwhile, your children watch you and learn from you. Do you give in to unjust authority and teach them to do so as well? Or do you voice your displeasure and let them see you do so? What type of ramifications will that have for my children in fifteen years when a police officer pulls them over in an act of racial profiling? These are material questions I, and other parents of color, are forced to reflect upon.

There was the visit Ayesha and I made to the DMV to renew our driver's licenses when we moved to Virginia. I had my picture taken; Ayesha followed behind.

"Ma'am you'll need to remove that rag from your head."

"Excuse me, what?" Ayesha said. My smile vanished and I looked right at the woman speaking to my wife, in disbelief.

"That rag thing on your head, you'll have to remove it for the picture."

Ayesha spoke up before I could. "Do you mean this scarf that I wear?"

"Yes, you'll have to remove it."

"Why?"

"Because unless it is for religious reasons, you have to remove all personal fashion items."

"But this is for religious reasons."

"What religion is that?"

"I'm a Muslim?"

The DMV attendant erupted. "A Mozlom? You ain't no Mozlom. Mozloms wear different and lavish colors. Mozloms are Ayrab. You're not Ayrab. No ma'am, please remove that thing so we can take this picture."

My jaw dropped. I was dumbfounded. Ayesha, however, wasn't silenced so easily.

"Do you have any idea what you're saying? Do you have the slightest idea of what you're even talking about? Do you know how ignorant and offensive you sound right now? I am a Muslim. This scarf is my hijab; it is not a rag. Do I have to take some religious test to prove it to you?"

"Ma'am, are you going to remove it or not."

"What does the law say?"

"The law says if it's religious you can keep it on."

"It's religious; I'm keeping it on. And frankly, had you just asked nicely I would've happily removed it for the picture, but now that I know I can keep it on for religious reasons, I will."

The woman finally took Ayesha's picture—with her scarf on. I shook my head as we walked away. "It's sad that this woman is a microcosm of what the world is right now."

Ayesha nodded. "Yes, it is a microcosm. That's exactly what it is."

By her tone I could tell she was trying to be lighthearted. "Are, are you mocking me?"

She smiled. "Not at all. I agree with your statement of micro-cosmness."

"You don't even know what 'microcosm' means, do you?"

"Of course I do!"

"Then tell me, please tell me what 'microcosm' means."

Ayesha pointed to Hassan who scampered ahead of us. "There, a mi-croqasim."

I was stunned at the sheer brilliance of it and laughed out loud—a much-needed laugh. "Well played, Ayesha, well played."

Ayesha and I have our postgraduate educations. We participate in the election process. We volunteer for local charities. We do everything any "real" American is "supposed" to do. And we do so not because we want to "look American" but because we believe it is the right thing to improve our surroundings and ourselves. But ignorance rears up all too often.

Personal experiences like these remind me that racism and ethnocen-trism are substantive problems in our country. It reminds me of the world I'm raising my children in, where Ayesha is looked at strangely for choosing to dress like Mary, Mother of Jesus. It reminds me just how crucial it is we maintain dialogue and open communication—which is particularly difficult when you see fellow Americans promoting slavery in 2009 or telling your wife she wears a rag on her head.

But in the end, the effort is what makes it worthwhile. Scottish au-thor Samuel Smiles writes, "The battle of life is, in most cases, fought uphill; and to win it without a struggle were perhaps to win it without honor. If there were no difficulties there would be no success; if there were nothing to struggle for, there would be nothing to be achieved."

All this weighed on my mind in a new light when I became a parent. What would I do when it came time to push my young son out of his bubble?

Chapter 17

Actions, Not Words

"Act that your principle of action might safely be made a law for the whole world."

—IMMANUEL KANT

As Ayesha and I sat across the table from a teacher at a Christian preschool, the elephant in the room was obvious.

"So here are our tuition rates for the year. You can pay up front or each month, whichever is easier."

"Thank you." I took the sheet of paper from her and looked over it with my wife.

"Now, as you probably noticed, this is a Christian preschool."

"Yep," I replied without looking up.

"And we teach a Christian curriculum as well."

"Uh huh." I was still studying the tuition chart to ensure I understood it.

"And, um, well, we..." She trailed off.

I looked up and smiled. "You want to know if we're Christian but you don't want to sound impolite."

She sighed in relief that I'd finally addressed the obvious. "You have nothing to be shy about," I said. "We're Muslim, and yes, we understand this is a Christian preschool. That's actually part of the reason we're putting him here. It's never too soon for him to learn about the diversity that is humanity."

"Are, are you sure? Because every single student in here aside from your son is Christian. And we teach Christian theology in class."

My wife spoke up. "Yes, we're sure. Do you have a schedule of classes and a curriculum?"

Somewhat surprised, she jumped into action. "Sure, here, here." She handed us the relevant materials and the conversation continued with much less tension than before. "Aren't you concerned he might be confused about what to believe?"

I smiled again. "No, we're not. He'll figure out what to believe."

Two weeks later Hassan attended as the only Muslim at a private Christian preschool, a southern Baptist school at that. I admit, at first it was a bit nerve-racking. But when I reflected that the alternative was to restrict Hassan's growth as a person, the choice became much clearer. That alternative was simply unacceptable. The experience paid immense dividends to Hassan in helping him understand that different people live with different worldviews, the need to respect those worldviews, and how to work together despite those different views.

For example, when Hassan came home one afternoon singing, "Jesus is light, Jesus is love," we smiled. I couldn't help but reflect that as a child I memorized nearly every Christmas carol imaginable. Far from confusing me, it helped strengthen my understanding of religion and culture and my sense of the wider world.

In one of my fondly recalled early "father-son conversations" with Hassan, he once pointed to a book and said:

"Look dad, a Qur'an."

I replied, "No Hassan, that's a Bible."

"Oh; what's it say?"

I replied the only way I could. "It says, 'God is love.'"

"Oh, OK, I love you too then."

That was the easy part.

The greater trial at this young age wasn't his, but ours. My wife and I were the only Muslim parents the teachers at our son's school knew on a personal level. And in that interaction we discovered just how much more interaction is sorely needed. It became painfully obvious one late spring afternoon in Richmond when the weather was finally getting warm.

Ayesha arrived a few minutes early to pick up Hassan from school. One of Hassan's teachers greeted her.

"Hi, Ayesha. How are you doing this beautiful day?"

"I'm fine; how are you?"

"I'm great. You must be so hot in that thing!"

"Sorry, come again?"

"That thing you're wearing, on your head, you must be so hot!"

"Oh, you mean my scarf. Well, no, actually I'm quite comfortable."

"Oh I don't know about that. It's almost eighty degrees. You must be boiling."

"I'm quite fine."

"Well, if you say so."

Ayesha didn't respond. It would not be fair to call the woman Islamophobic, bigoted, or malicious. You could call her ignorant, but even in her ignorance there was little to point to as arrogant. Simply put, this woman's ignorance had the best of her. Sadly, this exact scenario played out multiple times with Ayesha at our son's preschool. This woman, and others, could not accept that—despite Ayesha's insistence—Ayesha dresses modestly of her own volition.

Thus, in exposing our son to a different worldview, we exposed the different worldview to ourselves. The ensuing interaction could either have been a clash or a compromise in egos until we understood each other. In the grand scheme, no one can dictate to you how much you should, or should not, be willing to withstand. I've learned through experience, however, that relationships are not built overnight, nor are they built without one having to endure some potholes along the way. But to quote Rumi: "If you are irritated by every rub, how will you be polished?"

This woman's attitude was an example of one such pothole, one such rub. In the end Ayesha was able to explain the context and history of why Muslim women dress the way they do. And while the explanation made sense to the woman, it ultimately registered because of the practical example the woman had in front of her—i.e., Ayesha.

Indeed, meaningful conversations aren't just about words, they're about actions.

Earlier I mentioned that looking into America's history, I learned some painful realities no one ever talked to me about. Painful realities that changed my future and should change your future, too. Here's why.

Chapter 18

A Racial History We Need to Talk About

"We need to recognize that the situation in Ferguson speaks to broader challenges that we still face as a nation. The fact is, in too many parts of this country, a deep distrust exists between law enforcement and communities of color. Some of this is the result of the legacy of racial discrimination in this country."

—PRESIDENT BARACK H. OBAMA

I'd heard about white people before...though I'd never met one in real life.

I wondered what they were like, and whether they would like me. I heard they spoke this strange language called English and lived thousands of miles away...far too far to walk or take a train ride to. I heard that they didn't say "Peace be upon you" when they met one another. Instead, they said "Hi" or "Hello" or "How do you do?"

I remember thinking it was kind of a strange sound. Hi. Hi. Hhhi. I guess if you say any word enough times it loses all meaning. I was nearly five years old the first time I ever saw a white person up close. And this might sound strange for someone white or born and raised in America. But that was my reality. My family and I had just migrated from Pakistan to the United States. There aren't too many white folks in Pakistan.

But interestingly, even as a child I began to notice how certain people of certain races would "stick together" to the exclusion of others. And the older I got the more obvious it became. Thirty years ago there weren't too many Pakistani kids in my schools—first in Washington, DC, then in Chicago. I wasn't sure how I fit in. I was neither white nor black. And while many mistook me for Latino, I knew I wasn't Latino either. After all, I didn't speak Spanish like my one Latino friend, Alex, who was Puerto Rican.

Where did I fit in? Or did I?

Maybe I was destined to stay segregated—stuck between different cultures in a purgatory of sorts. In my early teen years I returned to Pakistan to visit family. I was shocked and embarrassed that—wait for it—all Pakistanis looked alike to me. I'd become so accustomed to not being around very many Pakistani kids my age that I literally had difficulty telling Pakistani kids my age apart.

Was I suddenly a self-hating Pakistani? Was I exhibiting a strange form of racism against my own race? Few things about life make immediate sense when you're a teen, and this episode only added to my confusion. It was around this time that I began to realize on personal levels how critical race relations actually are. In some ways it was ironic. Here I was returning to my country of birth where just about every person you see is Pakistani—and that homogeneity helped me recognize the need for and appreciation of diversity.

But when I returned to the United States several months later I once again realized I didn't quite fit into any neat and tidy demographic. On standardized tests they'd ask if I was "Black, White, Latino, Native American, or Pacific Islander." South Asian was never an option. I figured Pakistan was closest to the Pacific islands—even if that didn't quite make geographic sense—so I went through school filling in the little bubble that said I was a Pacific Islander. (Somewhere, an actuary's head just exploded.)

I graduated from high school, went to college and law school, and studied the civil rights movement. I reflected that after my kindergarten teacher, Ms. Wood, the next time I'd had a black teacher was in law school. Now, don't get me wrong, I've been blessed with some of the greatest teachers imaginable—but I found that reality odd, to say the least. As I studied Thurgood Marshall and Oliver W. Hill, my understanding of race in America shifted dramatically. I began to realize that America is not the melting pot of mixed races we were taught in elementary school.

I began to realize the horrible fact that there's no such thing as a "postracial America," at least not yet. And it bothered me immensely that I came to this realization so late. I felt lied to by our education system. I began to see racism manifest itself in numerous manners—sometimes openly, sometimes secretly, but always devastatingly and always to a far greater degree than I'd understood as a child.

We are simply not having the dialogue on race we need to. We have, to quote Robert Frost, miles to go before we sleep.

America today presents an increasingly racially polarized and segregated society. A May 15, 2014, *Washington Post* article reported, "That true school integration has not yet come to pass even sixty years later speaks to a complicated reality that has evolved far beyond the reach of traditional education policies: It's that much harder to integrate classrooms when the communities where children live are still so segregated."[5]

While segregation rates have seen some decline since the civil rights movement, the facts show we have light-years yet to go. A 2013 study reports:

> "Today, many black children still attend schools in racially and economically isolated neighborhoods, while their families still reside in lonely islands of poverty: 39 percent of black children are from families with incomes below the poverty line, compared with 12 percent of white children; 28 percent of black children live in high-poverty neighborhoods, compared with 4 percent of white children."[6]

And our religious institutions aren't much better. In fact, their apathetic approach is arguably making things worse. Many recall a painful observation by Dr. Martin Luther King Jr.: "It is appalling that the most segregated hour of Christian America is eleven o'clock on Sunday morning." In writing this book I met with black pastors who lead white congregations. On the surface this situation seems a step forward, and perhaps it is. But what does it mean when—to this day in 2015—such black pas-

---

[5] Badger, Emily, Housing segregation is holding back the promise of Brown v. Board of Education, available at:

http://www.washingtonpost.com/blogs/wonkblog/wp/2014/05/15/housing-segregation-is-holding-back-the-promise-of-brown-v-board-of-education/ (last visited January 1, 2015).

[6] Rothstein, Richard, Education and the Unfinished March, available at http://www.epi.org/publication/unfinished-march-public-school-segregation/ (last visited January 1, 2015).

tors face racism from their own white congregations? And we've already discussed the racism among Muslims in various Muslim congregations.

Consider Michael Emerson, a Rice University sociologist who tackles issue of racial segregation in churches in detail in his Multiracial Congregations Project.[7] Emerson defines a "multiracial congregation" as one where no one racial group is more than 80 percent of the congregation.[8] According to this measuring stick, "only 8 percent of all Christian congregations in the US are racially mixed to a significant degree: 2 to 3 percent of mainline Protestant congregations, 8 percent of other Protestant congregations, and 20 percent of Catholic parishes."[9]

So why does a Muslim care about the diversity—or lack thereof—of Christian congregations in America? Well, for two significant reasons.

First, I am fortunate enough to see firsthand how much more benefit to humanity a religious community becomes when it meaningfully transcends racial divisions with meaningful communication. I want to see that same reality of interracial harmony in American churches the way I've seen it and regularly see it in American mosques. As a Muslim I've enjoyed a racially and culturally diverse religious environment.

Muhaimin, whom I mentioned earlier, is a Muslim who comes from a multiracial background and has Muslim and Christian family. His ability to bring together people of different races and religions catapulted his effectiveness and helped people appreciate each other's culture, without diluting that culture. While most mosques I attend include Pakistanis, Indians, and Bengalis as more than half the congregation, a significant number of congregants are also black American, white, Latino, Indone-

---

[7] http://hirr.hartsem.edu/org/faith_congregations_research_multiracl.html

[8] http://www.phil.vt.edu/JKlagge/ConductorChurch.htm

[9] ibid.

sian, Eastern European, Arab, Ghanaian, Nigerian, and the list continues.

But while I've enjoyed a racially and culturally diverse religious environment, I've also seen the exact opposite in mosques. Mosques aren't immune from race issues. I've visited mosques where black Muslims profess they don't feel comfortable, or downright feel ignored and discriminated against. I've visited mosques where white Muslims profess they feel isolated. Ditto for Latino Muslims.

These are significant issues we cannot ignore, yet all too often we pretend they do not exist. Sometimes we disregard them due to fear of conflict. Other times, we're driven by the ignorant hope that maybe the problem will just go away on its own. Such thinking is not only foolish, but it also misses the dramatic benefit to humanity when we work together to overcome such serious issues.

Which brings me to the second reason I care that churches in America integrate: historically, they have played a significant role in breaking down racial barriers. Quakers, Catholics, Methodists, and Protestants, among others, have all worked to improve race relations. America is not a "Christian nation" from a Constitutional standpoint, but the vast majority of Americans—over 70 percent—identify as Christian. It is unrealistic to expect to resolve our race issues in America without the church taking a major or substantive lead. Indeed, despite all the means of communication in existence today, racial segregation plagues our religious organizations, and churches must take a hammer to these walls of division.

We've got an immense amount of work to do. For several years in Richmond I represented immigrant clients pro bono. A few years ago a client asked shyly, "Why do white people and black people in this country hate each other so much?"

I didn't know what to say. My client had emigrated from a war-torn nation that was drowning in racial division. Yet she was shocked and confused by the racial hatred in America, "land of equality."

Adding to the aggravation is how minorities are ignored in the public sphere. Roughly 97 percent of characters in children's books are white. Roughly 88 percent of the books the *New York Times* reviewed last year were written by white authors. We can't have a conversation about race if the racial demographic necessary to have a productive conversation is ignored. Thus, it is no accident that over 75 percent of the contributing authors to this book are women and members of racial minorities. We cannot improve race relations and address the struggles of minorities unless we listen to and learn about those struggles from minorities themselves.

The Charleston terrorist attack and the half-dozen black churches burned down in the weeks afterward are not mere accidents. Painful tragedies like the violent and unjust murders of Trayvon Martin, Tanisha Anderson, Sandra Bland, Eric Garner, Yvette Smith, Laquan McDonald, Mike Brown, Rekia Boyd, Tamir Rice, Kathryn Johnston, and Freddy Gray provide but a snapshot of the violence perpetrated against racial minorities in America—particularly African Americans. While I won't endorse riots, I will condemn the refusal to recognize the root cause of these riots. The reality is that the unrest in Ferguson and Baltimore are not instigations, but reactions. They are reactions to generations upon generations of unjust laws, discriminatory police, and social and economic deprivation. As Malcolm X aptly explained, "The American Negro never can be blamed for his racial animosities—he is only reacting to four hundred years of the conscious racism of the American whites."

The riots in Ferguson and Baltimore should not have been the first time people realized something might be severely wrong racially with our society. The epidemic murder of people of color by police should not be the first time we sense there might be a systemic miscarriage of justice in our systems. The incomprehensible economic disparities stacked against people of color in this country should not be the first clue that poverty is not a life choice but a life sentence.

Our country is better than this. Our humanity is better than this. This is a difficult conversation to have because emotions run high. No one wants to be labeled a racist. And it isn't necessarily outright racism that's the issue. It is the seeds of prejudice that creep in. It is the reality of things like white privilege, subconscious bias, and micro- aggression. If this is the first time you're hearing these terms, then you'll benefit most from this dialogue. Yes, this conversation is difficult, but far more difficult is the status quo for tens of millions of citizens living in America. That status quo cannot remain.

Step out of your bubble.

Bishop Desmond Tutu has remarked, "When the missionaries came to Africa they had the Bible and we had the land. They said, 'Let us pray.' We closed our eyes. When we opened them we had the Bible and they had the land." Racism in America today is the result of more than five hundred years of oppression and injustice. Nothing can undo that history, and no magic switch exists to instantly purge racism.

The real problem, however, isn't that we cannot undo the past; it's that we're not doing enough to change the future. We cannot be content in being "not racist." We must be antiracist—we must actively work against elements in society that perpetuate racism.

Those who've experienced a phenomenon called micro-aggression understand how common, and destructive, it actually is. Micro-aggression is unintended discrimination, which stems from a fundamentally wrong understanding of another race or culture. Again, it doesn't mean the person engaging in such behavior is racist. It means he or she is perpetuating racism and missing an opportunity to stand as antiracist.

For example, media interviewers generally don't ask white people if they condemn the violent riot that erupted after Vancouver's hockey team lost in 2011, or the violent riot after the San Francisco Giants won the 2012 World Series, or the violent New Hampshire pumpkin festival riot in 2014, or whether they condemn the violent riot in Denver after the Broncos lost the Super Bowl in 2014. No one questions whether such riots are an example of some inherently violent white culture. Exemption from such questions is an example of white privilege. In fact, media often refuses to label white riots as "riots," often defaulting to phrases like "taking to the streets" or "unrest." This word choice further ignores that the trigger for such violent riots can be flimsy indeed—sports games and pumpkin festivals.

But closely observe most every newscast that followed the Ferguson and Baltimore riots, and you'll see media talking heads repeatedly demand that black activists condemn the violence in those riots. Black rioters are called thugs, animals, and barbaric. Never mind that these riots are reactions to generations of social, economic, educational, and political injustices. Rather, all people of color are lumped into one monolithic category, and until and unless every black leader first condemns the violence without exception, nothing else they say is considered. As activist DeRay Mckesson put it, the Baltimore riots—sparked by the brutal police murder of Freddy Gray—should have shown the world that broken spines are more important than broken windows. We can replace broken windows. We cannot replace broken spines. And while he repeatedly and clearly stated that he does not condone the violence, he's still been maligned as a black activist who somehow condones violence.

Unfortunately, too little has changed to date. Pew surveys, government reports, arrest and charge rates all demonstrate that racism is not some peripheral issue today. It is a systemically ingrained and persisting cancer. As of 2015 we are not in a postracial anything, and we need to stop living under this misapprehension altogether. Rather than arrogantly believing we are above racism, we must act with urgency to purge this cancer from our midst.

The tactic for expunging this cancer is tried-and-true—learn from one another, have compassion toward one another, and talk to one another.

Don't wait for an opportunity to reach out to someone different; create the opportunity. Find a community service project to participate in and reach out to a person of a different race to work with you. Get out of your comfort zones and talk to those unlike you. Speak to your pastor, your imam, or your community leader. Indeed, one excellent strategy for connecting with people of different racial backgrounds is to connect with people of different faith backgrounds. Collectively, Muslims, Christians, Hindus, Buddhists, and those of no faith represent practically every racial demographic out there.

I now want to mesh our conversation about parenting from earlier with a conversation about racism. Lisa Thweatt—author of the next chapter—relates a reality millions of parents of color live through every day. Her story exemplifies the need to remain united against all forms of racism. It describes what it is like to live in a society that is slanted against people of color, deliberately or otherwise, and how to overcome those odds. It shows that teachers sometimes demonstrate preference for white students over students of color. And that this does not necessarily mean that such teachers are racist; rather, such behavior is often better understood as subconscious bias or the automatic bias some exhibit toward a long-stigmatized minority group.

Ample evidence demonstrates that teachers treat children of color differently than how they treat white children. A recent analysis found that "educators believed African American students were 47 percent less likely to graduate from college than their white peers." Hispanic students didn't fare much better: Teachers thought they were 42 percent less likely to earn a college diploma than their white classmates."[10] To undo this subconscious bias requires self-reflection and self-evaluation. It requires recognition that human beings have biases, and sometimes those biases are racial in nature. The refusal to recognize subconscious bias is a driving force behind why racism continues to thrive.

What is it like to raise children of color in an educational system that's all too often working against them? How do you help others recognize the reality of this struggle, and how do you overcome this struggle for the sake of your children?

Lisa Thweatt performs this task masterfully.

---

[10] http://www.takepart.com/article/2014/10/10/americas-teachers-still-dont-think-black-latino-kids-are-smart (last visited on July 2, 2015).

Chapter 19

Grades of Struggle

by Lisa Thweatt

"Racism is still with us. But it is up to us to prepare our children for what they have to meet, and, hopefully, we shall overcome."

—ROSA PARKS

No matter how much work I've put into it, no matter how much I've learned, no matter how impressed others are, nothing makes me more proud, more fulfilled, and more grateful than having my two healthy boys.

Sure, raising them can be stressful, worrisome, and frustrating. However, when I look into their eyes, their souls, and just watch them—especially when they don't know I'm observing them—I feel an overwhelming sense of joy, love, peace, satisfaction, and gratefulness.

Every parent feels this way about his or her children. Their laughter is transcendent music. Their well-being comes before yours. If they have what they need and are able to execute whatever it is that God has planned for them, only then do you feel complete. But sometimes I wonder if the struggle will ever stop. No, not the struggle of being a mom to two boys, but the struggle of being a black mom to two black boys in a world where racism still runs rampant. My journey as a mother of two boys, now fifteen and eleven, has brought with it ongoing grades of struggle. It has been a testament of determination to talk to and work with those who may not have the best interest at heart for my kids. I almost feel compelled to use the word "fight" instead of "work," only because of how difficult the struggle has been.

I know my husband, Al, and I aren't the first black parents to wake up to the reality that our children will face racism in their lives or in their schools. I also know we're not the last parents to wake up to that realization. I share my story with you if you're a family of color, to help you sidestep the potholes we've stumbled through. I share my story with you if you're not a family of color, so you can be an ally to those discriminated against on account of the color of their skin.

The Struggle Begins

So often we expect racism to raise its ugly head and declare, "Here I am and I'm comin' for you!" It doesn't work that way. I experienced this firsthand when my older son Albert was in elementary school. In speaking with his teachers I found that they set the bar low for him—painfully low. They informed me he was only capable of "average" results and that I was only a pest of a mother with "firstborn" syndrome.

I almost fell for it, but as I see Albert take honors classes in high school, I'm grateful I pushed forward. That struggle in first grade was just the beginning.

If you're a parent you well know the anxiety, angst, and bitterness when someone is being unfair to your children. Albert was in the second grade when I first noticed the disparity was more than just an anomaly with his previous teachers. One afternoon I happened to walk toward Albert's classroom before class ended. As I was about to enter I saw his teacher standing in front of the entire class, yelling at the top of her lungs at Albert. Albert stood silent, stoic, not responding, but clearly hurt.

I was stunned and frightened. I thought about stepping in to stop her, but to my immense regret, I walked away. I rationalized it was probably better to not cause a fuss. I didn't want Albert singled out even more, and besides, the teacher probably knew best, right?

I was wrong.

At the end of that school year that very same teacher's husband was in the news. He had spewed repeated racist remarks during meetings with people of color and as a result was facing demands to resign his position. At first, I remember, I'd felt so vindicated because I knew what I saw just wasn't right. When Albert was yelled at I'd talked to my husband about it. And while at first he thought I was overreacting, he now understood where I was coming from. But as I reflected, I realized what I'd done. I realized I'd let my son stay in a racially discriminatory environment absolutely destructive to his growth. When the news came out about the racist remarks from the husband of Albert's teacher, I called my husband in tears—cursing myself for letting my son suffer when I'd had the power to prevent it.

This struggle continued in the following years. The problem then was not necessarily outright racism, but subtle biases in one direction or another. Nothing, however, could have prepared me for what Albert's fifth grade teacher put him—and all the children in his class—through.

In fifth grade Albert was the only black student in his class, once again. In fact, he was the only child of color. As I reflect today on news stories about racist fraternities singing songs about "hanging niggers from trees" and schoolkids' pranks like hanging nooses in public places,

I'm not surprised that such things still happen. So picture your child as the only child of color in a nearly all-white school, and the following is the lesson plan for the day.

Albert's teacher had the class read the lyrics to "Strange Fruit," a song from the 1930s inspired by the lynching of two black men. Now, some might argue that since the song was antilynching, that makes it OK. Imagine your ten-year-old child of color is exposed to the fact that his forefathers were lynched for sport and from hate. And imagine you have no idea this is the burden suddenly thrust upon him.

If you don't know the lyrics to "Strange Fruit," here they are:

> Southern trees bear strange fruit.
> Blood on the leaves, and blood at the roots.
> Black bodies swinging in the southern breeze.
> Strange fruit hangin' from the poplar trees.
> Pastoral scene of the gallant South.
> The bulgin' eyes and the twisted mouth.
> Scent of magnolias clean and fresh.
> Then the sudden smell of burnin' flesh.
> Here is a fruit for the crows to pluck.
> For the rain to gather, for the wind to suck.
> For the sun to rot, for the leaves to drop.
> Here is a strange and bitter crop.

Once again I was left confused and angry. This time I didn't wait, didn't rationalize that the teacher "knew best." We met with the principal and an administrative representative along with another black family from the teacher's other class.

I'll never forget the look at the other mom's face. She had tears in her eyes. She was questioning the teacher and asking why he would do such a thing. My husband, Al, stated what we all were thinking. "What kind of impact is this going to have on my son? How are the white students going to take this?

154

Neither the school nor the teacher had any good answers or any answers at all. At the end of the year, that teacher no longer worked at that school. We never requested that he be terminated, but I wasn't sorry to see him go either.

The struggle continued when Albert was in the seventh grade. One afternoon his school left me a message at work requesting that I immediately call back. I did as requested, and in fact I called several times, worried something had gone terribly wrong. Each time, however, I was not put through to speak with the assistant principal. Each time I called, I was told she was unavailable. And worse yet, no one was willing to give me any information. I had no idea what was going on. I drove home, nearly frantic. Thankfully, there my son Albert awaited me. Breathing a sigh of relief that he was safe, I walked right up to him to find out what had happened.

"What's wrong, Albert? Why did I get a call from your school today?"

Albert looked confused and somewhat ashamed. "I got suspended, Mom."

"You got suspended!? Why? What happened?"

"Mom, they said I was stealing?"

"Why did they say you were stealing? Did you steal?"

"No, Mom, I swear I didn't steal anything. I don't even understand what I did wrong."

My head was spinning. I had no idea how to process the information. I know my children well enough to know when they fib—and Albert was telling the truth. By now I had learned the value of an immediate response. So, I pulled Albert into the car and we drove back to his school. I walked straight to the administration office.

"Hi, my name is Lisa Thweatt. This is my son Albert. He was suspended today for allegedly stealing. I need to speak with the assistant principal immediately."

Fortunately, this time she was available—though she never explained why she didn't return my repeated calls. "Right this way, Mrs. Thweatt." The administrator escorted us to the assistant principal's office and knocked on the door.

"Come in!" the assistant principal called out.

I closed the door behind us, and Albert and I sat down in the empty chairs in front of her desk. I didn't wait for her to initiate the conversation, but jumped in headfirst.

"Why was my son suspended?"

"Well, Mrs. Thweatt, I believe he would have told you by now, no?"

"I know what he told me. I want to hear it from you."

"Well, he stole. We don't tolerate stealing."

"What exactly did he steal?"

"Albert gave another student headphones, and then that student took the headphones home with him."

"I don't understand. How is that stealing on Albert's part?"

"Isn't it obvious?"

"No, it isn't. There appears to be some major misunderstanding here. I'm not understanding what my son did wrong."

"Well, if you disagree, you can appeal the decision. But the suspension will remain."

"Ma'am, Albert is going to his classes tomorrow. Your accusation is ridiculous and has left me dumbfounded." I paused for a moment. "And I need to speak with the school principal immediately."

"She's not available right now, Mrs. Thweatt."

"Is she still at the school?"

"Well, yes, but she's in a meeting with—"

"I'll wait."

With that, Albert and I left the assistant principal's office and stood out in the administration office. The staffer notified the principal that we were waiting for her. Before long, she came out of her office and walked to the administration office, looked right at me...and walked right past without saying a word. Surprised, I called out to her.

"Excuse me! I need to speak with you about my son's suspension."

She stopped and looked back. "Oh, right, his suspension. Look, I'm really sorry. I don't have time. I have to get somewhere. We can talk later. Really, my apologies. Just set up an appointment with my admin and we'll chat. Good-bye."

In a matter of seconds, she was out the front door. I stood there in front of the staff and in front of my son, hurt, humiliated, and speechless.

Indeed, I was hurt, I was humiliated, and I was speechless. But I was not about to quit. Albert and I left for home, and as we pulled into my driveway I picked up my phone and called our school board.

Shockingly, someone answered the phone. After what I'd been through that day, someone actually answering was a miracle in and of itself. And better yet, our school representative just happened to be at a meeting with other school board members. Fortuitously, a meeting was arranged with the principal the following morning. My husband, Al, joined Albert and me at the meeting.

Before we walked into the meeting room we saw Albert's principal. She wasted no time expressing her displeasure that we went "over her head" and contacted the school board directly.

"Mrs. Thweatt, I have to say I am shocked that you felt the need to go to the school board. I thought we have had a good relationship these past few years?"

My husband knew how angry I was and spoke before I could, in his calm, controlled manner. "Well, with all due respect, we thought we had a good relationship too, until you refused to speak to my wife last night on such a critical matter as our son's suspension."

She didn't respond, but just turned and walked quietly into the conference room.

I again wasted no time.

"I'm requesting this suspension be rescinded immediately and Albert goes to his classes."

The assistant principal declined, just like the night before. I insisted, once again relating the bizarre explanation of theft.

The principal sat silent, fidgety, and finally quietly choked out, "I believe there may have been a misunderstanding. Based upon the information provided, Albert's suspension should be removed."

Albert went to his classes that day, just as I told the assistant principal he would the day prior. The school principal dismissed the suspension. By the way, the other student involved in the made-up theft accusation was also black.

As I left the school with my husband, I smiled. But inside, I was furious beyond words. Had I not taken this fight to the school board, my son would have had "suspended for theft" on his academic record. I shudder to think how many other children of color in our academic system are unjustly disciplined, disenfranchised, dismissed, and disregarded due to overt or covert racial bias. How many parents of color innocently believe their student's teachers must have what's best for them in their minds and therefore don't dig deeper into these issues? How many parents don't know they're supposed to dig deeper into these issues? How many children are disadvantaged just because of the color of their skin?

The Struggle Soars

Now multiply that disadvantage every year, times twelve years of education before college even begins, and you'll begin to understand why consistently fewer black students go to college every year. You'll begin to understand why fewer black students graduate college every year. No, racism in our education system is not the only cause of such disparities—but racism is a significant and preventable cause.

Countless studies by universities, NGOs, and even the US Department of Education have shown that teachers in America disproportionately discipline students of color more than white students. Teachers are more responsive to white students' e-mails and inquiries. Teachers are more lenient with white students while grading. These are the realities of a disadvantage too many students of color face in America today, and I'm not sure if there exists a way to equalize the playing field. And as I see my younger son Matthew go through the some of the same things his older brother already has, I'm reminded once more that my children are but two precious drops in an ocean of opportunity—opportunity that we cannot afford to neglect.

I am a mother who loves my children, and I am speaking in particular to my fellow mothers out there. My children don't come from generations of college grads with multiple connections. They don't have "people in high places" so that upon graduation they will be able to cherry-pick their place of employment. We live in a world where people have advantages based upon their race, relationships, and socioeconomic status. This is not a just or fair world to give to our children.So how do I raise my precious children so they are proud and feel worthy and valued?

Embrace the Struggle

I know on a firsthand basis that they will have to work and perform twice or three times as hard to simply compete. I urge them on a daily basis to be strong and conscientious and to always do the right thing. I know that they are tired and maybe even angry. But I also know that it is up to me as their parent to look out for them. This is why I constantly remind them about their studies, about keeping their clothes and house clean, speaking professionally, walking straight, saying please and thank you, opening the door for ladies and their elders, putting their chairs back underneath the table, and the list goes on and on, ad infinitum.

Most of all, I tell them to embrace the struggle, because it is this struggle that will develop them into intelligent, compassionate, and accomplished men.

When I talk to my sons, I tell them I love them, and I tell them I'm there for them when they need me. And I know that no matter how much work I've put into them, no matter how much I've learned, no matter how impressed others are, nothing makes me more proud, more fulfilled, and more grateful than having my two healthy boys.

That's a struggle worth talking about and acting on.

Chapter 20

The Courage to Lead

"The leader of a people is he who serves them."

—PROPHET MUHAMMAD

One of the best pieces of advice I've ever received was during my first corporate leadership job: "the entire world is only as big as your leader."

I looked at my director with a blank look. "I'm sorry, I don't know if I understand."

"It's simple. If your leader wants you to succeed, you can become president. If not, success is virtually impossible."

This exactly is Lisa's struggle as she guides her children to experience the world, and dare I say, become presidents. Those who overcome the communication obstacles of today will become humanity's leaders of tomorrow. Humanity needs leaders willing to take charge with confidence, passion, and compassion. Leaders with thick skin and comfortable shoes—because the onslaughts down this long and lonely road require both.

"Avoid putting yourself before others" taught Lao Tzu, "and you can become a leader among men." This principle of servant leadership is the core pillar upon which we can resolve problems. Likewise, Khalil Gibran beautifully said, "I slept and I dreamed that life is all joy. I woke and I saw that life is all service. I served and I saw that service is joy." Thesaurus editors should seriously cite "servant" and "leader" as interchangeable terms.

And that is the definition of leadership we will use—a leader is one who serves others.

Look at the leaders in your own lives—parents and grandparents, aunts and uncles, siblings and coaches—and learn from their leadership. We need to be able to talk about such individuals and take lessons from their examples, because they are right in front of us for us to access and learn from.

Reflecting on my experience in the principal's office and Lisa's experience with her children's teachers, I come away with the shocking discovery that teachers are human too. They're prone to mistakes just like anyone else. And like any person in any industry, teachers can benefit from additional resources to advance their ability to lead students. Muhammed Ahmad Chaudhry (MAC)—the author of the next chapter—has dedicated his life to doing just that. MAC, as you'll recall, is an education icon in Silicon Valley. Specifically, he's the president and CEO of Silicon Valley Education Foundation. MAC's work is priceless. In particular, he supports students from historically underrepresented and minority backgrounds and guides them to unlock their full potential.

In doing so, he's become a leader who is using education to change the world as we know it.

Chapter 21

Leaders for an Educated Solution

By Muhammed Ahmad Chaudhry

"A child miseducated is a child lost."

— PRESIDENT JOHN F. KENNEDY

We have a problem in our country. An education problem. And we need an educated solution.

I've lived almost all my life in Silicon Valley. Most people think of Silicon Valley as a unique hotbed of innovation. A place that holds endless opportunity, where billionaires are minted daily, where everyone lives in mansions, and where all children are brilliant high achievers who attend top schools.

Not so in reality.

Silicon Valley, like many regions in the country, has many faces. There are vast areas where families live at the top of the socioeconomic ladder and children attend some of the best schools in the country. But just a six-lane freeway away from those wealthy enclaves are neighborhoods where families struggle in poverty and their children attend some of the worst schools in the system.

I care deeply about this stark societal and educational divide, because education and how to fix it has been a big part of my life for the last fifteen years as CEO of the Silicon Valley Education Foundation. I've always believed that education is the great equalizer, that getting a good education can open doors for all students and lift many out of poverty with the promise of a better future. I reflect on the students I tutored in math and English one summer in college at a San Jose recreation center.

Those kids struggled in school and, with behavior problems, had little opportunity or hope. I helped them with algebra, grammar, and reading problems. And when they asked me how I got into college I told them the basic truth—through hard work starting in elementary and especially middle school. I said I always had the goal of attending college right in front of me and I wasn't going to let it go. Finishing college, even if it was a two-year community college, was crucial in helping me achieve success in life.

But the reality is that our kids need more than just a word of encouragement to work hard. I didn't realize this at first.

I also didn't then realize that tutoring and mentoring those kids would eventually lead me toward the career I have today. After getting my college degree in business I worked in the private sector in industries that had nothing to do with education. But as I looked around me and became aware of the struggles of children in disadvantaged neighborhoods and schools, particularly children of color, I knew where I wanted to take my career. I wanted to work for causes that changed children's lives. I wanted to be a leader for kids and families, not consumer products.

And this is why I need you to talk to me. We need to do this together.

164

If we don't act now, these children, my children, and your children will fall further behind and never succeed. The data doesn't look good. Right now among the world's sixty-five developed nations, our kids rank twenty-eighth overall in science and thirty-sixth overall in math. We need more leaders. The future of our global innovation is at risk if we don't improve our schools and ensure that our workforce is prepared to take on the technological and business challenges that lie ahead. We need a better-prepared generation of educated youth to help the United States successfully compete around the globe.

But we still have a long way to go to make education equality a true reality. I'm working to close this economic gap and the student achievement divide between white students and students of color. I want a world where all students can succeed. Many schools are working hard at it, despite severe drawbacks. And many students who attend schools with low scores and poor resources also are fighting against the tide and defying the odds.

Luis Gallegos is one of those students.

Luis represents more than six thousand students I've met through my foundation's math intervention program. I want to talk to you about Luis because there are countless more like him who need our leadership—yours and mine. Like many students in low-performing schools, Luis was falling through the cracks academically. This problem was most obvious in middle school math—a foundational subject and critical learning juncture.

Luis is the kind of student who was "supposed" to fail. Surveys tell us that kids in his demographic have a slim shot at academic success: his of-color and immigrant background, poor early English language skills, and family hardships put him squarely in a category of youth who usually end up with the "at-risk" tag. But the very obstacles he faced also gave him the backbone to defy the odds.

Luis took on that challenge. Given his hardscrabble beginnings, that action is no small feat. Neither of Luis's parents graduated high school, and when Luis started school in the United States he did so not knowing how to speak English. So obviously, Luis entered kindergarten already at a grave disadvantage. That he attended an overcrowded and underfunded school in Oakland compounded his challenge. The school offered no tutoring or ESL classes to get him up to speed. Luis later told me his disadvantage with English made him feel like a failure with *everything* in school.

He simply had no confidence.

Remember that while this particular story is about Luis, he represents a struggle that millions of children face every single day. He represents what our children and a disproportionately large number of students from minority and lower economic class backgrounds face every single day. Right now the support offered by local, state, and federal government agencies is simply not adequate. People are quick to blame parents, and while parents must do better, we should not overlook the struggle parents themselves often face. In this case Luis's parents had already sacrificed immensely just immigrating to America. As a nation of immigrants we must support one another.

Despite his language hurdle, Luis soon learned he loved engineering and physics. But he needed to drastically improve his math skills to pursue an engineering path. And this is when I first met Luis—an encounter made possible by meaningful dialogue and communication.

Manny Villalpando, a math teacher at Luis's middle school, recognized Luis's struggle with math. Manny saw immense potential in the thirteen-year-old and urged him to enroll in SVEF's summer math intervention program. The math program pulled Luis into a setting with small classes and a teacher and teaching assistant who could offer one-on-one attention if he needed it. Luis started doing well, he began to learn, and most significantly he began to regain his self-esteem. And in

166

the fall, when he went back to his own school armed with new math skills, he was the "smart" one in his algebra class. That boosted his confidence, spilling over into his other studies.

Luis blossomed, both academically and personally. And the grades he's receiving now are proof of deliberate choices and an incredible work ethic. When I visited Luis toward the end of the math program I could see the difference in the once-shy boy. He stood with confidence and began to lead with confidence. Luis, now seventeen and a junior in high school, is the oldest of three children. He's well aware his acts are an example for his younger brother and sister. And he's setting a pretty darn good example as a 4.0 GPA student. Not long ago Luis and his family had immigrated to the United States from the poverty-ridden town of El Resbalon in rural Mexico. Especially given the seemingly insurmountable odds his family faced, what Luis has accomplished is incredible, and incredibly inspiring.

When I last met Luis he said something that indelibly stays with me. "You guys took the time to listen to me and understand me. It changed my life." Education isn't just about conveying information—it's about learning how to understand our children. That is what great leaders do. As Luis reaches for a top-tier university, he will be the first in his family to go to college.

I assure you he won't be the last.

Students like Luis are the reason why I do what I do. He is the reason my education foundation created our summer math intervention course and other programs that focus on academically struggling youth. These programs, now models for other efforts serving at-risk students, are recognized nationally for their success. They are life-changing programs and often represent a turning point in a child's learning, setting him or her on a course to college.

I talk about education being the great equalizer, the common denominator. Is that realistic? Can our education system make it possible for poor, disadvantaged youth to discover how intelligent they are, work hard, and have ambition to reach the top? Some might argue that the current system has become one of privilege. Some argue our system is not one that every child can succeed in—especially not low-income students and kids of color.

If that's the case, then we have a lot of work still to do. We can't accept being the wealthiest nation on earth and have our students perform at the middle and bottom of the pack in math and science. We need leadership that brings back the privilege as belonging to all students. We need leadership that holds everyone responsible for attaining the goal of providing every student a world-class education regardless of economic, gender, or cultural background. We need leadership in every state, every city, every school, and every home. That's why I ask each of you to lead. It isn't a one-person or one-organization job.

My organization is just one of the many focused on providing leadership, improving student achievement, and narrowing the racial divide. But we have to have more people step up. We can't do it alone. Come talk to me about your children, about their educational future. This is why I do what I do—to take the millions of at-risk students in our country and give them the opportunity to become the best version of themselves.

We have a problem in this country, and you hold the solution in your hands. Let's talk together, work together, and make our future our own.

After I had the chance to talk to MAC, only one thing bothered me further: how little attention we're giving girls as well as minority children in America—and the inadequate awareness Americans have of this gender gap. We face a massive shortfall today in how we educate girls and minorities, one that threatens to increase exponentially in the coming years yet is not getting nearly the attention it deserves.

Someone once reminded me that white privilege or male privilege or wealth privilege is the dangerous belief that something isn't a problem for anyone because it isn't a problem for you. Whatever you wish to call it, the education gap both girls and minorities are facing in America is dangerous and cancerous—and we need to act now to change the tide. The solution lies with courageous leadership, and that's where MAC's example of leadership is critical. Part of what makes MAC such an inspiration is his relentlessness and his refusal to pass judgment. He understands everyone has a struggle, and rather than assuming he knows about that struggle he positions himself to help a person overcome it. This is a fundamental goal of leadership.

Often in our society we have a preconceived notion of who a leader is or what a leader should look like. That can be helpful for determining the characteristics, values, ethics, and morals we want in a leader, but it can also be harmful. For example, close your eyes and think about how your ideal leader physically looks. Now open them. How many of you imagined a Pakistani Muslim woman mother and wife who wears a hijab, is a human rights lawyer, and helped create Serial and Undisclosed Pod, two of the most popular podcasts in iTunes history? How many of you even considered a Muslim woman as a leader? Let me introduce you to the prolific author of the next chapter—Rabia Chaudry.[11]

---

[11] No relation to Muhammed Ahmad Chaudhry.

Chapter 22

Leadership Grows in the Dark

By Rabia Chaudry

"I don't go by the rule book. I lead from the heart, not the head."

—PRINCESS DIANA, PRINCESS OF WALES

The first time I went to court, I was terrified.

For a number of years I had only worked on appeals and filings, never having had to step before a judge or respond contemporaneously to opposing counsel or make a case with a roomful of people behind me.

When our case was called, I herded my client to the table, sat to his left, and waited patiently as the judge shuffled papers. I adjusted the microphone, opened and closed my file, fiddled with my pen. My client, a diminutive Peruvian man, stared at his hands.

After a few minutes the judge peered over his glasses at me and asked me to state my name. I did. Then he asked me if my attorney was present.

I blinked, not understanding.

He repeated the question.

Then I got it.

"I am the attorney of record, Your Honor."

This scene repeated itself nearly every time I went to court over the coming years. In every instance, I would sit with my client by my side, a sheath of files before me, wearing a suit, looking official, and every time the judge would ask me where my attorney was.

There is only one explanation for what was throwing the judges for a loop: I wore a hijab.

It was throwing me a for a loop too, because I had only recently begun wearing the hijab and was still trying to figure out how to assert my personality and identity through this little piece of fabric that was now blinding people to me as a person. The irony is that it also exposed me to the difficulties my clients faced.

The bulk of my legal career, which is now in my past, was focused on immigration and civil rights. The complications, barriers, and outright injustice immigrants (both documented and undocumented) face in the "immigration system" are not well known to the public. I got to experience, firsthand, what it felt like to be an immigrant dealing with the system—not because I was one, but because they thought I was.

Like judges, immigration officers usually thought I was the immigrant in need, coming to the field office to ask about my case. Here I was, a very brown South Asian woman in a head scarf, biding my time in a waiting room with hundreds of other immigrants and a handful of very lawyerly-looking white attorneys. At other times, I would join clients for interviews and be asked if I was a relative or an interpreter.

I could be anything: an immigrant applying for benefits, an undocumented woman, an interpreter, a supportive relative, but never the attorney of record. And as such, I was treated like the others. Brusquely, sometimes outright rudely, dismissed until I made it clear that I was the attorney. Then attitudes would often change.

It incensed me to know what my clients and millions of immigrants were up against. And it was precisely at this time of my life that I had left an abusive marriage. The change had forced me to get on government assistance for a short time, become a single parent, and truly become aware of social justice struggles—of women, of immigrants, of Muslims post-9/11, of the poor in the United States.

My years in law school were harrowing. I lived with my ex-in-laws, a large Pakistani family who had tolerated the abuse my ex-husband doled out. A family for whom I had to prepare lunch and dinner daily, while working part time in the mornings, caring for my infant daughter, and attending classes in the evening. I rose at 6:30 a.m. to begin my day, give a bit of time to my baby girl, make lunch for the family, and head to work. In the short break between work and school, I rushed home to make dinner and give my daughter another couple hours of time. I returned from classes around 10:30 p.m. and then spent half the night studying and doing homework before having to start all over again. Though I attended a top-tier law school, I never had the time or opportunity to be involved in the activities or contacts that would have set me up for a cushy legal career. No time for law journal, no time for mock trial, no time for legal clinics.

Hence, no time to position myself for the kind of job most law graduates hope for. I didn't end up where I wanted, but I did end up where I was needed.

I wasn't the rich lawyer, removed by economic rank and culture from my clients. I was the financially struggling lawyer in the trenches with them, the new divorcee, fighting for custody of my daughter, a domestic violence survivor, struggling with single parenthood, crying with my clients, raging with them, knowing personally what it was like to juggle every dollar, weigh every penny, worry about paying for child care or electricity. I was the lawyer who kept taking pro bono work but couldn't afford to, the lawyer who said prayers for every case, who was propelled by the fear and fatigue in the eyes of my clients like something tangible persistently on my back.

The stories of clients haunt me. Stories of immigrants who have struggled in ways those of us born with the privilege (and believe me, it is a privilege that makes your life so much easier, and one that millions are fighting for) of being US citizens will never know. They've become part of me. I carry them with me every time I travel and pull out my blue passport. A passport I did nothing to earn, one that I take for granted, one that gives me access to things people the world over are starved for.

How do you rank vulnerability and tragedy? Who wins this contest?

Is it the man who has been stuck in the United States for two decades, defrauded by numerous lawyers, not able to return home because he has to earn and send money to relatives? Meanwhile, they die off one by one—loved ones he'll never see again? Is it the woman who was trafficked along with her kids, who were then taken from her, who has no idea what her immigration status is, but knows she can't leave the United States until she finds her children? Is it the young man who was brought here as a child, who never knew he was undocumented until he learned he did not have the status to attend the universities he was admitted to, who graduated top of his class in high school but is relegated to working for cash in gas stations, exploited by his employer? Is it the women, the countless women (God knows I've lost count) who were brought here as brides, abused by husbands and in-laws, papers taken away, threatened with deportation and separation from their children?

Who wins this real life "hunger games" contest? I don't know. I could no longer tell.

There came a tipping point for me, a point at which I was filling to the brim with stories of pain and struggle, stories no one ever heard. I spent years thinking about these stories and people. Many of them lived in shadows, ashamed of their status, afraid to be reported, unable to travel, working undercover if at all, avoiding being noticed at all costs. The last thing they could or would do was tell their stories.

So I tried to do that for them, and in many ways for myself. For me as a working mom, first as a single parent, and then later remarried with another child, life was demanding, overwhelming. The only tool at my immediate disposal and within my purview was the written word. I had a laptop and Internet access. It was scary, but I could do this.

In seventh grade my English teacher Mr. Richards told me, a painfully shy girl, in front of the class that if I wasn't a published author by the age of thirty, his name wasn't Mr. Richards. That seed of encouragement stuck with me, but hopefully Mr. Richards's bet included published pieces that were not actually a book. I began with letters to editors, short pieces in local papers, opinion editorials, then a humble blog on a small religion site, then a blog on a larger religion site. Over the years editors noticed and I was asked to write for many other blogs and sites and finally major publications like *Time* magazine and the *Guardian*.

I've gone from writing about faith and personal challenges to writing about anti-Muslim bigotry, national security, immigrant rights, domestic violence, gender equity, and criminal justice. My world has broadened and deepened.

Writing didn't just become my advocacy weapon of choice, it provided a healing mechanism for dealing with aspects of my own past, my grapplings with faith, with the pain I feel in the face of systematic injustice. It has led to openings, opportunities, connections, and one of the most unexpected things—the unplanned and unwanted title of "leader" in the American Muslim community.

It's a situation that makes me highly uncomfortable, to be considered a leader. Not least because while some will identify me as such, others will challenge that status and then look to me to defend it. Except, I won't. I don't self-identify as a leader. And whatever challenge is posed has to be from those who think I do.

This dilemma has restrained my writing. Whereas before I wrote to purge, inform, vent, and share, with little consideration of how my words might impact the people who look to me as a "leader," now there's a fear. A fear others have stuffed into me, by wagging their online fingers at every word I say, by threatening me with accountability for my opinions, by declaring me a leader and thereby beholden to the sentiments of my "constituents."

A leader to whom? I always ask. A leader of what? And if I am one, what does that mean? Are leaders just mechanisms to convey the collective opinions of their "followers"? Or do leaders make the way, whacking bushes of ignorance, forging new paths, waging new endeavors, without checking to see who is or isn't behind them? Without caring, if I dare say?

The more I've been identified as a leader, the farther I've found myself wanting to distance myself from the community whose worries and fears I've carried for decades. Because of course, they're my worries and fears too. This trajectory is an odd and ironic phenomenon: from wanting to give voice to the marginalized communities I'm connected to, to becoming widely read and heard, to questioning my connection to the very communities that I've always fought for.

But I recognize what's behind it and my growing discomfort. It is a sense of losing myself by becoming a "leader" to others, the resentment at needing to limit my engagement because I refuse to be accountable to strangers. I will not answer to people who have had no part in my life or struggle. Do leaders have to answer to anyone? That seems almost counterintuitive.

And a layer below that is the recognition that writing does not make a person a leader. Telling stories of others does not make you a leader. The world is full of keyboard warrior pundits who think their opinions, even devoid of any real-world experience, is valuable. But no opinionating is inherently valuable. It is the years of work that lead to that piece in a major publication that have value. It is overcoming personal and professional challenges. It is refusal to drop the ball on family, work, or school; staying up nights with sick babies or a distressed client; collecting enough coins to buy a few gallons of gas; trembling in front of a judge; clawing your way up from the bottom; leaving an abusive spouse; having your child taken from you; standing in line to apply for government assistance; helping a victimized woman and her children find a safe place to stay for a few days; spending hours and hours and hours with God in prayer asking Him to remove the burdens that are breaking you internally, and yet still moving forward.

These are the things that build character, and it is that character that builds leadership.

I know it's not what I say or do publicly in 2016 that's made me a "leader." It's what I was doing ten, fifteen years ago when no one was looking, when no one was there. It's what's done privately to help others, to pull yourself together time and time again. It's experiencing your own failure and pain and the pain of others and doing something to change it—that is what counts.

And to that end, there are millions of leaders in the world. We are surrounded by them. Not many of them will have public platforms; most of them will live private, quiet lives, having served others for decades, having struggled themselves for decades, having taken responsibility when others won't, full of the wisdom of having worked in the trenches and impacting the lives of others.

We live in a time and age when it's very easy to gain prominence on social media and young people clamor for the most followers, the most "likes," the most retweets, thinking this is the mark of leadership. But as the well-known leadership expert John C. Maxwell has said, "Leadership is not about titles, positions, or flowcharts. It about one life influencing another."

Rabia's example reminds me of something an old friend once told me: "It takes years of struggle to become an overnight success." It's easy to point to Rabia's success now and pretend she "got lucky," as her work has gone viral. Nothing could be further from the truth. Hopefully Rabia's example demonstrates to you what is possible if we invest the time and struggle when no one else is watching. Hopefully her example demonstrates what a real lawyer looks like as a person who works with compassion, love, and in servant leadership. A leader is a person who speaks for those who can't speak for themselves—and that's exactly why Rabia's leadership is so powerful. So next time you close your eyes and envision what a leader is "supposed" to look like, add Muslim women to that list.

When I launched *The Wrong Kind of Muslim* in June of 2013, I was overwhelmed with the response. As I posted on my Facebook wall in the days before launch, "Has there ever been a book written by a Muslim, launched at a church, emceed by a Jew, promoted by an atheist, and designed to destroy terrorism without a single act of violence? I couldn't find one, so I decided to write it myself. *The Wrong Kind of Muslim.*"

In the coming weeks I received calls and e-mails of support from every near and far-reaching corner of the earth—Canada and Fiji, South Africa and Indonesia, France and Sweden, Pakistan and India, Guyana and Germany, and Thailand and Australia, among many other places.

And I also received calls and e-mails from some not so far-reaching places—such as from Ohio. It wasn't long after launching that I received a message from a then stranger who has since become a dear friend: Pastor Leo Cunningham. Unbeknownst to me, he'd already picked up a copy of my book and had his mind made up that he wanted me to speak at his church. I couldn't possibly say no.

And that's when things got interesting.

Chapter 23

But He's a Lawyer Too

"People fail to get along because they fear each other; they
fear each other because they don't know each other; they
don't know each other because they have not communicated
with each other."

—DR. MARTIN LUTHER KING, JR.

Pastor Leo and I scheduled a date that fall for me to fly out to Ohio and speak before his congregation. I received a call about two weeks before my lecture from a somewhat concerned pastor.

"Qasim, we need to talk."

"Sure, what's up? Everything OK?"

"Well, yes, but I just want to make sure you're up for this lecture."

"Of course I am; why wouldn't I be?"

"It's just that I think it's only fair I be completely forthcoming about my congregation. You see, they've never actually met a Muslim before."

Considering some 60 percent of Americans have never met a Muslim, I wasn't entirely surprised to hear that. "Great. That'll make our meeting all the more important."

"Yeah, well, they're a great group, but this is southern Ohio we're talking about. They're quite a homogeneous bunch."

"Pastor Leo, is that just a nice way of saying they're all white?"

"Mmm, yes, yes it is."

I smiled. "I got it, Pastor. No worries."

He continued. "You see, this entire town is quite homogeneous. They might be really uncomfortable around you, and that can make some people react strongly."

"If you think they might be hostile or aggressive, it's nothing I can't handle."

"No I mean it is so homogeneous that I'm the only black guy in my congregation."

"Sure, I got it. No worries."

"No really, if you came to my town and asked, 'Where's the black part of town?' they'd point to the Cunningham residence."

I couldn't help but laugh. "Pastor, I'll tell you what. Consider yourself as having fulfilled your obligation of being completely forthcoming. You still want me to come speak, right?"

"Yes, yes, without a doubt. Just needed to get that off my chest."

"I'm on it. This will be a memorable lecture. We'll have fun. I promise." I bid Pastor Leo well and hung up the phone, not realizing how memorable the lecture would actually be. We kept up lines of communication as the lecture date approached. Less than a week before the lecture my phone rang once more. I answered to find, once again, a concerned Pastor Leo on the other end.

"Qasim, today I announced it."

"Announced what?"

"Today I let everyone know after my sermon that you'd be coming to speak next week."

"Well, why do you sound so concerned? What happened?"

"So I made the announcement that a Muslim would be speaking at our church about his book, and no sooner did I finish my sermon but several members of my congregation surrounded me."

"Were they upset?"

"They asked me what in the world I was thinking inviting a Muslim to come speak at their church?"

"What'd you say?"

"Well they caught me off-guard so I said the first thing that came to mind."

"Which was?"

"I told them, well you know, he's also a lawyer."

"Oh, brother."

"And so then one of them stepped back and said, 'A lawyer, you say?'"

"And?"

"Well, he said, 'You know, on second thought I'd rather have the Muslim come speak.'"

For the second time in as many phone conversations with a worried Pastor Leo, I threw my head back and laughed. I also reflected on whether it was wise for me as a Muslim to also become a lawyer at a time when Islamophobia is at an all-time high? Talk about a self-embraced uphill battle. I thanked Pastor Leo again for the heads up, and in the coming days I made my way to his congregation.

And then the bottom fell out.

In the days before the lecture we suddenly faced an obstacle that undermined the entire dialogue. In hindsight, maybe it was more expected than not. Pastor Leo's congregation continued its pushback against having a Muslim speak at their church. And it became clear—they simply didn't want a Muslim in their church. In the end, we were left with two equally unattractive options: cancel the event altogether and appease the congregation, or move forward solo.

If we canceled the event altogether we defeated the whole point of having a dialogue. You can't encourage someone to step out of their comfort zone if they won't even open the door. Alternatively, if we moved forward solo we invited the seriously probability of speaking to an empty church, thereby also essentially defeating the whole point of the dialogue.

I admit I was pained for a number of reasons. I wrote *The Wrong Kind of Muslim* in part to speak up, as a Muslim, for persecuted and silenced Christians in Pakistan. Yet, here in America, Christians weren't willing to hear me speak simply because I was a Muslim. Most of all, however, I was reminded just how powerful a motivator fear is, and how much more work is needed before we can overcome that fear.

But as pained as I was, I was also optimistic and not looking to give up so easily. I found inspiration in Pastor Leo's relentless push for interfaith dialogue. Resourceful as he is, he developed a solution that paid immense dividends. He found option three. Pastor Leo called me the day before the originally scheduled (now canceled) lecture, "Qasim, I'm giving you another address. Be there at the same time as we planned, OK?"

I didn't know what to expect, but moved ahead undeterred.

It was a drizzly morning when my brother Tayyib and I arrived at what I thought was Pastor Leo's church. It was a modest church in rural southern Ohio. We soon learned that another pastor, Pastor Brad, ran this church. Pastor Leo had called Pastor Brad and told him the whole story—about my book, the resistance we were facing from having the event at Pastor Leo's church, and the ultimate cancellation. Though only on last-minute twenty-four hours' notice, Pastor Brad graciously opened the doors to his church and his congregation.

We were back in business, but would we get any business?

At first the church was nearly empty. You could hear your voice echo off the far walls. But then a few members trickled in, then a few more.

And as the audience settled in and waited for me to begin, I began to realize how well Pastor Leo had described the congregation. Even though these folks had invited me to come speak and had come to hear me speak, the tension was undeniable. I couldn't imagine how much more uneasy it might have been at Pastor Leo's church. They were kind, they were all white Americans, and they all sat eerily quietly, no doubt wondering just what in the world I was about to say to them.

Pastor Leo stood up, briefly introduced me, and sat back down. And the small audience was suddenly mine for the taking. I took a deep breath and stood up. "Let me start with three things and then we'll get into our conversation. First I want to thank Pastor Leo for this gracious invitation and Pastor Brad for opening his church. This olive branch has allowed us to talk to one another and learn about one another from one another. Second, I want to make clear why I'm *not* here. I'm not here to debate which is the "right" religion. I'm not here to evangelize or preach Islam. And I'm not here to convert anyone to Islam."

As I said that I could feel a sigh of relief resonate through the audience. I smiled and continued.

"And third, after my short lecture we'll have a Q and A, and I want you to ask whatever is on your mind. Don't worry about hurting my feelings, don't worry about making me feel uncomfortable, don't worry about what some might call a 'stupid question.' You being here means you want to be here, that you want to learn. And I want to foster that learning with a candid and open dialogue. Sound fair?"

Again I could see heads nodding in approval. "Great! Let's get started."

With that, we began. Cautiously and carefully, I spent the next twenty minutes discussing *The Wrong Kind of Muslim*, why I wrote it, and whom I hoped read it. I spoke about the persecution of Ahmadi Muslims in Pakistan. I related the painful facts about Christians persecuted in Pakistan. I discussed terrorism and how to overcome it with education and compassion. I described how ordinary individuals are rising above the intolerance and conquering terrorism without violence of any sort.

The dialogue after my lecture at Pastor Brad's church proved the unique experience such sessions always are. At first the questions were largely predictable.

"Does Izlam teach you to kill the infidel?"

"No such concept."

"Why do terrorists claim so, then?"

"The same reason the KKK wrongly preaches that Christ taught racism—for power and corruption."

"Do you condemn 9/11?"

"Yes."

"Do you support our troops?"

"Well, let me ask my brother Tayyib to answer that question."

"Why him? Why can't you answer it? Are you afraid to?"

"Well, I can answer, but considering Tayyib is an honorably discharged United States marine who served for five years' active duty and three years' inactive duty, he might be better suited to."

I smiled as I saw several jaws practically drop to the floor.

It was shocking enough to meet an American Muslim for the first time—but an American Muslim marine was simply mind-boggling. The event was winding down. I looked over at Pastor Leo and Pastor Brad and smiled, thanking them for the opportunity. They responded in kind. I thanked everyone for attending and what began as a session with the tension of a tightly strung guitar ended with hugs, handshakes, smiles, and invitations to "come back soon ya hear?"

And then something happened that's never happened to me in person before. As I packed up my things a young man approached and asked if he could speak to me in private. We walked a few steps away from the crowd, paused, and then walked a few steps farther and sat down in a few empty seats.

He had a cup of water in his hand when he approached me and held on to it as we made our way out of earshot of the rest of the crowd.

"What's on your mind, friend?"

He seemed hesitant and a little nervous. After taking a deep breath he spoke up. "I was furious with Pastor Leo and Pastor Brad when they told me a Muzlum was coming here. I was furious that they actually invited the enemy to speak at our church."

I listened attentively. I knew this took courage for him to step out of his comfort zone.

"See, I was in the military too. I was gonna ask the question about whether you support our troops and never in a million years did I think Muzlums would join the US Marines."

He hesitated.

"I...I don't know if I should be saying this but you said nothing was off limits so here goes."

I nodded to reaffirm I was still listening. He leaned in and lowered his voice.

"I joined the army not long after 9/11, because I was angry at what your people did to us. I joined the military for only one reason..."

He took a deep breath.

"I joined because I wanted to kill as many Muzlums as I could possibly get my hands on."

His hands shook with nervousness as he spoke and the water in his cup nearly spilled. He didn't seem to notice.

"I was just so angry at all Muzlums. I wanted to kill every last one of you. And when Pastor Leo said you were coming, even though I've been out of the military for years, I was still furious at Muzlums."

I reflected on the two forces at work here. First was the reality that many Muslims will describe to you. The greatest intellectual tragedy of

9/11 was that hundreds of millions of Americans gained their first introduction to what they were told was Islam when the Twin Towers came crashing down. This false narrative of Islam seared a painful experience in the minds of many who otherwise had never heard of what Islam was or was not.

Second was the ignorance with which this young man joined the military, and the ignorance that had remained with him for well over a decade. He had not taken the initiative to learn about Islam from Muslims. He had not reached out to communicate with Muslims. Instead, he remained in his comfort zone this entire time.

But now there was also a third force at work that never existed before for this young man. That of a Christian pastor who understood deeply that extremists don't define any religion and that terrorism has no religion. And as the young man soon learned, that force was the most powerful force in this equation. He continued.

"I only came today because of Pastor Leo and Pastor Brad. Pastor Brad told me he didn't expect me to trust Muzlums for no reason, but that if he was my Pastor, he expected me to trust him. And Pastor Leo's a good man and so is Pastor Brad. I came because I trusted them. And..."

I looked directly at him to maintain eye contact, even though he spent most of his dialogue looking at the floor.

"And I never thought I'd say it, but Pastor Leo was right. I was wrong. I can't blame Muzlums for 9/11 just as I wouldn't want you to blame Christians for the KKK. And, I owe you an apology. I came here hating you, and I'm sorry, because I realized while listening to you that I didn't know who or what I hated. I'd never even met a Muzlum before, and frankly I'm ashamed that I hated an entire religion of people without ever meeting even one of them. That's not what Jesus taught us."

He paused again. I stayed silent, letting him vent. He continued. "Qasim, I'm glad you came here. I'm glad Pastor Leo invited you to come here too. I'm glad Pastor Brad opened up this church to you."

Without saying another word, and before I could speak, he shook my hand and walked away. I couldn't help but smile. That single conversation made the entire trip a success. He took the time to talk to me when he didn't have to.

I reflected again on the power that faith leaders hold when building bridges of understanding and dialogue. This young man would have gone his entire life hating and fearing 1.6 billion people out of ignorance. He was fortunate to have courageous Christian pastors who led by example, who refused to let others write his narrative, who chose to write their own narratives of tolerance and forge their own paths of pluralism and understanding.

But in this lesson is also an opportunity for Americans and Westerners in general to self-reflect. Let's do role reversal. Let's assume this young man was not an American Christian who joined the army after 9/11 to kill Muslims. What if he was an Iraqi Muslim who joined the Iraqi military after the 2003 Iraq War started "for the sole purpose of killing as many Christians as possible"?

Would we call him an Islamist? A jihadist? A terrorist? If so, would we call the young Christian man who confessed his history to me a Christianist? A Crusader? A terrorist?

I certainly hope not. I propose we call both individuals ignorant and frustrated, motivated by power, anger, vengeance—but not religion. Pastor Leo could have become a wedge to create further anger, distrust, and fear of Muslims. He chose instead to become a powerful adhesive, and as a result helped transform an angry and frustrated young man into an increasingly educated person, now willing to meaningfully engage with those he formerly feared. Pastor Leo took the time to talk to me, and it made all the difference.

And as that dialogue continued I further appreciated just how hard Pastor Leo worked to create that bridge. He has courageously fought the ghosts and demons of bigotry and racism his entire life. And his story deeply moved me. Earlier I discussed how Christian leaders must write the narrative on racial harmony if we hope to end racism in America. Pastor Leo's example brilliantly demonstrates the church's pivotal role in that healing process. Pastor Leo is the author of the next chapter. His story is painful, and critical to our progress.

Come talk to him next.

Chapter 24

Ghosts of the American Original Sin

by Pastor Leo Cunningham

"There comes a time when one must take a position that is neither safe, nor politic, nor popular, but he must take it because conscience tells him it is right."

—DR. MARTIN LUTHER KING, JR.

Racism is alive and well in many of the churches in the United States.

Please understand, I am not saying all churches in the United States are racist. But it is naive to think in a country with a historically proven foundation built on a variety of -isms (classism, sexism, elitism, and racism), there would not be institutions and organizations haunted by the ghosts of racism.

If we stay with the ghost imagery, then sometimes racism is a demon because it is raging, vulgar, controlling and evil from the onset. In some congregations, racism is out front and up front in policies, procedures, and preaching. In other congregations, racism is cloaked in code words and whispering phrases used to justify actions of people who claim righteousness (not bigotry) as the rationale for actions or inaction.

Residual racism is a ghost that lingers in the recesses of hearts and minds. In other congregations, racism is like a fable or a ghost story of days gone by—when in reality racism took possession and people were tricked into believing racism no longer exists. These congregations are deceived into declaring that this is a "postracial society" and they would never act like the people referred to above. People in these congregations become angry when accused of racism because of the now all-too clichéd mantra "We are not racist. We are color-blind."

I'm talking to you today about examples of racism in churches and with people of faith—examples I've personally lived through. In my opinion, the ghost form of racism is the most harmful and dangerous because it catches many people off guard.

One Story of Cross-Cultural/Cross-Racial Appointments in the American Church

I am a member of a "mainline Protestant denomination." Globally, this denomination is rather diverse in mission, ministry, outreach, and churches. That has not been the case with my church in the United States. The majority of the congregations in the US-based churches are European-American. The majority of the clergy are European-Americans. The majority of people in higher-level leadership are European-American. The sustainability of ethnic minority churches and development of ethnic minority leaders is an ongoing issue in my church.

As an African-American pastor in this denomination, I find race relations comes up as an issue or a topic from time to time, directly and indirectly. One of these times is when a pastor of one racial or ethnic identity is sent to lead a congregation that is of a different racial or ethnic background. These situations are called cross-cultural/cross-racial appointments.

What makes our church different from other denominations is that individual congregations do not hire or "call" a pastor to lead the church. Rather, a bishop and the cabinet appoint the clergy to the church. The cabinet consists mostly of district superintendents (DS), similar to district managers. The bishop and cabinet discuss and pray about whether a church and clergy is a match. If there is a match, the clergy (and family if the cleric has one) is sent or "appointed" to that church to serve and lead the faith community. It is almost like being called up for deployment.

A phone call is made and the DS and the potential new pastor talk. They set up a date to meet with the leadership of the church in question. There is a meal, along with a tour of the parsonage, a tour of the church, and one more meeting with a larger group of church leadership, and if all goes well, the clergy is appointed.

The whole process is called an introduction, which is supposed to mean that it is *not* an interview. The nuanced difference is that an introduction is not supposed to include an opportunity for rejection or denial, while an interview of course does.

One day early in my ministry, my phone rang—I was up to bat. It was the spring of 2000. Though still attending seminary, I had an opportunity to become the student pastor of a congregation. The DS called me at seminary and we talked about the church he had in mind. The conversation went well. We decided to meet early the next morning for breakfast to determine if I was going to be a good match for "introduction."

"You don't sound black. You are so articulate."

I got to the restaurant early. I didn't want to risk being late and instead wanted to show I can take the initiative and lead. Plus, I wanted to see the DS before he could see me. I knew he had not seen my picture because my ministry file was in another district. And for you young kids out there, there was once life before Facebook and Google, so my DS couldn't look me up online either.

But also, given the intent to be a "color-blind cabinet and church," race was not the first thing presented or discussed. "It is about the pastor's skills and abilities, not the pastor's race," a previous bishop had said to me after some trying incidents elsewhere. Meanwhile, I knew what this DS looked like thanks to the conference web page. I sat and I watched him walk up the sidewalk, enter the restaurant, and speak to the hostess. I could see and hear the conversation from where I sat.

"I am looking for someone but I don't know if he is here yet," the DS said.

"What his name? Do you know what he looks like? Maybe I can find him?" the hostess replied.

"I have never met him," the DS said, "but his name is Leo."

When I heard my name, I got up, walked over to the middle-aged white man, and extended my right hand. "Reverend [So-and-So]? I'm Leo."

And much to my dismay, the racism ghost appeared.

I recognized the shocked look; "Oh. You're a large black man." This facial expression is followed by a person realizing I can see the look and that I heard the nervous inflection in their greeting. These subtle cues speak volumes. These cues screamed at me, without saying a word, that I was not what he expected. And to compensate, he was trying overly hard not to appear prejudiced.

"Hey. Hi. Hello. How are you? Glad to finally meet you. Let's have a seat and talk more about this wonderful ministry opportunity." The DS shook my hand and walked over the table while clearly inwardly backpedaling.

He jumped right into the meat of the discussion, speaking a mile a minute. "This is a rural church but it is a few miles outside of a county seat. It is mixed in age. It is in a good school system. You would have to drive back and forth to go to seminary. But you sound the like the right person with the right energy to lead this congregation in a direction they want to go. There is a parsonage too." The parsonage is a house the church owns and is provided to the pastor. The DS was part recruiter and part salesperson.

I tried to slow the conversation down, to have us speak less and listen more. "What are the major challenges facing the church?"

"They have gotten smaller in number and can no longer afford a full-time elder. But they can afford a student pastor. This change in leadership staff is hard for some of the older people because it is a shot at their pride. They used to be able to do something but now they can't."

I nodded to show I was engaged and let him continue.

"The biggest struggle for them is you are going to be the first student they have ever had lead the congregation." The DS was sharing his perspective based on conversations with the church leadership and the profile information page.

I decided to play one of my cards. "So the fact that I am black isn't going to be an issue?"

With confidence and a hint of surprise the DS said, "Oh, absolutely not! It is going to be having to go from an elder to a student."

Forging ahead, I decided to play another card. "So the fact that my wife is white isn't going to be an issue either?"

With even more confidence the DS declared, "Absolutely not an issue. Actually, they asked for a young clergy family with kids."

"Well, then, it seems this sounds like a good opportunity."

"Great. I agree. I'll meet with the cabinet, tell them our breakfast meeting went well and then we'll have the formal introduction."

"I'll also meet with my wife and discuss this new and next step in my ministry and our lives." We set a date for my wife and me to meet the DS at this "wonderful ministry opportunity."

The DS and I parted ways and I headed back home. I knew my wife would be eager to hear how things went, and I was eager just the same to share with her this frankly exciting next chapter in our lives. "Well, dear, the meeting went well. It is a small congregation in a farming community. The church is about twenty to thirty minutes from your parents and about ninety minutes from my parents."

"Is there a parsonage?" My wife asked for an important reason. At the time we were living in a two-bedroom townhouse on campus with our son, who was four at the time. We'd had to give up our dog—which was not a popular decision in my family—when we moved to the seminary.

"Yes. There is a parsonage. We can have a dog. We will be close to both of our families." I tried my best to highlight all the advantages of this opportunity.

My wife, straightforward as she is insightful, asked what I already knew was on her mind. "Is there going to be a problem with you being black? I know how people in this county can be. Remember, I grew up there."

I could only tell her of what I'd been informed. "The DS said it would not be an issue. Apparently, the big problem is they can no longer afford a full-time elder, so they aren't sure how it will be with a student. I will have to commute to school and will have less time for homework. They are wondering what that is going to be like. He also said, because I specifically asked, that our marriage wouldn't be a problem."

And just to reassure her, I repeated again what the DS had told me. It was my first dealing with this DS and, being a student, I took him and his word at face value. I didn't have a reason not to trust him. My thinking was simple: "He is the DS. He is in charge. He knows the church. He knows the lay of the land."

My wife trusted me just as I trusted the DS and nodded. "OK. When is this meeting?"

Dinner and Discouragement

About a week later, my wife and I drove to the district office to meet the DS before our dinner meeting. He wanted to walk us through how

196

the evening would go. As I mentioned before, part of the church's introduction process is to go to dinner with two or three members of the congregation's leadership team, the DS and spouse, and the potential pastor and spouse. It is part first date and part job interview—but supposedly without the scary risk of rejection for which first dates and interviews are most known.

Everyone present at the meeting gets to ask a wide array of questions, some personal and some professional. I asked again, "Are you sure me being black is not going to be a problem?" Once again the DS said, "Not at all. They are not sure what is going to happen with a student pastor instead of an elder." Some people might call me paranoid to ask the same question repeatedly. I might call some people wrong. In any case, we left the office shortly thereafter and headed to the dinner meeting.

The conversation was pleasant. The questions were ones to be expected. My answers must have been satisfactory because I can say with all honesty that the dinner meeting went well. At least it went well enough that we decided to go on to the next phase of the introduction. The next step is the church leaders would call the other members of the "staff-parish relations committee" (the church's human resource team) to meet at the church. Meanwhile the DS, someone from the church, and my wife and I would tour the parsonage. I call it "company housing."

We toured the parsonage with high hopes, and they were met. My wife and I liked what we saw. We were especially pleased to be back in a normal house as opposed to the seminary campus townhome—I think deep down we both loved the thought of getting a dog again. After the parsonage tour, we went across the street to the church to meet the rest of the committee.

And that is when the introduction suddenly became the interview it wasn't supposed to become.

Those of us who toured the parsonage went across the street to meet the rest of the church leadership members. We walked through the doors and entered the sanctuary. A long aisle led up toward the front with its elevated pulpit. To our left was what appeared to be an overflow room for Sunday mornings. Tables were set up in a square. Several people of various ages, but of the same race, sat around the tables awaiting our arrival.

When we entered the room the congregants stood up to greet us. We exchanged names, pleasantries, and smiles, and an opening prayer kicked off our formal session. First on the agenda was a candid question-and-answer session. The few younger members were positive in their questions. They wanted to know about my ideas to grow the church. They wanted to discuss vision and possible directions the congregation could go. They wanted to discuss music, ministry, and mission.

The older members, however, were the exact opposite. Passive-aggressive in both questions and attitude, they wanted to know about my theology, my political leanings, and my Christology. They wanted to know about my childhood, my faith journey, and, considering I grew up in a different Protestant denomination, how I became a member of *this* denomination. They wanted to know the exact date I accepted "Jesus Christ as my Lord and Savior."

The introduction was long dead. We were in full-blown interview mode.

Eventually, my exhausting inquisition came to an end. Little did we know the end of my questioning only meant that now the older members turned their sharpened questions toward my wife. My wife and I both knew that process was uncalled-for. Their decision to ask her questions was borderline out-of-bounds—if not way out-of-bounds. After all, she was not going to be the one preaching or leading the church. The older members relied on a model for parish ministry from the 1950s, when the wife was automatically an extension of the pastor's ministry. She was the dutiful pastor's wife, who didn't work outside of the home, played the piano, and was seen but not heard.

This attitude was unhealthy in the 1950s and you better believe it is unhealthy in the 2000s. Still, many churches continue to uphold this gender-role stereotype to the detriment of the church and in many ways at the expense of the pastor's family. For example, in almost fifteen years of serving churches, I have never served a church where I made more money than my wife. Even though the church covers numerous expenses beyond my salary, my wife's career income trumps my income to this day.

During her inquisition, my wife remained direct yet respectful about how life worked within our family structure. Clearly, it was not the model the older members wanted to hear. The younger members remained understanding and empathetic. Frankly, many of them were also living in two-income homes.

After ninety minutes or so, the ~~introduction~~ interview came to an end. The DS escorted my wife and me to a classroom in the church and said he would be back momentarily. He needed to speak with the church members about the details and logistics of us coming to this church. The DS and the church leaders would discuss over the overall feel of the evening, the answers we gave, whether we were a good match, what it would cost to move us to the area, the salary, and benefit package— basically the entire career package.

This is standard procedure after the Q and A with the leadership team. My wife and I, though a bit frustrated over the hard questioning, spoke excitedly and dreamed about the advantages of being closer to family, how we would introduce ourselves to the community, and of course, finally getting another dog.

As we sat and planned for this next chapter in our lives, about twenty minutes went by. We kept talking...thirty minutes. "What is taking so long?" my wife finally asked.

"I have no idea," I replied. "I am just as new to this as you."

At this point we were caught between optimistic and concerned. Either we were going to get a great benefit package beyond our expectations, or something had gone very, very wrong. Nearly an hour later the DS walked back into the room. His nonverbal cues told me everything I needed to know. The look on his face, followed by an exasperated sigh, informed us the verdict would be the latter of the two possibilities. Something had gone very wrong.

Trying what I can only guess was his best to remain professional, the DS tried to speak calmly. "Well, in good conscience, I don't think this going to be a good fit for everyone."

My wife and I stared blankly, unsure what to say. He kept talking.

"They like the energy and attitude you bring. They think you would be able to attract the younger people in the community."

I waited for the "however..." or the "but..." to be spoken. That is when the blasted ghost of racism smacked us in the face so hard it left us shaken.

"But, after a long conversation, they know a lot of the members would have an issue with your wife being white. They are afraid people would cause problems or not react well to your marriage."

My jaw dropped.

The DS was trying to be pastoral and comfort us, but to no avail. In an instant my wife was devastated and crying. I focused all my energy to keep my emotions in check as I tried to comfort her while shifting into defense mode.

"I thought you said none of this was going to be an issue?"

"I didn't think it was going to be an issue. They never gave any indication about a racial preference or concern when they filed the paperwork. I was very surprised. They did say it would also be an issue if you were single." Once again, the DS was backpedaling.

"Wait. So if my wife was Asian I could serve here?"

"Well, yes it appears so."

"If she was Hispanic, I could serve here?"

"Yes."

"If she was black, I could serve here?"

"Yes."

"But I can't serve here because she is white and I'm black?"

"Yes. They are worried about the older members leaving the church and taking their money with them. Again, I am really sorry all this is happening. When I meet with the cabinet and bishop tomorrow, I will let them know that this appointment isn't going to work."

Still unable to process what was happening, I repeated my initial comment, "I thought you said this wouldn't be a problem." I was trying to voice my disappointment without being insubordinate. After all, the DS could still be my supervisor someday...though that didn't seem to matter as much at that moment.

"I am just as surprised as you, Leo. They never gave any indications race would be an issue. They requested a young family. I am sorry. I just didn't see this happening."

My wife was still in tears, and I was still beside myself. And then, casually, without missing a beat the DS added, "Well, it has been a long night. Let's go back in and close the evening in prayer."

The DS actually had the audacity to pull us to back into the room with these people. These so-called Christians. My wife was still in tears, her makeup smearing. Internally, I was in an absolute rage. Externally I focused all my energy on playing it cool, reflecting on the importance of being Christlike, especially now. My wife and I stood up and marched back into a room with the people who just said the woman I married, the mother of my son, and the reason I joined this denomination, was a detriment to my ministry. These people said our interracial marriage disqualified us to come to their church and lead them in the faith we claimed to share.

As we walked back into the room, it was clear to me how the power dynamic worked in this rural, white, small-membership church. The younger members were looking at the tabletop, hunched over, and not making eye contact with my wife and me. It seemed they were embarrassed and humiliated. The older members were sitting proud with their backs straight, confident, victorious.

Finally, one of the younger committee members spoke up, and she spoke loud enough so everyone could hear. "We really like you. We think you could do great things here." She hesitated as she came to terms with what she had to say next. She had to acknowledge that fear and racism controlled that church, instead of faith and compassion. "But we know there are some people here at the church and in the community who wouldn't handle your marriage in the best way."

My wife and I sat silent. I showed no emotion and gave no reaction.

Seeing we obviously weren't pleased with or convinced by that explanation, one of the older women spoke up. "Our church is already small and we can't afford to have any more people leave." She sounded more like she was trying to convince herself instead of us.

In one congregation, two ghosts of racism manifested. One ghost bewitched the DS into believing racism was not an issue and didn't exist in this church. Even though I would have become the first African-American pastor in the church's history and one of a few ethnic minority clergy in the county, the DS was caught off guard and surprised. The other ghost of racism was the demonic one, which had complete control over this church. The older people were convinced that through open racism, they were actually defending the future of the church and gospel of Jesus Christ.

My wife was sitting to my right with tears still in her eyes. I was trying to keep my chin off my chest. I was trying to show my resolve and inner strength to the people who tried to break it. I stared at the DS stone-faced. I wanted him to understand my anger at our having been placed in this wholly unnecessary situation. The DS offered a prayer about grace, love, and forgiveness—concepts apparently lost on too many of the people representing the congregation that night. After DS said "Amen," some of the younger people tried to speak to my wife to comfort her. Others just left and went home.

A few people spoke to me. "I was really looking forward to hearing you preach here. Maybe someday you will." I offered my honest opinion at the time: "I doubt it." I just wanted to get my wife, head to our car, and go see our son. As she and I made it to the car, the DS offered another apology.

"Look, Leo, I'm really sorry about tonight. I'll be sure to inform the bishop and cabinet about what happened. I'll check on you next week after our weeklong annual conference session of clergy and laity ends."

"That's fine. I just want to leave this church right now, get to my in-laws (who were watching our son), and take care of my wife."

That evening my wife and I would have to retell the story of that day to family and friends. I remember trying to explain to my four-year-old what happened but the words wouldn't come to my lips. I tried to put it in terms he would understand without robbing him of his innocence.

Finally I managed to sputter out, "Son, I love you. And I'm sorry, but we can't get that dog we promised."

Calling It Out. Having the Conversation.

I know some people are going to read this and think, "Well, that was America fifteen years ago and it was an isolated incident." Unfortunately, this was just one of the examples of the racism that exist in some of the churches in the United States. Am I saying all churches are racist? No. I am not making that kind of absolute statement. Are race relations and racial issues still a challenge in Christian churches in the United States? Yes, absolutely. I could keep sharing many, many more examples of my experience of race relations and racism in the church. Some are positive examples and other examples are completely baffling.

My account is just one example, from almost fifteen years ago.

There are situations when people must assemble and expel the evil of racism from aspects of communal life. There are moments when a choir of humanity must sing songs of freedom as they march, protest, sit in or shut down the environments that breed the poltergeist of prejudice. There are instants when the cries of the collective rise high enough that the final sound is historic.

Sometimes it takes more than one voice to call out the demons and ghosts of racism. In order to exorcise the ghosts of racism that haunt, torment, and disturb America, we must call it out by name. And just as important is the need for even a single voice to discover that receptive ear, one idea to be planted into a fertile mind, and one transformative act to impact a heart.

I've learned throughout my life that one-on-one conversations are a powerful path to effective change. It involves creating an atmosphere of grace and an arena of trust to overcome the screams and shouts of a thousand people. It takes a willingness to share, to be honest, to be vulnerable, and to be self-aware to venture into the difficult conversations about race in America and it required that those conversations be authentic. One of the wonderful examples of one-with-one from which I draw inspiration comes from the Book of Acts in the Christian New Testament, and I will paraphrase it.

One day an Ethiopian was in Jerusalem for worship. When the service ended he journeyed back to Ethiopia. While on the road, God told a man named Philip to head to the same road. When Philip arrived on the road he heard the Ethiopian reading from the book of Isaiah. Philip asked a question of the Ethiopian and the Ethiopian of Philip. The two men traveled, talked, and learned, and eventually the Ethiopian was baptized. (Acts 8:26-39)

The great thing about the Bible is the same story can be used in a variety of purposes. In this case, I am presenting it as what happened when two people from different cultures and ethnic groups spent time learning and journeying with each other. They talked. They asked questions. They shared. They were headed the same direction with a similar purpose. This willingness to see the value in each other's existence, and each other's experience, led to a transformative relationship. Each person went away richer and I want to believe each used the treasure of authentic vulnerability to bless other people.

Maybe Philip and the Ethiopian continued to reach out to other people of different cultures and ethnicities because of the one brief encounter. It was that brief encounter that changed their lives.

It is talking and listening, conversation and communion that have served me well in breaking down the walls of racism. This is one of the ways to start addressing the ghost of American's original sin. If we are willing to enter into authentic and honest dialogue, acknowledging our vulnerability and humanity with grace, we will discover so much more about one another and ourselves. This kind of effort is challenging but brings the priceless reward of promoting understanding and advancing peace and justice.

After all, as you finish reading this contribution to *#TalkToMe*, know that it all began with a simple tweet after reading an op-ed piece, which started the friendship between an African-American pastor and a Muslim-American lawyer.

Chapter 25

The Christian-Muslim Bridge at Richmond Law

"We are born of love. Love is our mother."

—RUMI

Meaningful communication through interfaith dialogue and strong race relations is demonstrably powerful. It isn't just a feel-good practice—it literally saves lives. Pastor Leo gets this, and this is what fuels his passion. At a time when black churches are still being burned, fear of Muslims is at record highs, and immense ignorance of Islam persists, the more bridges we can build, the better.

Recall what I discussed earlier: that meaningful communication is about actions, not mere words.

As mentioned earlier, I was in law school on the tenth anniversary of 9/11. The year prior, I had proposed and established my law school's first-ever Muslim Law Students Association (MLSA). Its formation was significant, considering my law school was then roughly a hundred and sixty years old and I was certainly not the first Muslim ever admitted.

Heartwarmingly, the law school faculty unanimously approved the new student organization; we were funded and well on our way.

Two significant incidents happened over the following two years that demonstrated just how important communication is when writing the narrative for tolerance and understanding.

The first incident occurred even before MLSA was official. Like any student organization, MLSA needed a faculty adviser. Dr. Azizah al-Hibri, a prolific Lebanese-American scholar, was the only Muslim professor at my law school. I admire Dr. al-Hibri immensely, and she seemed the obvious choice. However, enlisting her for that role was problematic, given her then-part-time teaching schedule and prior commitments to her human rights NGO called KARAMAH. (As a side, if you're interested in supporting women's rights—and every one of you reading this book should be—you should check out KARAMAH). Though not our faculty adviser, Dr. al-Hibri ultimately served as a brilliant mentor and led many of the scholarship events we organized with unmatched zeal.

For now I was left with the prospect of a Muslim Law Student Association with a non-Muslim faculty adviser. On initial observation, the thought seemed strange. Yet upon further contemplation I realized deep wisdom and opportunity might be found via such a bridge.

Indeed, history records that during Prophet Muhammad's lifetime, it was the Abyssinian Christian King Negus As'hama, son of Abjar, who offered refuge to persecuted Muslims when no one else would. Now, of course, neither I nor any other Muslim at my law school was facing persecution for my beliefs. But that historical precedent (law pun intended) helped affirm my conviction that a non-Muslim faculty adviser would reap long-term rewards.

I just didn't know how, or to what extent.

Most pressingly, I didn't know whom to ask to undertake such a role. Would the person feel comfortable taking on this duty, or would they see it as a problem? Would I want someone who required convincing and urging? What if the candidate was apathetic—or, conversely, overzealous? I was in uncharted waters. The deadline to submit my proposal for creating the organization was fast approaching. I had built a structure without a base to support it and, worse yet, had no clear idea where to begin.

I now reflect how one fine fall afternoon all my questions, concerns, and prayers were so wonderfully answered that to this day I sit in awe. I quote in part from an op-ed I wrote for the *Richmond Times-Dispatch* shortly after the incidents that transpired.

The first incident all started about eighteen months before the second incident—and the two were connected in a fateful yet wholly unforeseeable manner. Professor John Carroll passed me in the hallway and stopped. "I don't mean to bother you," he said, "but you're Qasim Rashid, right?"

I turned to see a well-dressed, handsome individual. He wore a suit and had a trimmed, graying beard. His piercing blue eyes matched his tie, and his smile was as authentic as they come. "Yes, Professor, I apologize—I'm afraid I don't know your name."

"I'm John Carroll," he said as he extended his hand. "Do you have a minute?"

I was actually running late to a class, but something about him drew me as I took his hand. "Sure."

He leaned in and paused, taking a deep breath. "I don't know how to say this, Qasim, but...I just want to apologize from the bottom of my heart for that lunatic threatening to burn the Qur'an in Florida. As a Christian, I want you to know that I condemn his act, and that I'm here to help however I can."

Earlier I cited Pastor Leo as an example of a courageous Christian leader working hard to build bridges. Professor Carroll was referring to a so-called Christian pastor in Florida threatening to burn the Qur'an. I was stunned, speechless, and heartbroken. Even now years later my eyes well up as I reflect on Professor Carroll's compassion. He continued.

"I think people don't understand that Muslims consider the Qur'an the word of God. As Christians, we consider Jesus the word of God. So, burning the Qur'an is actually not like burning the Bible—it's like burning Jesus."

"Professor Carroll, who are you?" was all I managed to mutter.

"I'm John Carroll."

"Yes, I know that, but, why are you doing this? You don't need to apologize for that lunatic."

"Maybe not, but maybe I just wanted to be sure."

That conversation reminds me that empathy is not a lost art in humanity. And when Professor Carroll pulled me aside "just to be sure" I knew how he felt; I learned how communication could overcome apathy and revive empathy. That very next day I needed to finalize our faculty adviser selection for the newly proposed Muslim Law Student Association. And now I knew my solution immediately.

I e-mailed Professor Carroll, asking him to accept the role, burden, and responsibility, writing, "I'm confident that our different backgrounds yet common goal will cater to the underlying theme of pluralism I hope MLSA will foster. I already know my own perspective as a Muslim, but I cannot possibly know the perspective of a Christian. I think this will be a great strength going forward."

Professor Carroll, with his patented humility and compassion, replied, "Thank you for your kind words. As I get to know you better, I am beginning to realize that I cannot understand even the Christian perspective without also understanding your perspective."

He graciously accepted the role. And suddenly those uncharted waters suddenly didn't seem so scary. As we collaborated on how to move forward as an interfaith team, Professor Carroll became the catalyst that changed countless lives. Under his leadership, MLSA hosted six unprecedented Islamic scholarship events and two interfaith community service events, including that "9/11 Muslims for Life" blood drive described in Chapter 13 that collected more than one hundred donations.

He helped create a new conversation at my law school and created bridges of understanding for hundreds of students—future scholars—where none existed before. Few know that Professor Carroll reviewed and provided invaluable feedback to one of the earliest manuscripts of *The Wrong Kind of Muslim*. How beautiful that a Christian professor helped a Muslim student find his voice to speak up for universal religious freedom for all people regardless of faith or no faith?

That was the first incident, and it is a moment I reflect on with immense pride. As far as the second incident...we'll get to that in Chapter 27. For now, I continue the theme of navigating uncharted waters. Taking that first step to attend a church, a mosque, a temple—or any house of worship you've never attended before—can be scary and daunting. But it is one thing to navigate an interfaith relationship in your own country and in your own school. That anxiety is elevated when you realize that attending a new house of worship often means immersing yourself in a different culture, with people of a different race, with a wholly different power dynamic, and in a new country halfway around the world.

How do we overcome this fear? Well, let's find out. To that end we ask, what happens when a Latino-American female Christian theologian attends an Indian all-male Islamic university?

I refer you to the author of the next chapter—Karen Leslie Hernandez.

Chapter 26

Uncharted Waters

By Karen Leslie Hernandez

"I love you when you bow in your mosque, kneel in your temple, pray in your church. For you and I are sons of one religion, and it is the spirit."

—KAHLIL GIBRAN

The scariest thing about exploring uncharted waters is the fear you've gone too far.

In the summer of 2006, in Varanasi, India, it was my turn to go deep into uncharted waters. And as a result of that leap of faith, I had a life-changing conversation—as meaningful as they get. I was researching Christian and Muslim communities for my graduate degree thesis in theology. Field research is never predictable. I learned this firsthand when a local interfaith activist, Father Santiago, arranged for me to go to a "Muslim college."

I was along for the ride. I simply thought it nothing more than a regular old school for Muslims, whatever that meant anyway. What I didn't realize until I walked through the gate into the all-white grand marble structure was that this wasn't just any old Muslim college—this was a madrassa, a religious college. Moreover, it was an all-men's madrassa attached to the mosque.

And as the icing on the cake, I was the first Western female ever allowed in to visit.

I cautiously entered the school. To this day I vividly remember the smells, the sights, the sounds. My first impression was how young boys and men stumbled to their classroom doors and craned their necks to see me. I guess they had been forewarned of my visit, because they didn't seem surprised at all—more intrigued than anything.

Our hosts took us on a tour of the school, into the library, the mess hall, the administrative offices, and some empty classrooms. The building was simply beautiful. Vibrantly white, with rich, green foliage, the structure was so large that it actually blocked out the normal sounds of India. I couldn't hear horns or people—it was as if I'd entered an oasis.

It wasn't long before I had the opportunity to talk to the students. Many of the conversations centered around simply understanding the school's academic structure and what the students were learning. I was pleasantly surprised to find they were learning the basics—history, math, English, and the Qur'an. Surprisingly they also had a class on the Bible where they studied both the Hebrew Bible and the New Testament. These Bible classes were mandatory.

Earlier in 2006, there were two bombings in Varanasi at the train station and at the Monkey Temple. Some renegade Muslims were responsible, and this madrassa had addressed the incident without delay—condemning the act and assuring the community that the acts of a few did not represent a whole religion. This was a great time to visit the school because I was able to have some honest dialogue about what happened. The students and I discussed what was occurring in the wider context, around the world. We likewise embraced the chance to discuss personal thoughts on religion and violence.

Stepping Out of My Comfort Zone

These conversations were not all full of daisies and rainbows. Some were immensely challenging. One student walked up and flat-out asked, "Excuse me. Why are you a Christian? Why have you chosen to remain in the wrong religion?"

How does one answer such a dogmatic question in the context I was in? Especially coming from a young Muslim man. It wasn't easy. I certainly didn't want to come off as defensive or dogmatic myself, and I had yet to develop the dialogue skills I have now. I remember sitting there, confused, thinking, "How do I answer this without sounding like I am pulling my third-grade Christian doctrine class lesson out of nowhere?" Despite my best efforts to the contrary—that's what I ended up doing.

"Well, I don't feel I'm in the wrong religion. I'm in the religion I feel comfortable in. I feel it is right for me."

"By why? Why are you a Christian? Your religion is not true. It is wrong."

"But I don't think I'm in the wrong religion. I am in the religion I was raised in, and where I feel I belong. For me, it is right."

That opened an avalanche. They came like a storm, the questions, peppered and incessant, from several other boys and young men.

"But have you ever really thought about your religion?"

"Well, yes, of course I have—"

"But why do you believe Jesus was the Son of God?"

"Because I think that—"

"Do you think Jesus was God? What about Mary? Is she a saint?"

I was in over my head and I knew it. This was way out of my comfort zone. I mustered up whatever answers I could. "Yes, I have thought about my religion. I was born a Christian."

A student interrupted, "So, you are a Christian because you were born a Christian, not because you chose to be after study?"

"Um, no, not necessarily. I am Christian because it is what I believe."

"So then do you believe that Jesus is the Son of God?"

"Yes, yes, I do."

"Why?"

I was forced to pause. I had to think about this. Why do I believe Jesus is the son of God? Is it because this is what I have always been told? Is it because this is what my parents believe? No one had ever asked me this question, and now, a young Muslim man wanted to know. And I didn't know if I had an answer ready.

"I believe Jesus is the Son of God because of what history tells me. And, deep down, in my heart, it is what I feel to be true."

"But you haven't thought about it?"

As I said, the questions were incessant. And in a way, he was right. I hadn't thought about it as deeply as they wished I had—as deeply I suddenly wished I had. As I was contemplating how to acknowledge this, another question came in and spared me from having to publicly admit my then lack of investigation.

"Mary, she is part of your trinity, yes? Why do you believe Mary to be God?"

This confused me, because he was confused. "Mary is not part of the trinity. Mary is Jesus's mother. The trinity is actually something I struggle with. The trinity is Father (God), Son (Jesus), and Holy Spirit."

"What is this Holy Spirit? It is Mary, is it not?"

I began to squirm, because I struggle with the notion of the Holy Spirit, as many Christians do. I didn't want to give him the wrong answer—both theologically as well as historically. I was venturing further

and further out of my comfort zone. Perhaps against even my own in-
stincts to stop, I decided to keep going.

"The Holy Spirit is not Mary. The Holy Spirit is in me, and in all
Christians. It is the One, kind of like another person who lives inside of
all of us, who bears witness to Jesus Christ."

Blank stare.

"The Holy Spirit is like a teacher."

"You mean, like a Helper?"

"Yes, kind of."

This dialogue continued for an hour. Trying to explain the Holy
Spirit to Muslim men was not something I was prepared for. The conversation remained fixated on Mary, in an agreeable way, in some respects. For example, we discussed the immense reverence for her in both
Christianity and in Islam.

But wouldn't you know it, one young man brought up the obvious
discrepancy.

"Mary is not that important in the Bible, I see. In the Qur'an, we
have a whole chapter dedicated to Mary, yet your Bible has only a few
verses. I feel the Qur'an says more about Mary than your Bible."

He was right. I had to admit it.

"You have a good point. I can't tell you why Mary is not revered in
the Bible more. The New Testament focuses much more on Jesus than
on Mary. I will say I appreciate how Mary is acknowledged in the
Qur'an."

"Did you know that in Malaysia and Indonesia, there are Muslim
temples dedicated to Mary?"

"Actually, I didn't know that. Thank you for telling me."

The exchange left me exhausted, disoriented, and frankly bewildered.
I felt I had lost in a way, and that felt wrong for a number of reasons. It
really wasn't a debate. At least I didn't think it was. But that was beside
the point. What bothered me most about these first exchanges wasn't

the Muslim students—it was I. I sat and wondered why I wasn't able to stand comfortably in my religion and not feel threatened. Why was I so jostled by these questions?

I remember leaving the school that day feeling a bit embarrassed, as if I hadn't thought of my religion all that much. And more, how did I identify myself? Was I a Christian first and foremost, or was I simply Karen Hernandez and all that makes me me? I ended up using a bit of this identity work in my thesis. I learned in my field research just how important identity is to some, while to others, it really isn't that important at all. I also remember thinking that I, after several years of study of Islam in school, knew jack diddly about the actual practice of Islam. I was book-smart about Islam, but I certainly had a lot to learn from Muslims themselves.

Over the coming weeks I made a few more trips to the madrassa, each bringing its own barrage of questions, summons from my comfort zone, frustration—and learning. But unquestionably my last visit was the most memorable one. It was during this visit that I had some of the most incredible one-on-one conversations with students I've ever had.

Everyone listened quietly. Yes, though these conversations were one-on-one, everyone else was present and watching. In truth, in India you are never actually alone. In a country with 1.5 billion people, privacy happens in your home, and that is about it.

My last conversation on my last visit was with a student named Noorolam, or Noor for short. Noor was wise for his age and spoke with much more maturity than your typical twenty-year-old.

Noor and I talked about everything from religious extremism and terrorism to the differences between our religions, cultures, and upbringings. I loved these conversations, as they involved fundamental belief systems, as well as the idea that most of us are born into our religion. They also made me reflect on why it is important to think about why we were born into that religion. Noor and I talked of my life as a Christian in the developed United States as opposed to his life in yet developing India and how different those lives are. The conversation got particularly interesting when Noor and I spoke of terrorism.

Noor talked of the recent attack in Varanasi. "I was part of the student body that spoke on panels and worked to calm the fear that gripped the city," he said proudly. He had a keen understanding of how important it was to be present to quell fear and eradicate misunderstanding. He continued, "You know of the ongoing tension between Hindus and Muslims here in India?"

I nodded.

"So you know that for decades, since the partition, we have had conflict. This is what is on our minds always. When the temple and train station were bombed, we had to be present, to show we care. My parents taught me this. They say the partition has caused too much death in our countries."

I nodded sympathetically. "I have had many Hindus and Muslims tell me there is constant worry that conflict will break out between the two groups. Do you believe this? Do you feel this?"

"Oh, definitely. There are many matters to this and much history, but yes, I do. We must be diligent in making sure we not allow communal violence to win."

After speaking to the Christian community in Varanasi, I felt compelled to ask Noor, "I have talked with several people in the Christian community here in Varanasi, and I keep hearing one thing—that the Christians in India as a whole get along quite well with the Muslim community in India. Do you feel this is true?"

Noor smiled. "Oh, yes. We have no problems or issues with Christians in India. They are a small group, and we see them as our partners, not as our enemies."

I felt I had spoken long enough and we had established enough rapport to ask hard-hitting and honest questions. I proffered a difficult one with the hope he would understand I had no intent to offend. "What are your thoughts on Islamic terrorism?"

I was pleased to see Noor wasn't at all offended, but eager to answer. "You see, there are two matters," he said. "There is no such thing as an Islamic terrorist. People say there is, but Islamic terrorism does not exist, because Islam does not allow for terrorism. And, second, Islamic terrorism is used as propaganda. I am not in favor of terrorism. The terrorists are not fighting on behalf of Islam and Islam says they are totally wrong. We must be realistic when reading the Qur'an. There is no ayah [verse] in the Holy Qur'an that makes an enemy of another."

I was then, and I am still today, struck by Noor's words: "There is no such thing as an Islamic terrorist."

In just nine words, Noor summed up every single point that the overwhelming majority of Muslims try to make on a daily basis. What he said hit me right between the eyes, proverbially speaking of course, and is the truth. Predictably, the conversation soon turned to 9/11.

As we both reflected on this atrocity, Noor recalled, "As I watched the images on the television with my parents, I remember thinking that Islam was not what drove those men to carry out such an act, but more, it was their ignorance and lack of compassion."

Again, I was struck by his candid remark, and it made me want to ask more.

"Did your parents explain to you what was happening, since you were younger, or did you understand the significance of what was occurring?"

"Oh, I understood and I was displeased. Allah does not approve of such actions. That type of violence is forbidden in Islam. Is it not forbidden in your Christian religion as well?"

"Yes, yes, it is forbidden. We do have just war theory, but, that is too difficult to discuss right now as we would need the theory in front of us to be clearer."

I found myself frustrated that there was so much we could talk about, but there was not enough time. And I also kept finding myself consistently in a position where I had to be careful to not push too much for information, while balancing that with getting as much out of these young men as I could.

Noor asked, "What were you doing on 9/11?"

"I was painting an office in my church, and I was in the exact place I needed to be—a place of worship. I felt safe and in the presence of God."

Noor smiled again. "I can see your light. I can see how affected you must have been on that day. Allah made sure you were near Him that day, so you could do His work today."

I was deeply moved. How could I not be? I had stepped out of my comfort zone weeks prior, not knowing what to expect. This comment, this point, this was the payoff. It was that moment that's been tattooed in my mind. That moment between a Christian woman and a young Muslim man who acknowledged her in a way no one in that madrassa ever had before.

It was a hard-fought step toward pluralism and understanding—made possible by talking to each other. Sometimes we can get lost on our path, and then someone says something so simple, and it brings us back as to why we are on that path in the first place.

This was that moment for me.

The Gift of Charted Waters

The conversations with these young Muslim men made me realize that I had to examine why I believe what I believe. Why am I a Christian? Were those students right? Was it because I was born into Christianity? That may be so; however, the reason obviously runs much deeper than that. And what of the questions about the authenticity of Jesus and his role as the Son of God?

For a time I questioned my faith, and I even wondered if I was in the "wrong" faith tradition. Theological school has been known to distress people. Your faith is obliterated and everything you learned in third-grade Sunday school is explained and you are left with this vacuum of information. Your safe "God loves me" bubble is broken, and you need to start over, building your faith back up again from the roots. The great thing about that is your faith becomes your faith and no one else's. Your faith comes from an authentic place, from where your heart lies, but only after it's been ripped out of your body, stomped on a bit, and thrown back in. Where I stood in 2006 isn't much different from where I stand now in my religious tradition; I am just more confident that I am in the right tradition—for me.

I often wonder what those students are doing now. Are they still fighting to wage a jihad of knowledge, or, have they given up? Are they teachers? Imams? Are they still alive? I will probably never know.

What I know is that my interactions with Muslims in India a decade ago has guided me here, to this very day. It has guided me to write about that experience and let these young men's voices be heard at this critical time. Such conversations matter immensely, because such conversations bring understanding at a grassroots level to a chaotic world. It is such conversations outside of our comfort zones that lead to continued dialogue. Dialogue that leads to ideas, that lead to action, that lead to collaboration, that lead to working side by side with the "other." Dialogue that can eventually lead to peace-building and peacemaking. Dialogue that can save one person, a group, or even a whole nation.

I still return to Noor's voice and words today in my work. I still remember his spirit and his sense of assurance and grace. I use his words in my teaching every day. I appreciate his continued presence in my life. And the amazing thing is, he has no idea that his voice is still ringing and making people think, as I do my work in the United States and elsewhere.

And as I reflect back a decade later, I realize the lessons from this time in my life are more important than ever. Uncharted waters can be frightening, but they can also be enlightening beyond expectation.

What a gift.

Chapter 27

The Second Incident

"Today a pious man has died. So get up and offer the funeral prayer for your brother Ashama."

—PROPHET MUHAMMAD'S
remarks at the sad demise of the King of Ethiopia, who as a
Christian provided Muslims refuge from their pagan persecutors

Karen's story is powerful because of the struggle she went through. There's no doubt that she was operating outside her element, but the payoff was immense. Karen has since worked relentlessly to advance interfaith dialogue and understanding—and in fact it was through her efforts of dialogue that we connected. She stepped out of her comfort zone and became visible. That visibility made our friendship possible. And now, countless more have read, and hopefully been inspired by, her example of meaningful communication.

When done right, such interfaith work builds such strong bonds that losing the friends you make in these endeavors often feels like losing a close family member. I believe this is because such bridges of understanding remind us by showing us the common humanity in all of us. When I was a young child a great man once told me that death is not the exception in this world, but the rule. Life, instead, is the exception. Everything dies, and it is only God Almighty who is ever living.

Earlier I mentioned two incidents at Richmond law school that were life-changing or me. By now, eighteen months after its establishment as an official student organization at the law school, MLSA was in full swing and the second incident had just occurred. And I was about to find out. I had just finished a lecture on sharia at a Richmond-area rotary club when my phone buzzed with an e-mail.

It was from the law school dean, Wendy Perdue.

"Dear Friends: We are all stunned and grief-stricken by John's sudden death. His abiding love of his family and infectious enthusiasm about all that he did was an inspiration for us all. We do not yet have information about funeral arrangements but will let you know as soon as we do."

The e-mail didn't make sense. I read it again, and a third time. And finally it clicked in. Suddenly my knees shook and my heart had that sinking feeling you get when you see an accident coming your way and know you can do nothing to avoid it. You brace for impact and everything moves in slow motion, but you fall apart knowing everything is out of your control. My knee-jerk reaction to learning of his death was, believe it or not, to call Professor Carroll to talk about it. He was a young man, only in his early forties. He wasn't supposed to die. But as God's plan would have it, this was his time. Indeed, life is not the rule in this world, it is the exception.

When Professor Carroll accepted the responsibility and burden as faculty sponsor for MLSA, I had no long-term relationship in front of me to know just whom I was getting involved with. From our initial communication, I only knew I was dealing with someone special. I just had no idea how special.

As I looked over the hundreds of e-mails we'd exchanged since that initial meeting eighteen months prior and pondered over the countless lengthy conversations, the stolen five-minute office pop-in discussions, and the grab-you-in-the-hallway rants—I couldn't help but reflect on the unique lessons I learned from him. Lessons all made possible by him taking the initiative to reach out and shake my hand—to talk to me.

I remembered how just ten months before Professor Carroll's death, my wife, son, and I were guests in his home for dinner, a privilege that my wife and I immensely cherish. As was our habit, he and I prayed together before eating.

I learned that Professor Carroll valued family more than anything. As a then-new father myself, I found his example priceless. He never canceled a meeting we had scheduled for work or business reasons—but he did for his children. To be sure, even those instances were few and far between, as I saw immediately that he viewed his students as extensions of his family. The lesson conveyed was simple, though it is often forgotten—work *supports* family, never the opposite. Family must always take precedence. Children must always take precedence. Professor Carroll had a brilliantly successful career, but he was an even more successful father—because he put his children first.

I recalled that six months before Professor Carroll's death, he, his wife, and his eldest daughter were guests in our home during Ramadan, to break fast with us. Again, as was our habit, we prayed together before eating. I recited from the Qur'an 5:70: "Surely, those who have believed, and the Jews, and the Sabians, and the Christians—who so believes in God and the Last Day and does good deeds, on them shall come no fear, nor shall they grieve."

Professor Carroll would often stop me in the hallway completely out of the blue and say, "Did I ever tell you that I'm married to the single most incredible woman in the world?"

I would smile and respond, "I think so, but remind me again why?"

Then, his piercing blue eyes would light up like the Fourth of July and he'd grin his patented grin (pun intended—Professor Carroll was an intellectual property lawyer) and say, "Well her name is Maria, and she's just outta this world." And then, without pausing he would add, "Can I tell you why?"

Laughing to myself and at the lovey-dovey look in his eyes, I would respond, "Sure, I would love to hear it."

Invariably he would throw his head back and start, "Ohhh, you're not gonna believe it..." a preface statement to him then telling me the latest and greatest thing he realized about her.

As my wife and I quickly approach a decade of married life, the lesson I learned from Professor Carroll is profound. Never be satisfied with merely having fallen in love years ago. Without saying it even once, and only leading by example, Professor Carroll taught me that if I can't find new things to love about my wife as the years pass by, then not only am I doing our marriage a disservice, but I'm doing my wife a disservice. A healthy and lasting marriage depends on continuously learning how to appreciate one another every single day, not merely in vows made years ago.

Two weeks before his death, Professor Carroll and I took one last stroll around the lake at the University of Richmond. "You know, this is my third year here, and I've never once walked around this entire lake," I commented.

"Really?" replied Professor Carroll. "I love it here, and on a beautiful day like this, it would be a crime not to enjoy it."

As we circled the lake we talked about where my career was headed. My path wasn't clear. With his years of wisdom he reminded me to reflect on God and family and choose the path best for both.

Suddenly he turned to me and said, "Did I ever tell you about my family history?"

I smiled. "No, but I'd love to hear it."

As we walked he told me that history in detail, all the way from the time of his great grandfather. In 20/20 hindsight, it almost feels like he knew another chance like that might not come. The honor I feel at having received that story is not something I can express in words.

His lessons live on through his students, because while Professor Carroll was a brilliant scholar, he was an even more gifted teacher. For example, he did not believe in memorization. Instead, he believed in internalization. It sounds simple enough, but his approach had a deeper meaning regarding life. We cannot memorize how to be compassionate, sincere, loving, and gracious. We cannot memorize how to communicate. We can only meaningfully internalize these behaviors and then meaningfully communicate them to others. Recognizing this principle, Professor Carroll made sure his students learned how to be compassionate, sincere practitioners, not rote replicators.

One week before his death, Professor Carroll attended our Christian-Muslim interfaith event that we hosted in conjunction with the Law Students for Reproductive Justice.

This would prove to be the last time I spoke to him.

And mere days before his death, I saw Professor Carroll's office door open and will never forget that I passed by, expecting but failing to say hello on my way back. Innocent as the lapse was, I failed to communicate, and it is a regret that tears me apart every time I think about it.

On the beautiful afternoon of March 8, 2012, John F. Carroll IV took his final trip around that lake, and physically stopped. His soul, however, continued. From God we are, and to God must we return.

Perhaps most remarkable about all of the above experiences I've shared is that I never once had Professor Carroll as my professor. Yet he maintained such robust communication with me, conveying that connection to his family and friends, that many simply assumed he was my teacher for numerous classes. As a result of him publicizing our interfaith relationship, I was asked and honored to speak at his funeral before over a thousand Christians. The thought of a Muslim speaking about a Christian teacher in a devoutly Baptist church before a thousand-plus

Christians alone demonstrates the power of overcoming ignorant fear in favor of educated communication.

Much like the first time he passed me in the hallway, Professor Carroll's entire life passed me by in an instant. And much like how he stopped me in that hallway, today I stop everyone reading this and ask you to continue to build that bridge of tolerance. Professor Carroll saw a lunatic burn a Qur'an, and rather than buy into the fearmongering, he reached out to a Muslim he previously didn't know and communicated his commitment to pluralism.

And because of his communication, we worked together on an interfaith bridge built on respect, compassion, generosity, and love—of God and of humanity. If we work together to help one another communicate "however we can," especially when that might appear difficult, we will continue to do what Professor Carroll has already magnificently done and leave this world a better place.

Don't let the opportunity pass you by.

So as I continue to reflect on examples of embraced opportunities in the face of fear and confusion, I'm reminded of my good friend William Wood, or Billy as we know and love him. Billy looks at racism from the point of view of a white family raised in the former capital of the Confederacy. One manner racism spreads is from the false belief that it doesn't exist beyond the individual random bigot. Indeed, racism is institutionalized in America today, but not enough white Americans understand this point for substantive change to occur.

How can white Americans recognize the institutionalized racism that is embedded in our society and thus become catalysts for pluralism and progress?

The author of the next chapter—Billy Wood—provides a powerful antidote.

Chapter 28

A Civil End to Civil War

by Billy Wood

*"Sadly, whites are rarely open to what black and brown folks
have to say regarding their ongoing experiences with racist
mistreatment. And we are especially reluctant to discuss
what that mistreatment means for us as whites: namely that
we end up with more and better opportunities as the flipside
of discrimination."*

—TIM WISE

Let me paint a picture of what you're about to read.

I grew up in the rural county of Hanover on the outskirts of Richmond, Virginia. Richmond was the second and permanent home of the capital of the Confederate States of America. Hanover County itself was the home of many slave-holding plantations before and during the Civil War.

After the war and emancipation, Richmond and the surrounding suburbs remained a center of haves and have-nots in regard to racial conditions. Hatred, fear, and jealousy developed between black people and white people. Even after desegregation in the 1960s the racial divide and tensions were clearly evident. This history was the canvas for my own experience with the subject of racism and hatred.

I attended Stonewall Jackson Junior High school and graduated from Lee-Davis High School. Both schools are named after confederate icons. In fact I was a Stonewall Rebel and a Lee-Davis Confederate. Reflect on that and remember that the Civil War ended more than a hundred and fifty years ago.

The majority of students were white. We were raised on the belief that we were simply better off than the poor blacks, who were slowly trickling into the county from the city. My own parents moved to Hanover County from the city because the Richmond neighborhood that they grew up in had "too many blacks" moving in. And this belief wasn't strange or socially taboo. In fact, this was the case with many white people my parents' age in Hanover County when I graduated from high school in the 1990s.

After high school I joined a volunteer fire department. I wanted to help people who were in need and I wanted to feel needed. Although my district was racially diverse, we had only white male firefighters. This was no accident. White people were treated as superior to people of color. People of color were not favored or even wanted for volunteer service.

I never considered my presumption of superiority a hindrance to helping people. I lived in an environment where heritage was important, so I easily rationalized my view as normal. It was white privilege in its finest example. Since I was a Lee-Davis Confederate in high school I proudly wore my Confederate battle flag sticker on my fire helmet. My foolish pride and my supercilious attitude meant nothing to me at my young age of nineteen. However, one fateful night would change my perspective forever.

232

There's Nothing Civil About Civil War

It happened on a day of celebration.

I was with my friends and we heartily congratulated one another on graduating from the volunteer fire academy. Grinning ear to ear, we patted ourselves on the back and held our heads high. We were hanging out in Richmond City on a strip called Leigh Street. Leigh Street was known to attract rural county kids, who came by to display their pickup trucks and muscle cars. It was a long-standing tradition. As a matter of fact, my grandfather, whom we called Papa Flinky, did the same thing in his youth just a few streets over from Leigh Street. Leigh Street was known both for drinking and fast cars when he was young. I never acquired his taste for drinking or fast cars, but I did enjoy Leigh Street.

But in addition to fast cars and drinking, Leigh Street was also becoming increasingly notorious for racial conflicts. As a result, my father, who happened to be a Richmond City firefighter, had warned me to stay away. My father grew up in a largely segregated Richmond, Virginia. During his youth he was taught to fear the influx of minority populations into the city. While serving in the fire service he was exposed to an environment of poverty and violence that was mostly associated with minority groups. Dad's fire station was the first response company for medical emergencies that covered Leigh Street. So when he told me time and time again of the fights, shooting, and stabbings that were occurring near Leigh Street, he spoke from experience, not paranoia.

Fearless as I was, I did not heed his warnings.

So there I was, walking down Leigh Street with my friend Adam. I had on my cowboy boots, flannel shirt, and camouflage hat. I proudly wore my Confederate flag sticker. I was proud of my heritage and of who I was. We soon came upon a group of people, most of them black guys ranging in age of twelve to eighteen and wearing dark clothes and hooded sweatshirts. The group blocked our way along the sidewalk. But as we got closer the group suddenly became very friendly and calmly parted so we could pass through.

I was blind to their true intentions.

We walked through the group and like a house of cards they collapsed upon us. That was my last clear memory because I remember what felt like a cinderblock hit me in the face. I was so stunned I could not focus. Fists began flying at me from everywhere. Suddenly I was forced to the ground. I remember one young black woman kicking me while yelling racial slurs. More and more kicking ensued from every direction. I looked up and noticed that most of the attackers had pulled up their hoods. Just before I blacked out I remember seeing a knife coming at me.

When I came to I had no idea what was happening or where I was. I saw a lone black guy defending me from the rest of the group. I wasn't sure if he was a part of the group or not. He told me to remember his face and explain to the police that he helped me. He pulled me up and told me to run. I did as I was told, to the best of my ability: I got up and away from there as fast as I could, literally running into an oncoming police car. The car stopped; the crowd scattered, jumped into vehicles, and fled. A white male police officer on a horse dismounted, took me into his arms, and told me to hang on. I was dizzy and couldn't even see straight. But as my focus came back another officer began questioning me, a black female officer.

"Young man, can you give me a description of the attackers?" she asked. Before I could respond she added, "And don't tell me they all looked the same!" She said it in the bitterest tone imaginable.

"What do you expect me to say?" I replied, exhausted and confused.

The officer, stomped off in a huff. The white male officer stepped in and looked at me dead in the eye to ensure he had my attention.

"Tell me what you mean. Talk me through this. What were they wearing? How tall were they? What color clothing?"

I described their clothing as best as I could, but didn't get far. "Officer, it was difficult to tell. It all happened so fast. I couldn't really distinguish between who was who."

He nodded. "Anything else?"

I was frustrated. "Look. When you're lying on the ground being beaten, everyone looks the same."

The officer left me and explained what I'd said to the other officer. They soon left the scene to assist another officer who possibly had the suspects in custody. A few moments later an ambulance arrived and took me to the emergency room.

Although still delirious, in the ER I quickly became aware of my condition. I had a severely swollen black eye, bruised ribs, and a broken finger, and I had soiled myself. I was frightened, angered, and humiliated. To make matters worse, I had to answer to my father. Much to my relief, my dad wasn't angry or upset. Instead, he told me that he loved me, and he reminded me of that over and over again. After I calmed down some, he informed me that the people who did this to me had been taken into custody.

My father was right about a lot of things, and not going to Leigh Street was one of them. I never liked it when he said "I told you so" if I made a mistake after disobeying him. But on this occasion he never said those words. He was mostly teary-eyed and continued to remind me that he loved me. It was a side of him I'd never seen before.

As my father drove me home from the hospital, the police asked us to make one stop along the way. We had to go to an area near Leigh Street and identify my attackers. The gentleman who'd helped me was there too—but not of his own accord. The police had him in custody despite his pleas that he'd done nothing wrong, that he'd actually saved me from far worse injury or even death. The police didn't believe him; they finally let him go only after I told them he was telling the truth. I thought that was odd, but never considered they may not have trusted him because he was black and from the same neighborhood as the attackers. The reality is in my ignorance I simply hadn't considered, or was then willing to recognize, racial bias from the police.

The others denied what they had done. A horse-mounted white male police officer informed us that we would be going to court in the near future. The officer knew my dad and even though I did not realize it at the time, he was one of the officers who had helped me.

My wounded eye healed slowly as we waited the long months until our court date. For the first few months prior to the trial I was angry. I trusted no one of color. I remember being utterly confused about why this had happened to me. I was a nice guy who helped people. Why would someone want to hurt me? What had I done to those guys to trigger the attack? Was it my cowboy boots? Was it my flannel shirt and blaze- orange hat? Perhaps they mistook me for some other redneck? Or, maybe it was something else. What if they just assumed that I did not like them or that I felt as though I was better than them? Eventually the anger turned more and more to speculation and theory.

After what seemed like an eternity the court date finally arrived.

A Change of Heart

It struck me as odd that we were in a juvenile court.

As I entered the courtroom I ran into two white females I knew from high school. One of them quickly said hello and began speaking to my mother (my family knew this girl well). I quickly realized that they were there with the defendants. This blew my mind. These two girls were old friends from high school. I had been on the swim team with one of them since I was thirteen. The other girl was more of an acquaintance. But either way, I could not understand why they were here in juvenile court with the defendants. Needless to say, the conversation soon came to a screeching halt and we moved on to take a seat. I felt betrayed. I was angry.

There were approximately ten defendants. None of the defendants was older than fifteen. I was only able to recognize one defendant—a thirteen-year-old also named Billy. Billy was the one who made me think I got hit with a cinder block—he hit me with brass knuckles. My anger quickly turned to confusion. How could this kid have done this to me? What was his motive? As these questions rushed through my mind one of the defendants suddenly blurted out the answer, "We did this because he's white."

I froze with an emotion that I cannot explain. I tried to collect my thoughts but I couldn't. I was numb. This was a problem because right away the state called me to the witness stand for my testimony. The prosecutor spoke directly to me, but loudly to ensure everyone could hear.

"Billy, will you please tell the court who it was that hit you with the brass knuckles? Can you please point him out?"

Nervously I looked at that kid and his grandmother. I was confused. For some reason I found myself feeling sorry for him, but it made no sense. "How can I feel sorry for him?" I scolded myself. What did he hold against me that he felt so compelled to hurt me? I thought about what type of horrible world he lived in that made him think what he did was OK, where he thought he was better than me because of his race. This was a kind of racism I had never seen before.

And that's when I realized something that had been staring me in the face all along—I had seen this racism before; I'd lived it. I realized maybe we weren't so different after all. Sure, I hadn't attacked anyone. Nor had I wanted to harm anyone. But this certainly wasn't the first time I'd borne witness to racism. This was simply the first time I'd been the victim of racism.

Meanwhile, the proud white Confederate heritage I wore as a badge was responsible for the most horrific war ever fought on American soil. It was responsible for centuries of slavery, racism, oppression, and terrorism. It was responsible for racism existing in my own family some hundred-and-fifty years after the Civil War. And like another brass knuckle punch to the face it hit me: How would I feel as a minority teenager if after all that violent history, I saw someone who felt their race was superior trotting about my neighborhood? How would I respond? I suddenly hoped I would never have to answer that question.

That strange type of compassion I felt for this kid took hold. I'd remained silent for too long on the stand. The judge spoke up and demanded an answer from me. "Son, speak up; answer the prosecutor's question."

I didn't know what to say. "I don't...I'm not sure, Judge."

The lawyer for the defendant chuckled. My father cursed quietly. The police officer for the prosecution stared at me blankly.

"Son, I'm asking you one more time. Please answer the prosecutor's question."

I gave the same answer. Immediately the lawyer for the defense moved to have the case dismissed for lack of evidence. With no other witnesses willing to testify, the judge dismissed the case. All defendants were cleared.

I left the witness stand and slowly walked back to my family. As we left the court, the same police officer as before approached me.

"I'm sorry, Officer. I just couldn't get myself to point him out."

"It's OK, Billy. I understand." He looked at me with sympathetic, non-judging eyes.

My parents were sympathetic to me, although I knew my dad was screaming on the inside. We quietly left the courtroom that day and did not speak about it for some time.

Writing a New Future

Weeks later as I reflected on the events of that night, I realized I had a choice—remain angry and stubborn, or change. I chose to change. I removed the Confederate sticker from my hat. I started to embrace friendships with the few black people I knew. As time went on I began to question the racial tensions and notions that I had been exposed to for most of my life. I realized that hatred, fear, and jealousy were at the heart of the matter. I realized that I would not stand for it anymore.

This lesson in hatred would change who I was. I did not fully comprehend the change at that time. Instead, this change has come gradually and has been part of my growth as a human being. I have learned tolerance, learned to be different, and learned to love even those who may not love me. I no longer judge a book by its cover. I appreciate our differences and see the strength in our human diversity.

Today people see this change in me. It is reflected in the way I teach and raise my children. Not all of my friends and family agree with me. If I have to change each one of them one person at a time, then so be it. I am up for the challenge. I feel that it is my duty, my mission, and my burden to create a society where everybody respects one another regardless of skin color, social, status, religion, or sex.

Since that I time I have grown so much in my love and understanding of my fellow human beings. I have made a promise to myself not to let my children grow up with the same mentality I was exposed too. Tensions in this arena may never completely vanish, but I will never stop trying to end the racial divide.

I know I have a long way yet to go, and so does our society. But I hope we can paint that future, tolerant society together.

Billy's story is inspiring because of his conscious choice to step out of his comfort zone despite every motivation to retreat within it. He could have used his experience as evidence to validate preconceived stereotypes that black people are violent. Instead, he reflected internally and changed himself. He took personal ownership over his own future and of his children's future. As a result, Billy is leading not just with his words, but also with his acts, to create a more tolerant future. This doesn't mean he's "made it," as ultimately we are talking about a journey, not a destination. It does mean, however, that he's taking a step in the right direction.

I've seen Billy's work to lead a conversation on race relations and interfaith dialogue pay immense dividends. In the same spirit, I turn your attention to the author of the next chapter—Brandon Jaycox. Brandon is a lawyer and Pennsylvania state prosecutor. Brandon leads by example to serve the underrepresented and abused and takes that effort to a new level.

Some naysayers might say he wasn't "supposed" to be here—and perhaps that is exactly what makes his story all the more amazing and inspirational.

Chapter 29

Black Lawyers, Black Leaders, and Changing the System

By Brandon Jaycox, Esq.

"In recognizing the humanity of our fellow beings, we pay ourselves the highest tribute."

—THURGOOD MARSHALL

Reporting officer responded to incident location in reference to a complaint received regarding a black male subject lying in the road.

Upon my arrival I observed a black male subject lying on his back in the middle of the roadway. He had foamy blood coming from his mouth. There were several areas of blood on

the road near the victim. Blood was coming
from back of the victim's head. The victim
was not breathing. He was warm to the touch.
I could feel no pulse.

Excerpt, incident report, page 1 of 3, Officer M.D. Murdaugh, Hanahan Police Department, South Carolina, 11-14-1986.

Every morning I walk two blocks from my office to the Juanita Kidd Criminal Justice Center—the courthouse in Center City Philadelphia. On the way, City Hall with all of its impressive stateliness is on my left; on my right I pass a Dunkin' Donuts, a department store, a 7-Eleven, several hotels. There is a tourist souvenir shop too. There's always a crowd walking with me: city hall employees, police officers, schoolchildren, commuters, the homeless.

And there are lawyers.

There are varying degrees of pedigree and morning demeanor. There are the well-dressed stoics—typically the civil lawyers who cross the street over to City Hall just after the 7-Eleven. There are the efficient workhorse general practitioners, with well-pressed suits but well-worn shoes. There are the high-powered criminal defense attorneys, striding in look-at-me ties and monogrammed sleeves.

And then there are the assistant district attorneys of the Philadelphia District Attorney's Office. Prosecutors, I am one of them. I'm also a black man.

"You know what makes me proud?" A middle-aged black man was saying this outside 7-Eleven the other day. "Seeing all these young black DAs walking to court in the morning." I smiled in disbelief. Such validation was rare.

You can pick us out by the boxes of files we carry. Or some of the newer DAs have taken to wearing lapel pins with a particular amount of

242

pride. That day I was walking with several DAs. I don't wear the lapel pin, but I am proud of what I do.

Two types of buses I see on the way to the courthouse. The city buses carrying people on their morning commute. And the buses from Curran-Fromhold Correctional Facility, carrying the incarcerated to the Criminal Justice Center. Not everyone is happy to see DAs in the morning.

Some people are disappointed. I usually get it in the stairwell when I'm running from floor to floor and room to room. The stairwell smells of smoke, and desperation.

"Hey you a lawyer?"

"Yes." I never stop walking. There is no time and people always want to divulge incriminating hypotheticals in the stairwell before they know what I do.

"You got a card? I got a quick question for you."

"I'm out of cards and I'm a prosecutor."

"Oh, OK." Then the disappointed look. Occasionally I'll hear "*sellout!*" as I round the next flight of stairs.

I've learned how to win people over too, though.

"Hey you a lawyer? You got a card?"

"Yes, I'm a DA."

"Oh so you be *sending them up.*"

"Only the ones who deserve it." I say with a smile.

"Oh, all right."

"You still want my card?"

They take it about a third of the time.

"Brandon Jaycox on behalf of the Commonwealth. Good morning, Your Honor."

I say this every day. If I'm running behind, I might begin to say it as I push past the waist-high gold gate that separates the gallery from counsel tables before the judge's bench. I'm rarely the only black person in the courtroom. But I'm often the only black person on that side of the gold gate.

Other than the defendant.

```
Coroner Smith discovered what appeared to be
an entrance wound in the back of the victim's
head, an entrance would to the center of his
back, and a grazed area on the right side of
his chest.

No exit wounds were discovered at the time.

Excerpt, incident report, page 2 of 3, Of-
ficer M.D. Murdaugh, Hanahan Police Depart-
ment, South Carolina, 11-14-1986.
```

During my time at the Philadelphia District Attorney's Office, I have been assigned to the Family Violence and Sexual Assault Unit, where we handle domestic violence, sexual assault, and child abuse cases. These cases are arguably the hardest to prosecute. They often require civilian witness testimony. The facts are rarely as straightforward as many think, and victims of domestic violence and sexual assault need specialized advocacy. But such cases are also the most rewarding to prosecute for all the same reasons.

Recently a child molestation case I prosecuted went before the jury. The victim was a black adolescent teenage boy named Kevin, who was autistic and verbally delayed.[12] The defendant was a family member Kevin stayed with during the summers.

---

[12] Note that the names and facts in some of the cases mentioned have been altered to protect the privacy of victims and their families.

I was honest with Kevin and his mother before trial about the difficulties of trial. I told Kevin I'd ask him—on the stand and in front of fourteen strangers in open court—to recall how the defendant sexually abused him. I explained to Kevin that he would be subjected to a rigorous cross-examination by a skilled defense attorney.

Victims often feel betrayed by the criminal justice system. At the beginning, their hurt and pain are the focus. Then the shift happens. The focus is now on the accused and his constitutional rights. The defense attorney discredits the victim. Suddenly there is only sympathy for the man seated beside his lawyer, wearing handcuffs, looking pitiful and in peril. My job is to refocus the narrative away from the defendant and onto the defendant's crimes and the victim. I often contextually address this with jurors in closing arguments like this:

Now the defendant sits in peril, perhaps you have noticed that being on trial has weighed on him. But also considered that when he took Kevin down in the basement all those times, the defendant didn't think he would ever have to face judgment before you fourteen. He thought no one would ever find out—that Kevin would be too afraid to tell anyone and even if Kevin did tell someone, no one would believe an autistic teenager. And the defendant certainly didn't foresee Kevin—despite his disability—having the courage it takes to disclose sexual molestation before strangers in open court. The look on the defendant's face, you may have noticed, is one of a man about to be held accountable for his terrible actions.

After I gave my closing statement on Kevin's case, I went into one of the side rooms and prayed. I prayed for justice and I prayed for a conviction. The jury deliberated for a two days and ultimately found the defendant guilty of two out of three leading charges.

For victims, the criminal process is lengthy and stressful. It often seems at times not to be worth the emotional cost. I had a case where the defendant, after a dispute with his wife, pointed his firearm at her. He then held, let's call her Jessica, hostage for several hours inside their house. It took a year and a half for the case to come to trial. I remember Jessica's apprehension about coming to court. She talked of wanting to move on.

"I just want this to be over," she said. "It has been so long. Every time I think about the court date coming up I start to relive what happened. I don't want to have to see him again in court."

That's where meaningful communication becomes critical. That's where I invest long hours outside the courtroom, to talk to the victim, reassure her, and let her know she has someone in her corner. No amount of coercion can resolve these concerns—only patience, compassion, and meaningful dialogue. I'm fortunate to work with professional victim/witness coordinators who provide crisis counseling and intervention. These professionals walk victims through the difficult emotional journey before, during, and after trial.

According to a 2014 Bureau of Justice Statistics report, about three-quarters of victims of serious violent crimes—including those involving firearms—report moderate to severe emotional distress, increased relationship problems, or disruptions at school or work, all as a direct result of the victimization they faced. Even in cases that don't involve serious physical injuries or weapons, half of victims report similar levels of distress and life disruptions.

But there can be an extraordinary liberation for a victim at the conclusion of a domestic case. Jessica ultimately did come to court on the day of trial. I was poised to the pick the jury. No doubt having been told by his defense attorney that Jessica was in court and was ready to courageously fight, the defendant pleaded guilty to the lead charges.

Not long thereafter. I received the following e-mail from Jessica. "Thank you so much. Last night was the first night I slept peacefully in two years. May God continue to bless your career."

It was a simple one-line e-mail. Insignificant in length, compared to the hundreds of papers of documents and paperwork generated to bring the case to trial. But that one meaningful line was more valuable than anything else.

```
Name: Stephen Jaycox

Date of Death: 11-14-1986

City, Town Location of Death: Hanahan, S.C.

Immediate Cause: Internal hemorrhage and res-
piratory insufficiency due to, or as a conse-
quence of: 38 Caliber distant gunshot wound
to back.

Excerpt, incident report, page 3 of 3, Of-
ficer M.D. Murdaugh, Hanahan Police Depart-
ment, South Carolina, 11-14-1986.
```

My father is Stephen Jaycox. He was murdered in 1986. I have only a few memories of my father. I remember the smell of his cologne. I remember his arms. And I remember the day I was told he was dead. I was four years old. I was in day care.

I remember there was a faint odor of stale apple juice and sugar cookies. My mother worked there. I was in a playroom, the walls decorated with elementary graffiti, the floors sparsely scattered with Legos, Lincoln Logs, and other children's toys. The playroom was adjacent to the main entrance.

A woman rushed in through the center front door, sobbing. I watched as my mother came to comfort her. The woman's hair was matted and wet. Had it been raining outside? The playroom doorway perfectly framed the scene, like I was watching on some oddly shaped wide-screen TV. Suddenly my mom's face changed—like something deep inside broke.

She melted into the floor.

They were talking, but I did not comprehend their words. I turned away for some reason—maybe I wanted a few more seconds of normalcy. Then a boy, slightly older than I, whom I may have been playing with in the playroom, spoke to me: "She said your dad is dead." The little boy said it plainly. His eyes met mine.

I felt nothing. I just took it in—for later recollection, I guess. My mom hoisted me onto her hip. I remember her tears wet my face. I remember hearing my infant sister crying in a car seat. My mom, my sister, and I were going over a bridge. My mom's eyes were filled with tears. I did not know how she was able to drive. Either she said, or I heard from somewhere, "Life is going to be much different now."

My father had been murdered. If I'm honest, this experience has informed my career choice. My decision to become a prosecutor is in part because my father died a violent death at the hands of another.

A few years back I got ahold of some of the police paperwork in his murder investigation. As I read Officer Murdaugh's narrative, I couldn't help but wonder what my father's thoughts were in his last few moments. The foamy blood coming from my father's mouth indicates he was struggling. It was mid-November in South Carolina. Was the concrete cold?

The man who took my father's life needed to be locked up and sent up regardless of his race.

But see, I know the statistics. Blacks make up about 12 percent of the US population yet about 44 percent of America's prison inmates. According to a 2014 Sentencing Project report, roughly 10 percent of black men in their thirties are currently incarcerated. In the juvenile system we are also singled out. Blacks under eighteen years old comprise only 15 percent of their age group, but they account for nearly 44 percent of the national juvenile jail population.

But to those who would call a black prosecutor a sellout, I'd also point out the following: we are also more likely to be victims of crime. I serve the often forgotten interest of those victims. According to a 2013 Bureau of Justice Statistics report, violent offenses, including murder, rape, and assault, make up 24 percent of arrests made in the largest counties in the United States. Consider that property offenses, including burglary, motor vehicle theft, and fraud, made up an additional 29.1 percent of arrests. Therefore, more than half the arrests were made as a result of someone being hurt, physically, emotional and/or economically. Those are real victims who deserve advocacy.

Following recent grand jury decisions against indicting police officers for the deaths of unarmed black men, some of the anger stemmed from a very real perception that white police officers working with white prosecutors don't give a damn about black people. Where a system of power employs few of the minority people it most negatively affects, it is natural and logical to perceive bias and injustice. People see prosecutors as oppressors instead of as protectors of the community.

People want a criminal justice system that is working for them, not against them. I wish I had stopped to ask the man outside 7-Eleven why he was proud to see young black district attorneys. I think he saw protectors and not oppressors. I believe he saw people who would represent his community. And this gave him a sense of pride.

I'm honored to serve as an advocate for victims. Kevin and Jessica deserve someone to fight for them and hold their abusers accountable—just as my mother my sister and I needed someone to fight for us. I feel called to be an advocate for victims and hold accountable those who preyed on them.

According to the American Bar Association, blacks make up only about 4 percent of the lawyers in the United States. Among the few blacks who are able to and choose to pursue a legal career, the most common perception is that justice is best served sitting at defense counsel's table rather than prosecuting.

But is it not easier to change the system if one has a seat at the table?

Are there institutional biases in the US criminal justice system? Absolutely. And these must be addressed in open and action-oriented dialogue. We must understand that those who are supposed to be protectors are justifiably seen as the oppressors. But in our conversations about how to fix the broken system, while we should consider the plight of the incarcerated, we cannot be afraid to also address their wrongs and the victims they affected.

I am a black man who is a prosecutor for a reason. Not solely to convict those who deserve it by their actions, but also to be an advocate for victims. I am also a black man who serves as a prosecutor in order to address biases and injustices in the criminal justice system. I endeavor to be a protector and not an oppressor. We all deserve a criminal justice system that works for us. I invite anyone with a passion for justice to come talk to me.

I'm here both to talk to you and to serve you.

Chapter 30

We Owe One Another

"It is that fundamental belief, I am my brother's keeper, I am my sister's keeper that makes this country work."

—PRESIDENT BARACK H. OBAMA

Brandon is an inspiring leader because he lives to serve. His mentoring of others, his advocacy for victims, and his relentless pursuit of justice have literally changed countless lives. He has accomplished a great deal and will no doubt accomplish much more. But he didn't get here by accident or with a silver spoon. He consciously chose to invest his time wisely, respond to racism with education, and ultimately lead by example. Brandon serves others effectively in part because he exemplifies a critical characteristic of every great leader—he values his contribution to humanity.

And let's be clear on something. This is not about simply "learning about other races" or "other faiths" and calling it a day. We owe one another much more than that.

We cannot live with a people in peace unless we know the people personally. And we cannot know a people unless we make the effort to get to know them. This truth seems so obvious, but the effort is so often ignored. We need not repeat the mistakes of history to learn from them.

Earlier, in Chapter 8, I mentioned the anti-Islam rally in Orange County, where, among other things, an elected official threatened to send Muslims to "an early meeting in paradise." Unfortunately, this violent rhetoric has only increased in recent years. Islamophobia and anti-Muslim bigotry has become mainstream in the political landscape. We've all seen a certain ignorant billionaire politician advocate torture and murder of Muslims with "pig-blood-dipped bullets." And he's merely the latest in a series of candidates who are actively demonizing Muslims to win votes. The question then becomes, how do we meaningfully communicate in the face of such intimidation and threats of violence?

I turn to a friend who recognizes that we owe one another more than mere pleasantries. What does that "more" look like? I'm confident you'll find immense wisdom in the remarks of one of the most compassionate and loving people I know—who is the author of the next chapter—Lee Weissman.

Or, as he's popularly known on the Internet, Jihadi Jew.

Chapter 31

Abraham's Tent Had No Walls

By Lee Weissman

"None of you will believe until you love for your brother what you love for yourself."

— PROPHET MUHAMMAD

In 1982, an idealistic twenty-two-year-old sat in front of the White House.

I sat with a bunch of older, more seasoned idealists and lifelong protesters. We sat next to a sign that read "Wanted: Wisdom and Honesty." In the many hours I spent talking to people in that collective search for wisdom and honesty, I discovered that most people don't have "a cause." They mostly eat, sleep, work, raise their families, worship, and do the stuff of daily life. They often desire to help others and do so. It is not a passion, just part of life. Then there are those who have a cause. For those people, and I am among them, that passion is ignited by very specific experiences, radicalizing life-transforming moments. My experiences led me to my personal mission of creating bridges of understanding and friendship between observant Jews and Muslims. It hasn't been easy, but it is necessary.

So at a time when Muslim-Jewish relations seem more strained than ever, I'm grateful that you've taken a moment to talk to me.

The little *dargah* (shrine) in Chennai always smelled of roses. Professor Habibullah Shah would sit there for hours every evening, doing *dhikr* (remembrance of God) or talking with students. I mostly sat and listened in. Hanging around religious stuff was my profession and I was a great observer. Professor Shah finally asked me one night, "What are you doing here, Lee?" It wasn't an informational question. It was an existential question. He wanted to know what lay under my seeming obsession with all things religious.

I kind of sputtered something or other about my "intellectual curiosity." He stopped me.

"So has it ever occurred to you," he said, "that what you really want is your own way of serving God, not just to watch everyone else?"

It was in the sheer light of that question, and in my answer, that I found both my observance as a Jew and my appreciation for the beauty of Islam and my Muslim brothers and sisters. My interfaith work has always been and continues to be my homage to that man and those moments with him when I saw the beauty of faith in full bloom. I moved from Chennai to Irvine. Irvine smells like sage bushes, not like roses. Irvine, California, is a comparatively bland planned community. It houses a commuter school where not much seems to happen. Yet in 2006 and for a few years, Irvine became famous for its Muslim Student Union's Anti-Zionism Week—an annual flash point for passionate and sometimes violent conflict between Muslims and Jews.

I derided what I heard and what I saw. Adults in both communities urged students, both Muslim and Jewish, to fight the battles of the Middle East on a suburban California campus. Fiery speakers told Muslim students that their Jewish student counterparts, universally branded as "racist Zionist Jews," were the "new Nazis." The Jewish community branded the Muslim students as "battle-hardened jihadis."

Finding it a little hard to imagine battle-hardened jihadi on the campus of UC Irvine, I went there to witness Anti-Zionism Week for myself. The speakers that year were two prominent imams from Washington, DC. The fiery invective of these speakers left me shocked, not so much for what they said but for the way they said it. I had known many Muslim scholars in India, and they were some of the most softspoken and tactful people I had ever met. These guys were something entirely different.

The big surprise for me was the students. I didn't encounter "battle-hardened jihadis." I encountered decent immigrant Muslim kids on a search for meaning. They had found meaning in religious observance and in action for social justice. Like most people at that age they were sometimes over-passionate, less than completely informed, and naively self-righteous. More shocking, however, was the reaction of these "vicious anti-Semites" to me, the most Jewish-looking person most any of them had ever encountered.

Within minutes of my arrival at any MSU event, a mini interfaith dialogue would begin. Students would ask me questions about Judaism, about Jewish practice and belief. They'd immediately notice the incredible similarities between our religions. As the events progressed, I rarely got to hear much of what the speakers said. Mostly, a ring of students talking about faith surrounded me. It was so refreshing to talk to kids who really were taking their beliefs seriously and struggling not only to understand their own, but now to understand mine.

They were polite and kind and respectful. Not at all what I had been led to expect. Recognizing that I was an older religious person and that I might not be totally without wisdom, students began to talk to me about more personal things. While the battle over Zionism raged but a few feet away, I found myself making friends. My relationships with the MSU students extended well beyond Anti-Zionism Week. It soon included Shabbat dinners with my families, attending classes in "tazkiya" spiritual purification with the Muslim students, and long talks over coffee about things that really mattered.

I had discovered the power of religion as a language in common between Muslims and Jews. Observant Jews and Muslims, to a great extent, share a common worldview. They are uniquely able to understand one another and to appreciate the common struggle to live in society, to contribute to society, and yet to live, to an extent, above and beyond it.

One afternoon, the MSU president sat with me in my backyard, having tea and a bite to eat. Oh the table he saw a small booklet that contained the "Birkat ha Mazon," the Jewish grace said after meals. He read through the English translation and looked a little astonished, asking, "What is this?"

"That is the *du'a*, the prayer, we say after eating."

"But it's all about Israel and Jerusalem. What is that all about?"

"Well, when we eat bread and other special foods, we imagine that they came from the land of Israel and thank God for the land and for all He gives us from it."

He looked surprised. "So, wait a second, Israel is a holy place? Like are there religious obligations that you can only act on there? Or prohibitions that only apply there?"

"Yes, that's exactly right."

"But, how come nobody ever told me this before? *This* I understand. They tell me about Israelis inventing cell phones and having discotheques that you can see anywhere...but this...this I can understand."

In all the yelling and screaming this young man had heard on campus, no one had spoken his language before. I wasn't trying to convince him of anything, I was just sharing my faith. And he and I were able to make sense of each other. But I'm constantly reminded of how much work remains before us.

The anti-Muslim protest on February 13, 2011, in Yorba Linda, California felt like Germany, 1933. Or like the scene in *Frankenstein* where ignorant villagers pursue Frankenstein's childlike "monster" with torches and pitchforks.

It was a charity fund-raiser, and two controversial Muslim speakers were going to speak. I had gotten an e-mail asking me to come out and represent the Jewish community in the "fight against Islamic anti-Semitism." The truth is that I didn't much like one of the speakers speaking that night. This notorious incendiary figure was already well known from his speeches at UC Irvine. I really wanted to know what the attraction was with speakers like this and I figured I would come and talk to some of the Muslim folks about it. I didn't attend to tell them what I think, but to ask what *they* think. I attended to talk to them, and I hoped they might be willing to talk to me too.

What I found instead was a crowd of ordinary-looking middle-class white people screaming at the top of their lungs, "Go back home! Go back home! Terrorists! Terrorists!"

One man (who later identified himself to me as a "minister of the Gospel") stalked behind two absolutely terrified little Muslim children shouting into their ears obscenities against Prophet Muhammad.

Another woman screamed into a small group of women in hijab, "Go home to your husbands and let them beat you."

A man carried a sign saying "No Sharia Law" and mused out loud that he wished he had brought some fried pork skin so that he could powder it up and make the Muslims inhale it. He looks at me sheepishly. "Uh, sorry, Rabbi, guess you don't much like pork either." I was glad that for one brief second he felt ashamed that by mocking their religion he was also mocking mine.

Sandwiched between the police line and the crowd of screamers, dressed in my long coat and yarmulke, I looked ridiculous with my folding table, two chairs, bowl of dates, bowl of candies, and proudly displayed sign: "Not here to protest. Here to communicate. Let's sit down and talk."

My good friend Omer Hendler joined me, and he and I tried desperately to be a little wall of Chassidic love in front of a rising wave of hate. We didn't get much dialogue going that night. We ducked under the police barricade to offer greetings of peace to the frightened Muslim families as they ran the gauntlet of hate.

Yorba Linda provided a stark moment of clarity that this was not the America my Eastern European parents fled to—this was the world they fled from. As a child in suburban Philadelphia, I was a regular victim of anti-Semitic attack and hatred. Kids would chant "Hitler, Hitler!" and drag me off the bus and beat me up. I remember their faces. I saw the same ugly inhumane faces in Yorba Linda. The Torah teaches that we are created in the "image of God." In their hate, the Jew-haters of my childhood and the Muslim-haters of Yorba Linda had lost the divinity of their faces. This was not just about politics. This was about the spirit.

In my own community, I found that the outrage over Yorba Linda was underwhelming. In our community, expressions of contempt for Islam and for Muslims had become commonplace and accepted. I sincerely doubt that any of my efforts are going to bring peace to the Middle East. I am idealistic but not stupid. I do believe that my efforts can bring peace to our dinner tables, whether Muslim or Jewish, and curb the mutually misguided gossip on the parking lots of our mosques and synagogues. I have discovered that the key to achieving that is not in anything that I can really do. More than by what you do, you transform hearts by what you are. The best I can do is model what it looks like for Muslims and Jews to live in peace, mutual respect, and even love.

Whether in social media or singing around my Shabbat table, that has really been my goal.

Hate, even in its most seemingly benign and accepted forms, is a spiritual disease of the heart. It is a blockage that prevents us from seeing the commonality of humanity in others. A strong identity is not the problem. It is my fierce pride in my Jewishness that allows me to appreciate the fierce pride of others in who they are. Faith is not the problem. It is the solution. Judaism and Islam share a marvelous vision of what it means to be a good human being: mercy, kindness, charity, respect, discipline, modesty. Many of us do a great job at being these things within our narrow sphere. The moment we learn to be these things to one another, together, we will not only see a new us, but we will see a new world around us.

Jewish tradition teaches that thousands of years ago, Abraham had a tent that was open on all four sides. He never preached. He fed people and conversed with them about the one God he had come to know. He built relationships and modeled a path of love. All I have done is taken a few steps on that well-worn path.

I'm now an idealistic man fifty-five-year-old man, but I'm not just sitting in front of the White House. I want to invite you to my house and join you in yours. I still seek wisdom and honesty with the same passion as that twenty-two-year-old.

Only now, I know that we can get there, together, if only we take the time to talk to one another.

Chapter 32

Building the Partnership

"The lightning spark of thought generated in the solitary mind awakens its likeness in another mind."

—THOMAS CARLYLE

In the years I've had to pleasure of knowing Lee, we've spoken on interfaith panels together and broken bread together, he's been a guest in my home, and we've now joined in our written efforts to advance Muslim-Jewish relations. Lee's wisdom and honesty is infectious. I've seen firsthand how his compassionate approach to talking to others—aiming simply to learn about them—has been the antidote to extremism.

But we have immense work yet to do. Lee compared the scene at the anti-Muslim rally in California to Nazi Germany's anti-Jew rallies. Sadly, these anti-Muslim rallies have continued, with an armed hate rally in front of a Phoenix-area mosque as recently as May 2015. The 2016 election season has spurred unprecedented anti-Muslim hate, violence, and bigotry against American Muslims. The work we face is plentiful, and it is imperative we keep our tents open.

By now you've probably realized something. Having the courage to be a strong parent who teaches children to think for themselves and to become leaders in interfaith and race relations is not easy. Having the courage to educate those around you is not easy. Having the courage to have meaningful dialogues is not easy. You will get burned. You will be ridiculed. You will be brushed aside, insulted, and threatened. These aren't reasons to back down. Rather, they're reasons to expand your network and increase your efforts of compassion and tolerance.

Sometimes, even when you think you've made zero progress, you have no idea who is watching and building his or her own courage to talk to you. I watched as two unlikely activists built a partnership to advance freedom of conscience.

I turn your attention to the concept of God. Not whether He exists or not, but whether belief in God is a requirement to talk to one another. Can believers and atheists work together for a common cause, or are they inherently pitted against one another forever and ever?

I refer you to my friends and colleagues and authors of the next chapter—atheist and religion scholar Kile B. Jones and Muslim and scientist Dr. Kashif N. Chaudhry.

Chapter 33

Ahmadis, Atheists, and Awesomeness

By Kile B. Jones & Dr. Kashif N. Chaudhry

"In the long history of humankind (and animal kind, too) those who learned to collaborate and improvise most effectively have prevailed."

—CHARLES DARWIN

Hi, I'm Kile. These days—now as a grown man—I still vividly recall my first philosophy class.

The story goes like this. I was a youth pastor at the time, trying to make my way to seminary and higher education. I felt that if I were to be an honest believer, I would have to look the skeptical monster in the face and cultivate an intellectually sound weltanschauung. "Weltanschauung," for you non-German readers out there, means I was seeking wider perceptions, broader horizons. Feel free to use that word.

So anyway, there I was at a community college, with the whole world ahead of me. I was a mere stripling at the time, but I remember diving into the history of philosophy with Mr. Bertrand Russell. Here was a man who had become my surrogate grandfather. The Englishman's *History of Western Philosophy* was something of a second Bible for me, and it was not unusual for me to bring it to church on Sunday. Feel free to read that book.

Russell, the ethical reincarnation of Spinoza, sparked in me a zealotry for knowledge. Spinoza, by the way, was an amazing Dutch philosopher way ahead of his time, as I suppose most legendary philosophers are. Feel free to quote his work.

The fire that burned inside Russell had lit my torch. As a result, my appetite for education and learning had become ferocious. But it was more than a faint desire. It was a Dionysian passion. Feel free to Google Diony—OK, I'll stop doing that. I developed an insatiable passion for throwing myself into projects, creating something novel, and leaving an impression on the world around me. And although I had somewhat of an "otherworldly" focus, I deeply craved temporal significance. I wanted my life to inspire others. I wanted to matter. I wanted to drink in life—to absorb and be absorbed—while finding unique ways to bring people together.

But enough of philosophical poetry; where am I going with this?

As this biographical clip illustrates, I found joy and meaning in engaging with others to harness the potential that exists within all of us. I'm no Tony Robbins, but I need to stay busy. "The more things a man is interested in," Russell states, "the more opportunities of happiness he has, and the less he is at the mercy of fate, since if he loses one thing he can fall back upon another." I memorized these lines and reflect over them often. Russell adds, "Life is too short to be interested in everything, but it is good to be interested in as many things as are necessary to fill our days."

264

So here's the twist to my story. Some see my intent to become a minister as insincere when they discover I'm now an atheist. Some write me off as insincere because I am an atheist. In my inner circle, the manner in which I was compelled to navigate my Christian family and friends as a newly minted nonbeliever was indeed difficult. Here I was, holding degrees in theology and all too familiar with Christianity. I could and still can quote the Bible backward and forward. But I was now an atheist.

What could I do?

I often mention my de-conversion (or "enlightenment," depending on the way you frame it) but I never write about it. I feel narcissistic and echoic talking about such a personal and private matter. So rather than delve into why I became an atheist, I want you to talk to me about something far more important.

This is where I believe life choices matter the most. I could spend my time as a herald and an apologist for atheism. And in perfect honesty, for a while I did just that. I wrote critiques of various religious beliefs and practices for *Free Inquiry* and *The Humanist*. I debated Christians at universities, on YouTube, and on the radio. I spoke at secular conferences and promoted my tribe above others.

But eventually, I found this orientation unfulfilling.

It wasn't that my appreciation for debate and criticism fizzled—in many ways I still participate in them. But it seemed to lack the kind of constructive productivity I had previously envisioned. Once my blind fury relaxed and I realized that difference in the world is not only honorable, but also essential, I redirected my unique passions toward other goals.

One of those goals was to humanize both nonbelievers and religious persons. I've watched almost every debate Christopher Hitchens partook in. In doing so, I couldn't help but realize that the animosity and conflict inherent in the way these debates were framed didn't help counteract popular misconceptions about the groups represented by the participants. In other words, these debates did nothing to build bridges of understanding. Instead, they largely worked to burn down the frail bridges that remained.

I found this animosity unacceptable—both because as an atheist, I see how negative stereotypes have made atheists among the least trusted demographic in America, and because in my contact with atheists I see how little they trust they feel toward believers. So I decided to take a different route. Instead of setting up debates, where feces are flung and straw men are set up, I would fashion what I consider a much healthier manner of dialogue: interviews.

Thus began "Interview an Atheist at Church Day." On this platform I create opportunities for atheists and Christians to engage in meaningful dialogue based on respect for one another—not condemnation or insults. So far it has been a hit, and opportunities to grow continue to present themselves.

My PhD program weighed on me in that it pushed me to dream up other academic ways to express myself. I had always loved the idea of art journals. I remember my stepfather Jimmy's *Juxtapoz* magazines lying around the house. I also remember his passion for art.

So how could I create something intellectual, while also allowing a place for more emotive expressions? Answer: I started *Claremont Journal of Religion*. Besides our wonderful art, interviews, and articles, we have the most amazing team of editors and referees. Kyle Thompson, a friend and colleague whom I've entrusted with the journal and made editor in chief, is the perfect man for the job (even if he spells his name wrong).

The fact of the matter is that people in different social groups can work together to counteract stereotypes, create positive change, and imagine a brighter and more colorful future. It is this belief that I have seen manifested through the various projects I'm involved with. And that's no utopic naivety; it's an optimistic reality. We can transcend our tribes

266

and reach out to one another with the goal of leaving the world better off when we depart.

But theory is one thing—practical application quite another. Not long after Qasim asked me to write for this book, the horrific Charlie Hebdo atrocity happened in Paris.

My firebrand atheism flared up. "*Je suis* Charlie!" I declared. And as the world was being torn apart over free speech and whether or not to be respectful to religion, I made sure to emphasize my commitment to the secular ideals of liberty, critique, and the slaughtering of sacred cows.

Months earlier I'd "e-met" a physician, activist, and blogger named Kashif N. Chaudhry. Kashif is an Ahmadi Muslim who moved to the United States after facing persecution in Pakistan. Like me, he is a vocal activist for universal human rights and freedom of conscience. He was passionate about Islam and adamant that the Islam proffered by the Taliban, ISIS, and their ilk was as foreign to Islam as the KKK is to Christianity. We disagreed on theology, on the existence of God, and most importantly, whether cricket is the worst sport in human history or the greatest sport of all time.

But even after Charlie Hebdo I saw him, as a Muslim, advocate for free speech and universal freedom of conscience. This in many ways was new to me. I wanted to find out more.

In his actions, Kashif did not identify with the magazine. But while I noticed that Kashif was condemning the violence of it all, I also saw that he reacted in a different manner than most believers I knew. He emphasized the virtues of mutual respect and intellectual dialogue—while maintaining that religious beliefs were not above criticism. Kashif went on to note the double standards the West has regarding free speech and racism. Or how one of the first police officers shot dead was, in fact, a Muslim.

As was the case in the Charlie Hebdo attack, atheists and Muslims alike actively responded to self-described antitheist Craig Hicks's shooting of three Muslim students in North Carolina. I was shocked at both the horrific murders, but I was also shocked to learn something I didn't expect.

Hicks ran in many of my same atheist circles I do. He and I had many of the same friends on Facebook. And while many of my atheist friends were focusing on how this was an issue over a parking space—meanwhile mentioning all the good "liberal" stuff Hicks preached—Kashif was emphasizing the role Islamophobia played in the taking of the three innocent lives. "Islamophobia takes lives," Kashif said. "Rather than defending bigots who espouse it, antitheists must show some humanity and condemn Islamophobia loud and clear. Sadly, some are still refusing to acknowledge the very existence of this dangerous evil. What a shame."

I do not consider myself an "antitheist." I may not believe in a god, but I certainly am not antireligion. I believe in the age-old principle of "live and let live." That said, I apparently shared many of the same positions as this cold-blooded killer. It was in this case that I felt like Kashif did after the Charlie Hedbo shootings: stigmatized, caricatured, and ashamed.

But there is an important difference between the way Kashif and I responded.

Firstly, Kashif was clear that the terrorists who committed the Charlie Hebdo attack were not following true Islam. Regarding Hicks, however, I would not say Hicks was not following "true" atheism or that in killing people he somehow departed from "true" atheism. As far as I'm concerned, there is nothing inherent in atheism that says not to kill. It is a lack of a belief in a deity and nothing more. Atheism is not an ethical framework like secular humanism or ethical naturalism. But when self-identified Muslims kill innocent people, Kashif is quick to condemn their actions as un-Islamic. And as much as I understand his position, we disagree on whether there is, or whether we can know if, there is an essential core to Islam or religion.

But it wasn't just that Kashif and I parted ways about whether or not God or a soul exist: we tended to find different meanings in these horrific events. We genuinely saw a great many things differently. And while that difference in opinion is OK, it once again got me thinking about something greater and more important.

That is, is that all we are—a bundle of differences? Does our marrow inherently shout against the marrow in one another?

Well, besides the fact our marrow is composed of the same material: in my talks with Kashif we both began to realize that we share a great many things in common. He was the only Muslim I would let hijack my cause, as I would hijack his. It was a sense of benevolent co-opting. And why not? If we share similar goals we might as well nonviolently hijack each other.

So we decided to formally reduce our e-meeting to the e-world and started an online group called Ahmadis and Atheists for Freedom of Conscience.

Our lively group tries to find ways for atheists and Ahmadi Muslims to work together for social good. Our strange connection cultivates fields that might otherwise be left barren by rigidity. Our group works through issues surrounding theocracy, blasphemy laws, free speech, civilized speech, and social activism. Through it, we raise our voices for universal freedom of conscience—especially for marginalized belief communities. We campaign against religious persecution of Muslims in Burma, Christians in Iraq, Shia and Ahmadi Muslims in Pakistan, and atheist bloggers in Saudi Arabia and Bangladesh. Rather than spend time hurling accusations at one another, we have made our little corner of the Internet a refuge for people who seek out honest paths to be constructive. Indeed, we joke that we seek to create weapons of mass construction—by talking to one another.

And while our forum still has the occasional flare-up, we ensure we continue to talk to one another with a sincere intent to understand, not undermine. For example, there have been quite a few examples of people trying to evangelize through our group. We'll find atheists who want Muslims in a bunker, and Muslims who want atheists on a prayer rug.

When these situations occur, Kashif and I politely redirect people to our primary focus: finding ways to think, work, and live together—while respecting our differences. And even though this group contains a plethora of difference, there is a unique magic at play when you witness the capacity for strange connections to flourish.

There's no superficiality at work here. There is nothing worse than fake interfaith flattery. Kashif and I agree that in order for genuine communication to occur, both parties must be willing to face their radical dissimilarity. Despite our common focus on our similarities through this group, Kashif and I do not shy away from discussing our differences with a smile. "No, this verse does not prove that there is a Creator of the Universe," I responded to a post on his Facebook page. He had quoted a verse that alluded to the big bang and the nature of planetary motion. "Let's agree to disagree on this, Kile," he responded with a smiley-face emoji.

Kile began this chapter and I, Kashif, will close it out. Kile and I realized we could only get so far focusing on our disagreements, and that is why we instead use our similarities as our platform for growth.

The fact that we are always able to respectfully disagree on theological issues only adds to the beauty of our partnership. It was this respectful correspondence that inspired Kile to write a scholarly rebuttal to ignorant anti-Muslim memes alleging the Qur'an preaches violence against non-Muslims. I know I can count on Kile as an example of a nonbeliever who respects people of faith and does not dismiss them as naïve, ignorant, or weak. Kile knows he can count on me to speak up for atheists persecuted for their nonbelief. Our honest relationship is proof that we can disagree and yet come together for causes that matter much more than our disagreements.

And to exemplify how powerful this attitude is, consider this.

I had never once met Kile in person, at least not as of the writing of this chapter. We live three thousand miles apart, yet we share that singular goal of mutual respect and freedom of conscience. We finally met several months after this chapter was written, and long after we e-met.

Kile has invited me to visit him when he comes to the West Coast. "God willing," I reply, "God willing."

He smiles back, because life's too short to avoid building bridges with friends of a different belief.

Chapter 34

Misteaks Happen

"Success does not consist in never making mistakes but in never making the same one a second time."

—GEORGE BERNARD SHAW

The struggle to find that gem of a person subscribing to a different faith or belief, willing to work with you, can be long and arduous. But when that person is found, the results are powerful and constructive. Kile and Kashif have both faced immense backlash for their efforts, but they'll gladly tell you it's been a worthwhile struggle. As repeatedly mentioned throughout this book, that struggle to build bridges isn't easy—nor should you expect it to be.

Along the way, you'll make mistakes. As the title of this chapter suggests, "misteaks" happen. I mentioned earlier that I don't believe anyone has made more mistakes than I have when it comes to building bridges of interfaith relations. So what happens when you make a mistake? It is game over only if you let it be game over.

Bert Musick was one of the great leaders I've had the pleasure of working with. And the simple but profound wisdom he shared extends, like the value of dignity, beyond the differentiating factors we each bring to the table. It all started one afternoon early in my career as a lawyer.

"Qasim, we need to talk."

Few phrases cause as nervous as a reaction than when someone pulls you aside unexpectedly and says, "We need to talk."

Suddenly your mind races over every second of your life since birth. Though you'll know in mere seconds by virtue of that person just telling you, you insist on trying to figure it out on your own. "Oh no, he found out I got suspended for two days in the seventh grade for fighting." (True story.) Or, "Crap, I hope that guy I cut off on the way to work wasn't some executive." (No comment.) Or, worst yet for a lawyer, such as yours truly, "My life is over because I committed legal malpractice and he's coming to tell me I'm fired, will lose my law license, and am going to jail forever." (Hypothetical.)

It's only added anxiety when the "we need to talk" comment comes from a supervisor, a leader. So when my new director, Bert Musick, pulled me aside just four months into my legal career, I knew I was done for. Bert wasn't just any old seasoned litigator. He was also former Secret Service, which made him all the more intimidating to those who didn't know him. He later told some amazing stories about protecting our presidents, which heads of state had annoying spouses, and the time he accidently pushed former Iranian president Mahmoud Ahmadinejad in an elevator but played it off like he meant to do it. In my time with him I learned just how great a lawyer, person, and leader Bert was.

But for now I saw a stern-faced, brisk-walking, former lethal killing machine, escorting me to a conference room to have "the talk."

"Hey, Bert, should I bring a notepad or anything?"

"Nope, this'll be quick."

Oh, man, it's worse than I thought. I'm getting canned right now. I must have screwed up big time. Was it that contract matter out of Texas? I bet it was. You screwed me for the last time, Texas!

I walked into the small conference room and Bert followed me, closing the door behind him. I sat down while he remained standing and paced back and forth. This only added to my uncertainty about what was coming next.

"How are you doing, Qasim?"

"Um, fine."

"How's your son Hassan?"

"Also fine."

"When was the last time you went bike riding with him?"

By now I began to realize either I definitely wasn't getting fired or this was going to be the most awkward firing in history.

"I...I don't really remember."

"When was the last weekend you were home and not on your book speaking tour?"

"I guess maybe a couple of months ago."

"Do you know why I pulled you in here?"

"I honestly have no idea."

"It's for two reasons. You're a new laawyer and going through a steep learning curve." Bert never said lawyer, his slight Southern twang always elongated it to "laawyer."

"Right."

"So I need you to stop worrying about something for me. Stop panicking if you make a mistake. Mistakes happen."

I wasn't sure how to respond, mainly because my mind was still somewhere else.

"Wait, did I mess up on a case? What happened?"

"No, Qasim, I'm telling you the opposite. You need to stop worrying about things out of your control."

"I don't know what to say. I get that mistakes happen, but I want to avoid them, right? What if I cost our clients money, or make a recommendation that loses a case, or worse yet, commit malpractice?"

"All possibilities, some inevitabilities, and while there are no promises—mistakes happen. Right now you're more worried about not making mistakes than you are about learning from your mistakes or, dare I say, learning from your successes. Look, mistakes will happen. You will make mistakes. Every great leader has made mistakes. You'll send that e-mail you shouldn't have sent, make that comment you wish you hadn't, and give legal advice that will seem terrible in hindsight. But a good laawyer doesn't panic and doesn't pull his hair out, a good laawyer pauses and learns from those mistakes, and moves on."

He paused and finally sat down.

"Right now you're so uptight and worried about making mistakes it's impeding your progress."

"Paralysis through overanalysis."

"Yes, exactly. And because you're so close to your own work you don't see it. At a certain point you have to realize that the facts you have are the facts you have, and the applicable law is the applicable law, and you have to pull the trigger and move forward with the best information you have at that time. Good laawyers are the ones who can recognize that with confidence and execute with confidence. And despite that, mistakes happen. Don't get so caught up in trying to take the perfect step forward that you forget altogether to step forward."

"So I'm not getting fired, right?"

"Fired? What? No, you goofball, why would you think that?"

"I don't know; I guess I'm just being paranoid, what with that sudden 'we need to talk' comment. I thought you were upset about something."

"Actually, that reminds me of the second thing. And this I am upset with you about."

"Rats, what?"

"You're a laawyer for us and you're traveling on the weekends, seems like every weekend, right?

"Yeah."

"So you've got your full load of work here, and you're trying to balance that with your speaking and media and advocacy stuff."

"Yeah?"

"And I know you've had to take a few days off work here and there to tend to your book and media stuff."

"Bert, if you want me to cut back on the speaking stuff, I understand. I'll find a way to make it work."

"No, you're not listening, Qasim. You're in here every morning early, and most days you're here later than most."

"Wait, I'm confused; I thought this was about me missing too much work?"

"That's why I'm saying you're not listening. Are you getting much sleep?"

"Yeah, I guess."

"How many hours?"

"I don't know, like four to five or so."

"No wonder you look like hell. You need to get more sleep. Are you going anywhere this weekend?"

"No, not this weekend."

"Good, go home now. That's an order."

"Wait, why? It's only 11:30 a.m."

"Go home, and go bike riding with Hassan. I want to see a picture as evidence."

"Seriously?"

"You're not allowed to log in to work for any reason. You're not allowed to be on your computer for any reason. If there's an emergency it can wait."

I thought back to the wisdom Professor Carroll gave me several years prior. Work supports family, never vice versa.

"You know, my son is about Hassan's age, too," he said. "I know how important your book and advocacy stuff is and I support it 100 percent. But right now I can tell you your son needs you at home. That's where you need to be. So go on; get outta here before I have to fire you to get you to leave."

I couldn't think of anything to say. There really was nothing left to say. So, I did what any self-respecting man would do in my shoes.

I went home and took my son for a bike ride.

I wasn't yet done learning from Bert, not by a long shot. His communication skills, his emotional IQ, and the compassion with which he spoke taught me volumes about handling difficult and volatile situations. He was an amazing leader and a brilliant communicator.

Little did I know then that time was fleeting, and that the real inspiration from Bert was yet to come.

Chapter 35

Value Your Contribution

"With confidence, you have won before you have started."
—MARCUS GARVEY

Bert reminded me that whenever we start a new endeavor, we can't let fear of mistakes paralyze our progress. Part and parcel of overcoming the fear of mistakes, and of making mistakes, is recognizing your own value. Remember, this stuff isn't easy. Race relations and interfaith relations, leadership, parenting, death—none of these matters are easy. Oftentimes people quit when they stumble because they don't realize what value they bring to the table. I've made a ton of mistakes in my time, many of which I've elaborated on in this book. And I'm sure I'll make more.

But as I learned years ago from another amazing leader, Carol Rick Gibbons, successfully and consistently overcoming such mistakes stems from first recognizing your self-worth.

It all began over lunch during law school. "Look," she said, "we're really glad you're here, and I don't want to get your hopes up, but the chances of this internship turning into a full-time job are basically zero."

My heart sank, but I tried to take it in stride. "Sure, yeah, I totally understand. I'm just grateful to have been selected."

It was March, 2010. About two months earlier, on a whim, I'd applied for a corporate law scholarship. My application must have been the very last one to arrive before the application deadline, and I thought I had no chance. After several weeks of interviewing, waiting, praying, and more waiting, I'd been selected as one of the scholarship recipients. Part of the award included an internship in the legal department of a major corporation. It was a dream opportunity, especially in the terrible job market through which everyone in law school was suffering.

I was now having lunch with the lawyer who would supervise me during the internship—Carol. She'd also interviewed me during the selection process.

Carol was kind, sincere, ridiculously intelligent (which was kind of intimidating because I didn't want to say anything stupid, though I knew I would eventually), and had a great sense of humor. This sense of humor was especially helpful when the inevitable stupid remark left my mouth. Deep down inside I'd hoped for even the slightest possibility the internship might turn into a job, but Carol's clear statement left no doubt. Still, I was grateful for the internship itself. And frankly I'm not sure what impression I left with her during that lunch. I felt everything I said was remedial, irrelevant, and uninteresting. Still, Carol was gracious and we soon parted ways, with May 24th planned as my first day.

In law school all you hear about are the cutthroat partners at law firms who demand you work eighty hours a week. We'd hear stories of first-year associates arriving at 7:00 a.m. and staying until 2:00 a.m. as a matter of expectation. We'd also hear stories of associates being let go for not working the long and demanding hours. At the time I was a struggling law student, supporting my wife and our fifteen-month-old on loans and scholarship money. Job prospects were weak in a recession economy. My current situation and the aforementioned horror stories—

real or otherwise—added to my confusion, as I soon realized Carol was the antithesis of what I'd been told to expect.

I felt a bit shy at how genuine and deep an interest Carol took in my thoughts, opinions, and recommendations. Carol was and is a seasoned attorney, yet I felt like the center of attention when speaking with her. I couldn't figure out why my views mattered so much to her, but they apparently did. It was humbling as well as empowering.

The internship carried on and soon ended, as all internships do. Carol and her team took me out to lunch on my last day. We said our pleasantries and Carol asked me to keep in touch. I of course promised I would, but still didn't know what entirely that entailed. Do I call every week? Once a month? Is e-mail more appropriate? Unnecessarily overthinking it, I wasn't sure exactly what "keep in touch" meant until a few months later.

I was in class in early October of my second year of law school when I felt my phone buzzing. I stepped out of class to answer the call. It was Carol, asking if my wife and I were free for lunch with her and a few colleagues I'd met during the internship.

In my ignorance, I still didn't understand why she was going out of her way to reach out to me. My mind was still stuck on preconceived notions. She was an accomplished high-ranking attorney in a major company. I was a fumbling law student whose internship was long over. The internship was over. Her accepted responsibility of managing me those ten weeks was fulfilled. What was in it for her?

We met, and I saw the same sincere Carol and colleagues I'd met during my internship. They weren't there to offer me a job. They weren't there to ask me to come back and intern once more. In my ignorance I simply couldn't figure it out. We parted ways once again with the expectation that we'd keep in touch. And much to her word, we did, throughout my second and third year of law school. All the while I couldn't figure out what was in this dialogue for her. I was benefiting by learning from a mentor, a legal scholar, and, to be perfectly selfish, someone with strong connections in a still terrible job market. She was—as far as I could tell—wasting her time with a broke law student who thought a paralegal was a disabled lawyer.

Finally, in one lunch meeting during Ramadan 2011, I decided I had to ask Carol the question that had mystified me the better part of two years. We sat in a Chinese restaurant in Richmond, Virginia's West End. I sat with an empty plate because I was fasting, while Carol waited on her meal, and I wondered, why I didn't just tell her it was Ramadan so we could reschedule for next month? We later joked that she not only took me out to lunch but also picked up the tab.

"Carol, I need to ask you something that might seem a bit obscure, so don't mind it."

"Sure, what's going on?"

"I enjoy these lunch meetings. I enjoy the opportunity to learn from you, network with you. I have a great deal to gain by spending time with you as I build my legal career. And I am gaining a great deal. Everything, from the internship to the people you've introduced me to to the time I get to spend just picking your brain—it's all immensely valuable to me."

"But?"

"But, what I don't get is—and this is the part that might sound obscure—what's in it for you? What do you get out of all of this? There's literally nothing I can do to benefit you. And I know how busy you are with work and family and such. So why sacrifice all this time talking to me?"

Carol smiled and paused for a moment to collect her thoughts. "I'm glad you find our meetings valuable. But, believe it or not, you're wrong. Whatever you think you're getting out of these meetings, I feel like I'm getting more out of them than you are." She paused for another second and leaned forward. "Don't underestimate what you bring to the table."

I didn't know what to say.

I genuinely hadn't considered the wild, inconceivable possibility that maybe, just maybe, she found value in simply talking to me. What began as a scholarship I had impulsively applied for had turned into a memorable internship that had now transformed into an invaluable friendship. All the while, I was missing the obvious in front of me, because I wasn't willing to consider the value my mentor was ascribing to dialogue.

This experience was my giant flashing neon sign of a life lesson, a directive to shed my inhibitions and insecurities. You never know how valuable you are to others, so don't shortchange yourself. Instead, reach out to those you aspire to become like. Find those mentors, leaders, and friends who appreciate and know your worth—even when you don't.

And as far as that internship that wasn't supposed to turn into a career? Wouldn't you know it; I joined Carol's company several years later. It began with the relationship we'd built in years prior, strengthened with the communication we maintained throughout, and cemented with the trust that ensued as a result.

You are invaluable. Surround yourself with leaders who recognize that and are willing to lend you their shoulder, not just to lean on in times of need, but also to stand on in times of progress.

Chapter 36

Bert Never Let Me Buy Him Coffee

"Our dead are never dead to us, until we have forgotten them."

—GEORGE ELIOT

Bert was one such leader who let me lean on his shoulder in times of need and stand on it in times of progress.

It was a warm September day in 2014, with clear blue skies as far as the horizon.

My flight left Chicago O'Hare late, and thus it arrived late at the Richmond airport. When the pilot finally turned off the seat belt light, I didn't wait for others to exit but instead literally sprinted off the plane and out of the gate as fast as I could. I carried my computer bag and travel bag while sliding across the dusty terminal in dress shoes. Down the terminal, out the front doors, across the street, and down to the same spot where I always parked my car in the Richmond airport garage.

Today was just about six months to the day in late March when Bert left work early, complaining of headaches. That March, Richmond had been hit with an unseasonable snowstorm. Bert wasn't one to complain or make excuses, so he marched into the office without flinching, while most people worked from home. Bert had a high pain threshold, too. But the previous few weeks at work he'd mentioned throbbing head pain on more than one occasion. Thinking it was a sinus issue, he'd brushed it off.

I'd e-mailed Bert a few hours after he left work that day, but he didn't respond—unusual for him. That evening I texted him, both to check on him and also to reschedule a meeting we'd planned for the following day.

His wife responded almost immediately. "Bert's not doing well. I'm taking him to the ER. Can you let me know Bert's supervisor's number so I can tell him Bert won't be in tomorrow?"

I sent her the information she requested, but something didn't sit right. Bert wasn't one to complain. He wasn't one to ask for help or favors—even on small things. I'd known him almost a year-and-a-half now, and he'd never once so much as let me buy him lunch or even coffee.

Something was wrong but I couldn't put my finger on it. I wanted to text back to ask for more information but knew I was only being selfish if I did. When someone is rushing a family member to the ER, the last thing she wants is more obligation or distraction. I forced myself to remain patient.

That night in March was a long night. I texted my coworkers, and while everyone knew something was wrong, no one quite knew what. We had no one to talk to about what was happening to our coworker and friend. The sun rose the next day and I stumbled in to work, hoping against hope to see the top of Bert's bald, glistening head poking out above his cubicle.

286

Nothing.

As more coworkers arrived, we all looked to one another for answers. No one had anything concrete, but one fact was for sure—Bert wasn't in good shape. We just didn't yet know how bad a shape he was in.

Now, in September, I raced down the highway as fast as I could. I was set to give a short speech and I couldn't afford to be late. I was battling a severe cold. My throat was sore, in part due to the cold. Also, I'd just delivered eleven lectures before large audiences—each lecture almost an hour long—in the previous forty-eight hours at various high schools and community centers all over the Chicago area. I was exhausted, but I also knew I couldn't miss this talk.

I was about fifteen minutes from the garden where I'd be speaking. I called a coworker to let him know I just might make it after all. Earlier I'd texted him saying there was a high probability I'd be late. As I weaved through traffic while maintaining caution not to speed past a police officer, it suddenly hit me. What was I going to present? I hadn't at all prepared my talk. I had no script, no outline, not even notes. In the hustle and bustle of the last few days I'd missed what was most obvious and most important.

Compounding the nerve-wracking situation, Bert's entire family would be there, along with dozens of other family friends. After all, my talk was in honor of Bert's accomplishments. I'd been asked to speak—something I will always consider a unique privilege. So I felt all the more furious with myself that I still didn't know what to say. I had to think of something, fast. I reflected on some of the wisdom Bert had already imparted to me in the short time I'd known him.

There was the constant and inspiring reminder he gave me, as well as several others who reported to him: "You deserve to be where you are. Don't let anyone tell you that you don't belong. You belong. Own it." There was the humorous jab at himself when we joked about male pattern baldness. "Bald is beautiful!" he'd declare proudly. I thought of the candid legal advice he gave me while discussing someone he had to sue on a business deal: "Only a fool represents himself in court, Qasim. Always hire a laawyer."

I can't forget Bert's default view of the world when talking to people. "Qasim, remember, it's not just what you say but how you say it. Always err on the side of kindness. You won't ever feel sorry that you did." And because Bert was so attuned to people's feelings and sensitivities he'd usually tack on, "Oh, and joking around is great, but be mindful of whom you're joking with. Sometimes people can be hurt but won't tell you. And you never want to put someone in that situation."

When Bert discovered Ayesha and I were buying our first house he looked me right in the eye as if about to reveal an eternal truth and said, "A home inspector in Virginia is only liable up to the cost of inspection, so make sure you trust but verify." And boy, did this advice come in handy when we soon discovered our home inspector had missed a massive gas leak, one that could have resulted in a major explosion. But rather than sending him a scathing letter—which my ego wanted me to do—I erred on the side of kindness. As a result, our home inspector was profusely apologetic and saw that our entire system was replaced at no charge to us.

And as I mentioned earlier, Bert's eternal bottom-line truth was his unending focus on family. "Family is your first obligation, Qasim; everything else can wait."

I thought about Bert's selflessness and leadership, his ability to communicate with those different than him—of different races, religions, and cultures. His contemplative decision-making and his bright smile. Bert never let me buy him coffee. He never let me do anything for him because he saw himself as a servant. But now, finally, this was my chance to talk to everyone Bert knew about how great he was, and there was nothing he could do to stop me.

I arrived at the location where the small ceremony was being held. Everything was already set up. I was one of the last ones to arrive but thankfully made it just in time. The microphone stood alone in front of about a hundred chairs, most of which were filled. Another hundred or so people stood behind and around the chairs. A few speakers addressed the group first; then I was asked to step up and deliver my talk.

As I walked up to that microphone that day I felt butterflies. My breathing and heart rate increased and my throat suddenly felt even drier than before. Reflecting about Bert triggered a host of emotions, and now I stood, trying to control them, in front of two hundred people.

In March of that year, just forty-eight hours after Bert left work early, he returned to his Maker. Despite emergency surgery, the cancer had simply spread too far. He was only thirty-eight years old. Bert was a brilliant lawyer, a compassionate human being, and a loving family man. He was an incredible leader.

It wasn't the first time I'd given a eulogy, and it may not be the last. But something about looking at Bert's beautiful children, his beautiful family, and his incredible friends that day—something about it all was overwhelming. I still didn't quite know what I was going to say, so I did what was natural—talk to Bert's family like I talked to Bert.

"Hi everyone. My name is Qasim. Bert was my supervisor and I think I worked with him longer in the legal department than anyone else." The crowd silently listened.

I suddenly blurted out, "Bert Musick...never let me buy him coffee." I paused as I saw a few people crinkle their eyebrows at the random comment. I looked down for a moment to gather my thoughts.

I repeated myself. "Bert...never let me buy him coffee." I looked down again. "I tried several times. I'd say, 'Hey, Bert, let me get this one.' And he'd respond, 'Nah, it's fine. I got this. This one's on me.' And I'd say, 'Come on, just this once.' And he'd shake his head no and tell me to hurry and order." The crowd still seemed lost. I couldn't blame them.

"So I thought about how I could repay Bert for everything he did for me, for all of us. And I wanted to gift him something that would be of benefit to those who are most precious to him—his children." The largely homogeneous white Southern Christian crowd sat silent and listened to the only Muslim speaking that day. That was relevant because of what I said next.

"You see, as a Muslim I'm bound to two duties. One is my duty to God. To worship Him and trust in Him. And two is my duty to humanity. To serve all humanity and to alleviate suffering. And I can't do only one—I am obliged to fulfill both duties to the best of my ability."

I saw a few surprised faces. It was clear to me by their body language that several had never heard this point of view before. With increasing confidence I continued. "And when I look at the way Bert lived his life, there's no doubt that he exemplified both of these duties. You see, Bert was a man of faith but Bert also never let me buy him coffee, and now I understand why. Bert's focus on his service toward humanity was so strong that he refused to ever be served. Bert lived to serve, and that's why his death has left such a gaping hole in all of our hearts."

I looked up to see a warmly attentive, closely listening crowd .

"So when I thought about how to fill that gaping hole, I could think of no better way than to capture just how much Bert meant to all of us. I wanted to create something that his family and children could look at next year, ten years later, thirty years later, and know their father was a good man, a great man."

I'd gathered all of Bert's coworkers and asked them to record their thoughts on camera to convey to Bert's family. What was supposed to be a short video ended up an inspiring compilation telling of amazing things Bert did for people without ever asking for anything in return.

"Bert ner let me buy him coffee. And I just wanted to say thank you for letting us get to know him and love him, and be loved by him."

I stepped away from the microphone and retook my seat, finally feeling that sense of calm I usually have after I speak. The pain of losing Bert remained, but the burden of sharing just how grateful I was for his service didn't sting as much anymore.

Just a few months before Bert died, he and I carpooled to a funeral. After the service, as we pulled away from the church, Bert turned to me and asked, "Q, do you have a will?"

"Sure do, Bert."

"Good. Only a fool doesn't have a will prepared. Because you never know when you're gonna go."

As I walked back to my car that sunny September day I couldn't help but smile. Bert may have been tragically taken from us, but the inspiration of his compassionate nature will live on far beyond his lifetime. It falls to us to focus on that compassion, seize the opportunity to learn from it, and carry it forward.

And as I learned one day, that is true whether you've known someone a lifetime or but a few hours.

Continuing this theme, I turn to my friend, colleague, and author of the next chapter—stand-up comedian Salaam Bhatti. Salaam's powerful story emerges in the backdrop of an obliterated city after Hurricane Sandy. It's all the more inspiring when you learn of the dying young man who inspired Salaam to serve.

Chapter 37

Reviving the City

by Salaam Bhatti

"Service to others is the rent you pay for your room here on earth."

—MUHAMMAD ALI

I volunteer for the charity Humanity First.

My cousin Musawar, aka Sevi, from England, got me into it. He is seven months younger than me, but better than me in everything. When we were in school, he aced exams by barely studying, whereas I studied for hours, hoping to match him. When we played video games, he beat me without breaking a sweat, whereas I ended up smashing the buttons in a humiliating loss. As a child, he was cuter; as an adult, I found my wit was nothing compared to his. After graduating school, I thought, "I need something to fill my time and to compete with Sevi in." Volunteering became the next competition. Sevi was one of the top youth fundraisers in England for Humanity First. He single-handedly raised over $7,000. The bar was set high, but I was up for a challenge. So I said, "Game on."

No sooner had I agreed to this than Hurricane Sandy came with an uppercut to the Eastern Seaboard's face. I know Qasim already quoted Mike Tyson, but I'm going to quote him again, because I gave Qasim the idea: "Everyone has a plan until they get punched in the face." And boy, did we get hit square in the jaw. In the New York/New Jersey area, we were essentially leveled. The greatest city in the world, the city that never sleeps, paused an impatient pause.

Humanity First, Red Cross, all the first responders came to Long Island. Many might be surprised to hear it, but Long Island is an island. When I think about islands, one of the first things that comes to mind is John Donne's poem "No Man Is an Island."

> No man is an island,
> Entire of itself,
> Every man is a piece of the continent,
> A part of the main.
> If a clod be washed away by the sea,
> Europe is the less.
> As well as if a promontory were.
> As well as if a manor of thy friend's
> Or of thine own were:
> Any man's death diminishes me,
> Because I am involved in mankind,
> And therefore never send to know for whom the bell tolls;
> It tolls for thee.

Donne wrote this poem hundreds of years ago, but I saw how volunteering transposed its core insight onto today's practical world. People from all walks of life came together to help out complete strangers. Charitable efforts showed those of us living on an island that we were a piece of the continent, a part of the main.

A week after Sandy, conditions were calm enough for the volunteers to come out en masse. Three of us met at another volunteer's Pakistani restaurant to make hot meals to serve thousands of people across Long Island. I thought, "There's only four of us. We seem a little understaffed." But, I reasoned, "I'm a New Yorker; let's roll up our sleeves and get to work." An hour later, a group of volunteers appeared out of nowhere. Well, not like Dr. Who out of a TARDIS time machine. They came from Manhattan and Queens. Timewise, that was about forty minutes from our Hicksville location. (Yes, we were in a Pakistani restaurant in a city called Hicksville.)

But remember, during Sandy's aftermath, gasoline was at a premium. The odd/even rationing license plate rule was in effect. We could only purchase gas on odd-numbered calendar days if our license plate ended in an odd number, and the same for even days with even license plate numbers. This was a moment when gas became black gold. Yet these men and women from Manhattan and Queens came and used that black gold just to help their fellow humans.

About twenty minutes later, a group of volunteers arrived from Connecticut. My jaw dropped. They'd traveled two and a half hours to help. They even brought five-gallon cans full of gas. I did not think this could get better. Yet five minutes later, a group of volunteers came from central New Jersey, which is another two-hour hike from Hicksville. This display was overwhelming. Five minutes before we left for Nassau Community College to distribute these hot meals, a group of volunteers came from Maryland, which is about four-and-a-half hours from Long Island. At this point, my heart leaped out of my chest at such an awesome display of humanity. I was so upset that Sevi never told me about the heart of a volunteer. I had no idea what I was getting into, and this was just all so fantastic.

We traveled to Nassau Community College. At this point, four volunteers had grown to forty. The Red Cross ran this shelter. Forty of us walked in with hot meals for more than three thousand people. Alison, a

Red Cross manager, said with tears welling up in her eyes, "This is amazing."

She had no idea.

I volunteered again a week later. This time it was on Long Beach, a barrier island that shields Long Island. In the middle of November, I slowly drove down a worn and battered Long Beach road to help the Sandy relief effort. When I was several miles away from our skating arena meeting point, I began hitting red light after red light after red light. It was frustrating; I wanted to get to the arena and volunteer. Sandy had ripped through the area a full two weeks earlier. Yet heaps of garbage, furniture, and unusable appliances continued to pile up on sidewalks throughout every neighborhood.

Portable toilets were on each block. It was heartbreaking to see that just a stone's throw away from the world's capital, New York had slowed down. At this point, there were no aid trucks rumbling through the streets; major media networks had long since left and moved on to other stories. I thought, "Well, I guess everyone has forgotten. If the news isn't showing it, people probably think they no longer need to volunteer and the crisis is over." I was disheartened, but not about to quit.

I reminded myself once more, "I'm a New Yorker; let's roll up our sleeves and get to work." When I arrived at the arena, nobody had forgotten. In front of a makeshift headquarters, a long line of people waited to register as volunteers. A long line and it was only 9:00 a.m. Despite all the junk, dilapidated buildings, and worn-out faces I'd seen on my drive here, this crowd sure was a sight for sore eyes. Sevi never told me about this feeling. I vowed vengeance the next time I saw him.

The mission was simple: gut houses. This was my first time gutting houses and I had a vague idea of how the process worked: walk into people's homes and rip off their drywall. Turned out, I was right. Being right felt good.

The first home we gutted and cleaned belonged to Daniel and June, a married couple. We helped them organize their belongings into items to toss or keep. Fishing poles, keep. Magazines, toss. China, keep. TV, toss. Then we came across a box. When June saw it, she hesitated. She opened it and brought out her wedding dress. She cried for a moment, "Oh David, my wedding dress...it's ruined." Then, she composed herself and soldiered on. "Toss."

Kim owned the second house we visited. She had three feet of wet sand in her basement. One week in and that sand had not dried at all. We carried out two waterlogged leather sofas. With the water, the sofas weighed a lot; I couldn't help carry them with my lack of upper body strength. So I stood outside with Kim. I saw the depression covering her face. While my crew lugged out the ruined couches, I advised, "Don't scratch the upholstery." Kim cracked a smile. I asked her what she planned to do. Hope shone in her eyes as she passionately related her plans and her fears. How would she work full time and also keep her family warm with the fast-approaching New York winter? I didn't quite have an answer. Instead, I said, "There are hot meals at the skating arena. It won't stop winter, but it can take the edge off. Help yourself, OK?"

She smiled. We worked and moved on.

I cherished helping at each house. I realized why there were so many red lights in the city. It's because the city does not want people to just pass on through. The red lights make you stop, look around. They make you park your car and help out however you can. Long Beach's old self had died. Its rebirth was painful but would be worth it. Donne also wrote in his poem, "Any man's death diminishes me because I am involved in mankind."

You see, about eight months before Hurricane Sandy struck, Sevi died. He was only twenty-five years old.

It broke my heart. The world may have lost an irreplaceable personality, somebody beyond genius and so quick-witted and charismatic, but the world did not need to lose such an incredible volunteer. I took up the mantle of being a volunteer in honor of Sevi.

Months after Sevi's death, our homes in New York were rocked, flooded, and leveled by Sandy. It was time to honor that promise I made.

Game on.

Chapter 38

Leadership Matters

"Every one of you is a shepherd and is responsible for his flock. The leader of people is a guardian and is responsible for his subjects."

—PROPHET MUHAMMAD

By now we've established quite clearly the simple principle that leadership matters. Salaam became a leader by serving his community, regardless of differences in faith, color, or creed. He learned from Sevi's powerful and selfless example by serving for the sheer sake of humanity, not for any reward or credit.

I've been fortunate to have learned—and to still learn—from many great leaders in my lifetime. One leader, however, stands out because of his international burdens, responsibilities, influence, and unmatched compassion for all humanity. He exemplifies perhaps the single most important element of good leadership—self-reflection. Just how critical is self-reflection? I believe it is literally the key to peace on earth.

I don't get nervous meeting famous celebrities. I don't get nervous speaking live before a thousand people. I don't get nervous on live television before millions of people.

But put me in the room with the world's greatest leader and my stomach is in a knot of epic proportions.

He's a scientist, a philanthropist, a scholar, a humanitarian, and he leads the world's single largest Muslim community as the Khalifa of Islam. His name is Mirza Masoor Ahmad. I'll refer to him going forward as Huzoor, which is a term of love and respect in the context of His Holiness.

Leadership matters. And Huzoor's leadership is such that while leading tens of millions of Muslims in more than two hundred nations worldwide, he makes it a point to tend to the personal matters of each Muslim who follows his lead and of countless human beings in need, regardless of their faith. Huzoor invests a significant amount of time into meeting with people individually to impart personal or professional guidance. He masterfully maintains open and two-way communication and responds to every one of the thousands of letters he receives each day.

I don't understand how this is practically possible.

But the reason I know it is true is because I experience his leadership personally, intimately, and consistently. Huzoor is the Islamic Khalifa who has inspired tens of millions of Muslims to pledge their lives to the service of humanity. He is the Islamic Khalifa who has ensured not a single member of his tens of millions of followers ever engages, endorses, or approves of any form of terrorism—no matter the opposition. He is the Islamic Khalifa who champions separation of mosque and state, women's equality, education, universal freedom of conscience for all people of all faiths and no faith, and relentless service to humanity for all humanity.

He's the Islamic Khalifa and world Muslim leader whom major media ignores because he doesn't fit their narrative. For example, Huzoor is the fifth Khalifa in a worldwide Islamic caliphate that has advanced uninterrupted for more than a century—dating back to 1908. Huzoor leads upward of sixteen thousand mosques worldwide, more than five hundred secular educational institutions offering free education to all people, and dozens of hospitals offering free health care to all humanity. But when I said caliphate, chances are you've only heard of that terrorist in Iraq and Syria who came to light in 2014, right?

Well, let me shift your focus ever so slightly to an unprecedented world leader you've not yet encountered, but should.

In March 2015 I requested a meeting with Huzoor to gain his insights on leadership. Huzoor most graciously granted my request.

Huzoor is a world-famous figure and VIP, but he does not live as you might think. His residence is in modest quarters in Southfields, United Kingdom, next to the Fazl Mosque. Erected in 1924, the first mosque ever built in London, it's a small white building with a green dome and a stunningly elegant simplicity.

Arriving at the guesthouse the day before my meeting with Huzoor, I met Muslims from Syria, Iraq, Egypt, Kenya, Pakistan, Kuwait, Palestine, Sweden, Germany, and France. Each had traveled from around the world to meet the leader and seek his guidance, prayers, and direction.

Some came from war-ravaged countries, others from nations where Islamophobia grows seemingly exponentially, and yet others from nations where Ahmadi Muslims are specifically targeted and murdered for their faith and spiritual allegiance to Huzoor.

Yet none of them expressed the slightest desire to engage in anything other than resolute service to humanity. Each one, despite the violence they faced and witnessed, desired nothing more than to continue to help the less fortunate, the suffering, and the downtrodden.

Leadership matters. What was it about Huzoor's leadership that created such Muslims from nations that in some cases were facing total obliteration?

I'd never met these Muslims before, but under Huzoor's leadership we instantly connected like long-lost family. These Muslims were amazing scholars, religious and secular. Most of them were converts to Islam Ahmadiyya. I was the sole American present. But as one of the youngest in the guesthouse, I was treated like royalty, to the point where I felt embarrassed. I was literally hand-served dinner by world leading scholars.

"Brother Qasim, you're so skinny. Here, eat, eat!" scolded the president of the Palestine chapter of the Ahmadiyya Muslim Community, filling my plate with more food.

"My friends, why are you doing this? I can get my food. Please, you're my elders; let me serve you."

"And here's some more juice." I looked up to see the president of the Sweden chapter pour me a cup.

I gave up trying to argue; they were resolute. "Brother, the Khalifa has appointed us to lead our respective nations," they said. "And that means we are servants first. Now stop talking and eat."

I smiled and ate to my fill. And while I could have stayed up all night learning from them, I wanted to rest up for my meeting with Huzoor the next day.

Forcing myself to relax, I finally closed my eyes for the night. What felt like mere minutes later, my alarm sounded to wake me for Fajr (predawn) prayer. I leaped out of bed and made my way across the street to Fazl mosque and offer prayer behind Huzoor, then returned to my room and prepared for the meeting.

Huzoor's secretary had instructed me to arrive by 9:00 a.m. After breakfast, gathering my notes, questions, and concerns, and dressing up probably better than I did for my wedding, I headed over to Huzoor's office.

In a small room outside the office we waited. The president of the Palestinian chapter nervously paced back and forth, as did several others. Each moment with Huzoor is priceless; one waits nervously not from fear, but anxiety to make sure not to miss a golden opportunity. No one wants to conclude a meeting and regret forgetting to seek guidance on what burdened them. No one wants to leave without transferring their worry.

That deserves an explanation.

I sat in contemplation and prayer outside Huzoor's office and reflected on his leadership style. You see, Huzoor demonstrates the main difference between secular and spiritual leadership. It's a concept I call "worry transfer." At your place of work, your supervisor gives you an assignment and trusts you will complete it: all worry about that task getting done transfers to you, who now handle all the problems associated with it. You own that worry and get the job done.

With Huzoor it works in the opposite direction—worry transfers up to him. His community members convey to him their concerns and problems, and Huzoor owns and helps resolve them. That's why it is possible for Huzoor to lead tens of millions of Muslims in more than two hundred countries worldwide without any of those people ever resorting to a single act of violence. When you trust your leader in all good things, you look past the violence, terrorism, and discrimination you might suffer through, because you are no longer burdened by them. It becomes impossible for unjust thoughts to cross your mind as a viable response to injustice, no matter how grave the injustice. You see your leader lead by example, in service to humanity and service to God in peace, and you find comfort in that service. The inevitable result is internal peace and humanitarian progress. You follow Huzoor's lead, and you transfer your worry to him.

"Qasim, Huzoor will see you next." Lost in my thoughts, I was startled when the secretary called my name. I stood up and walked through Huzoor's office door.

Radiant, Huzoor sat at his desk and looked up from his work. "Assalaam alaikum, Qasim, have a seat. How are you today?"

My heart beat rapidly and I had to consciously calm myself. "By God's grace I'm well, Huzoor. How is Huzoor today?"

Huzoor nodded and motioned for me to take a seat, then got right down to business.

"You've come all the way from America. What's on your mind?"

I had my first question ready to go. It focused on the rising levels of violence and prejudice against minorities in America. "Huzoor, when dealing with racism, Islamophobia, and prejudice, how do we best respond?"

"With compassion. In the media, stay calm and do not get angry for any reason. Remember that this is our community's approach and perspective. The Prophet Muhammad[sa] has taught us to stay behind the imam. Our policy is compassion; my policy is compassion. Stay with this approach."

I took notes as fast as I could and listened attentively. Huzoor continued.

"Follow my lead. You'll note that I do not speak angrily when I respond to antagonistic people. There is immense benefit in responding calmly. Stay coolheaded and speak with calmness. Be always sober in your approach."

I reflected that after the May 28, 2010 terrorist attack in Pakistan when the Taliban murdered eighty-six Ahmadi Muslims in cold blood, Huzoor responded calmly while urging calm. When the police stood idle and did nothing, Huzoor reminded Ahmadi Muslims that their focus must remain on service to all humanity. That day, as thousands of Ahmadi Muslim families suffered through that horrific act of terror, and as millions of families watched helplessly from around the world, Huzoor reminded us all that their refuge was with God alone. That no form of violent response was permitted. Indeed, no such response remained in the minds of any Ahmadi Muslim.

I continued. "Huzoor, what is the endgame? What is the result of what we're trying to do?"

"Justice. Establishing justice should be the end goal of everything we do. Without justice we cannot have peace. Unfortunately, the promotion of greed has become Western policy, and to achieve its goals the West is ready to promote chaos and create wars."

I continued taking notes, reflecting over the illegal Iraq war, illegal drone strikes, unjust treatment of racial minorities in America, and illegal detainment of prisoners in Guantanamo Bay.

Huzoor continued:

"This thinking must change. Fortunately, the West well knows that the Ahmadiyya community is capable of advancing Islam with justice alone. You must continue to tell people that they must be fair in their behavior."

Huzoor paused and waited for my next question. "Huzoor, I'm writing a book called *Talk to Me*."

"What is in the book?"

"The book discusses five important topics: parenting, racism, interfaith work, leadership, and death. What is Huzoor's advice on how to approach these subjects?"

"We as a worldwide society have shifted our focus over the past years. Today parents are far more focused on making money. There is not enough interaction with kids. Kids come home, make their own food, and go to sleep. Parents come home tired, and marital relationships are already not very strong. Families perhaps interact on weekends but there is no genuine interaction. Kids are home by themselves as if in a hostel, and there is no consistent teaching of morals and ethics. This approach must change. We must have better communication within families."

I reflected on that word again—communication—and its fundamental reliance on strong family relationships. Huzoor continued.

"On interfaith conversations, you must have ongoing interfaith dialogues. Instead of staying away from one another, everyone should participate. This entire interfaith disharmony is happening because we have forgotten our basic human values. Those who want religion destroyed altogether are benefiting from this lack of dialogue and interaction."

In just ten seconds Huzoor had summarized the crux of why people fear one another—we don't talk to one another.

"The founder of the Ahmadiyya community, the Messiah Mirza Ghulam Ahmad[as] said over a hundred and twenty years ago that we must have interfaith conferences and dialogue. We must talk to each other and learn from each other. We must appreciate the good things in each other's faiths. One beauty of Islam is that it accepts all the beautiful aspects of all faiths."

There it was again—the critical need to talk to one another and learn from one another. Huzoor continued and I kept taking notes as fast as I could to capture Huzoor's wisdom.

"When I was in Germany I met with the mayor of a town I was visiting. I related to him the hadith of Prophet Muhammad[sa] that 'wisdom is a Muslim's lost property and he should pick it up wherever he finds it.' The mayor responded that this teaching is capable of making us victorious all over the world."

I sat quietly and listened, still taking notes as rapidly as possible, not wanting to miss a word. I felt grateful both for the opportunity to glean Huzoor's wisdom and for the ability to type over one hundred words per minute. Huzoor continued.

"I advise you to read the Messiah Ahmad's book *A Message of Peace.* The Messiah Ahmad said that he wrote this book as a solution to the fighting between Hindus and Muslims. The solution that Messiah Ahmad provides is that both sides adjust and reform themselves. The Messiah Ahmad told Muslims that if Hindus do not like it when Muslims eat beef, because cows are sacred to Hindus, then Muslims should avoid eating beef for the sake of peace. Likewise, Hindus should not speak against Prophet Muhammad. You see, give and take is needed. Compromise is needed."

I found this an interesting trade-off and was about to ask Huzoor to elaborate. As if reading my mind, he did just that before I could open my mouth.

"You see, we are even ready to go to this extent that we are leaving halal and permissible things so that chaos does not exist. As long as we insist on these things by force then we cannot have peace."

Huzoor paused to let me catch up and gather my thoughts, then added, "Once you've finished writing your book, send it to me."

"Huzoor, I will, I promise."

"What else is on your mind?"

"Huzoor, I'm speaking at Harvard University next month to deliver a lecture on intra-Muslim relations. How should I approach this? How should I talk to my audience?"

Huzoor smiled. "This is what I've been telling you! Read *A Message of Peace* and follow the Messiah Ahmad's guidance. Be compassionate."

Our entire meeting lasted nearly forty minutes. Throughout every topic of discussion Huzoor insisted on three fundamental principles in everything we do—focus on reforming yourself instead of trying to reform anyone else, maintain absolute justice in all affairs, and communicate with the utmost compassion and love.

When I had no more questions on my plate I asked Huzoor for his prayers for my family and showed him family pictures. As our meeting concluded Huzoor remarked, "Write to me and come see me regularly. Perhaps it is of some benefit to you and it is of immense benefit to me."

My heart broke. There's an old saying: "Humility is not thinking less of yourself; it is thinking of yourself less." Despite Huzoor's worldwide responsibilities and soul-crushing burdens, his entire focus was on my well-being and my needs. It is that personal leadership and personal attention, I realized, that has elicited such love and dedication for Huzoor among tens of millions of people worldwide. It is that love and dedication that conquered violence, hatred, and greed.

Prior to his election as Khalifa, Huzoor served as a principal of a high school in Ghana and as an agricultural scientist. He is credited with being the first person to successfully grow wheat in Ghana. Huzoor often muses that he considers Ghana his home, and though he himself is Pakistani, one can only marvel at the love he has for the people of Ghana and indeed all of Africa and the reciprocal love Ghanaians have for him.

Earlier, we discussed the racism that exists in some mosques in America. The reality is this racism exists in these mosques for the same reason racism exists in some churches, which is the same reason why racism exists in general. Failed leadership, failed communication, and a failure to work together with compassion. Racism is not a religious teaching; it is a cancer that emerges among some ignorant people and is perpetuated by arrogant leaders.

I reflect on how beautifully Huzoor leads and unites Muslims in more than 207 nations—people of all races and cultural backgrounds. This is no accident. This feat is achieved by focusing on race relations, leading with compassion, and talking to one another.

I left Huzoor's office that day in awe of Huzoor's leadership and, thankfully, worry-free.

Indeed, leadership matters.

Chapter 39

Finding the Gem

"If you hit a Talib with your shoe, then there would be no difference between you and the Talib. You must not treat others with cruelty and that much harshly, you must fight others but through peace and through dialogue and through education."

—MALALA YOUSAFZAI

I consider myself immensely fortunate that all those years ago, I was verbally ambushed about my faith. While I wouldn't wish such an incident on anyone, that event triggered a change in my life's trajectory. And while I've learned a great deal in the near two decades since, what I've learned most is how much further we have to go. Indeed, despite everything, a day doesn't pass where I'm not reminded of the struggle.

Sometimes, it takes repeated failures to find that gem, a struggle that presents you with a choice once more: Give up in frustration, or find a way to enjoy the ride, maybe even find some humor. Whether dealing with parenting, leadership, interfaith relations, or race relations, finding that gem of a person willing to talk to you isn't always easy.

It's like getting hung up on, over and over and over again.

One of the worst jobs I had was a gig I had right after high school. I was the dreaded telemarketer. Or, as we called it, "vacation specialist." Seriously, who were we kidding?

"Hi, my name is Qasim; is Mr. Smith home?"

"Your name is what?"

"Qasim. Ka-Sim."

"Casey? Scott?"

"Scott? What? No, it's Qasim."

"That's a strange name."

"Erm, sorry. Is Mr. Smith home?"

"Are you a telemarketer?"

"I'm a vacation specialist."

"What the hell is a vacation specialist?"

"It's a...well, I'd be happy to explain to Mr. Smith if he's available."

"He's not. Don't call back, Casey." Click.

I thought about changing my name to Casey—at least for the purposes of the phone calls—but resisted the urge. Still, that was my routine for eight hours a day. And then suddenly, right when all seemed lost, this would happen.

"Hi, my name is Qasim; is Mrs. Jones home?"

"Yes, this is Mrs. Jones. What can I do for you?"

"Hi, Mrs. Jones. I'm a vacation specialist and I'm calling about a discounted vacation."

"Oh, my goodness; you know, that is exactly what I need right now. Hold on; let me get my husband on the phone and let's see what you have available."

Somewhere in heaven an angel would get its wings whenever that happened. My heart would leap for joy—and not because they actually cared about buying a stupid vacation from me. But because they actually cared to talk to me. They didn't hang up. I'd found the gem I was look-ing for all day long. I finally had a real live person to talk to.

Over the years, as I continued to engage in interfaith dialogue, I real-ized how similar interfaith dialogue was to telemarketing. Finding the one person interested in talking to a telemarketer is much like finding the one person genuinely interested in interfaith dialogue—it can be an exhausting process.

But that's really where the similarity ends. People avoid telemarketers as an annoyance. People avoid those of a different faith for all the signifi-cantly bigger reasons I've mentioned—fear, ignorance, uncertainty, and aversion to being pushed outside their comfort zone. As you're on the hunt for that gem, remember to approach with patience, prayer (if you pray), and, frankly, by seeking the humor in tense situations.

Enough of theory, let's get to practice.

The Miami International Book Fair is an excellent place to start. I've attended for several years now, but my most memorable one was the first I attended. If you've never been, you're missing out. I've been fortunate to have participated in book fairs nationwide. Miami's is my favorite. The level of diversity, the sheer size of the fair, and certainly the Miami weather make it a premier event.

And as I was reminded once more, finding that gem isn't exactly easy.

Day 1

We set up our booth on Islam, complete with thousands of books, plen-ty of free giveaways, and snacks for anyone who walked by. It wasn't long before a decent-size crowd engulfed us—people from all walks and back-grounds. Some merely glanced, while others stopped to say hello. Almost out of the blue, a black woman who looked about sixty walked up to me and asked bluntly, "Are you Rashid? Did you write this book?" She held up a copy of The Wrong Kind of Muslim.

"Um, I'm Qasim Rashid, and yes, I wrote that book."

"Rashid, I have a few questions; can I ask you directly?"

"Sure; Qasim would love to answer."

"Who's Kasam?"

"I'm Qasim."

"I thought you were Rashid."

"Well, I am Qasim Rashid. And you are?"

She ignored my question and continued without missing a beat. "Rashid, I want to know why you wrote this book?"

"OK, sure. Well, I, Qasim, wanted to tell a story of persecution and perseverance that I believed no one else was telling. I wanted to give voice to those denied the right to speak, and invite all people to join me."

"But why do you feel it is OK to tell these wrong kind of Muslims they're wrong? Why would you shame them publicly like that?"

I chuckled. "Um, well, the title is actually satire. I'm not actually shaming them. When you read the book it'll make more sense."

"Oh, I don't read books. Books are beneath me. I'm not a writer either, but I'm writing a book. But it's dangerous. A publisher told me it's dangerous, that it could destroy America."

At this point I couldn't tell if she was serious or if she was trolling me. Either way, I was beginning to sense something wasn't quite right. When you step out of your comfort zone and make a call you otherwise wouldn't, much can happen. I wasn't sure how to respond.

"Um...OK. So anyway, ma'am...any other questions?" It was silly to ask such a question, because, obviously, she had many more questions. And her next one was a doozy.

"Would you not agree that you are not unequal to me?"

I paused and repeated the question in my head, trying to process just what exactly she was saying. I had no idea where she was going with this but took a stab at an answer. "Uh, sure?"

"So then tell me, why does Izlam condemn being happy? Why are you commanded to stone me for being happy?"

Still clueless as to where she was going, I responded, "Yeah, so the problem with that statement is...everything. But what's your point, ultimately?"

"My point is I don't need books of any sort. I have an intuition where a higher power tells me about a book. And we should burn the Koran."

"Oh, really?"

"Oh don't get me wrong. I'm not a bigot. I also want to burn the Bible."

"Oh, that's much better!" I tried to sound as dry as possible but I'm pretty sure she missed it entirely.

Undeterred, she continued. "Don't you think life would be better if we just burned all books and went by our intuition?"

"Well, no, actually I happen to not think that at all. But if that's your thing, great!" Outside I smiled, but inside I was wholly lost as to where she was going with this.

"Well, Rashid, I don't want you to think I'm crazy."

"No, no of course not. Not at all. I can't imagine a reason why I would think something so outlandish."

"You see, I'm not a writer but I'm writing this book about humanity and how Europeans are cannibalistic by nature and how Izlamics condemn being happy and how we can reconcile it all by burning all books."

"Wait, let me make sure I understand. You're writing a book about...all that stuff...calling for the burning of all books? You don't see the contradiction here?"

"Well, I don't want people to burn my book, because that's what will guide them on what to do!"

As I was trying to fathom how in the world I was going to respond to this person, my friend Khalid walked up.

"Oh, there you are Qasim, we need you to—"

"Coming! I'm sorry, ma'am, good luck with your burning and cannibalism-combating. I have to go now." I literally ran ahead of Khalid in some arbitrary direction. As I turned back, I saw her begin to grill him with questions.

The first day of the book fair was rough, as the conversation with the strange woman was likely the longest conversation I had. Coming into day two, I had higher expectations. I figured it couldn't be any worse.

Day 2

Though it had rained on and off most of the day, things were going well overall. Well, that is, until a young Latino guy probably in his twenties showed up. He had a scruffy beard and long hair pulled back in a ponytail. He walked up sort of shy but warmed up quickly. After looking through some of the books on display, he looked up at me.

"Sir, do you speak Spanish?"

I smiled politely and replied, "No, sorry, I don't speak Spanish."

"Oh, OK no problem. I speak English."

"Great; what's on your mind?"

"Are you Muslim?"

"Yep."

"Is this a picture of Prophet Muhammad's tomb?" He pointed to a random picture near our booth.

"No, that's a picture of a hotel."

"Oh, how come?"

"How come what?"

"How come it's a picture of a hotel?"

"Um...I...what?"

"OK, you sure you don't speak Spanish?"

"Yeah, pretty sure..." We entered an awkward pause and literally stared at each other for about ten seconds. I finally spoke up again. "By the way, did you say you were Christian or...?"

"No, it's kind of complicated."

"Oh, I understand—you're searching? Well, I wish you the best of luck."

"No, no, it's not that."

"Oh, OK, sorry. Didn't mean to assume."

"It's just that, I know truth, I am truth."

"Pardon?"

"I am truth. I am God's prophet."

"Ah, of course, how obvious."

"You see, Jesus stole the truth from God."

"Jesus did what?"

"Jesus was a Jew. And all Jews are thieves. And he stole the truth because he was a Jewish thief."

Inside I died a little. Nothing like open bigotry to kill a dialogue. "I can honestly say my mind is blown."

"And God sent me to steal the truth back from Jews and give it to all mankind, and I'm here today to give it to you."

"Oh, well, I don't know what to say; this is all so sudden."

"As a sign of my truth, I am going to pray that it doesn't rain today, and then you will know I am from God. It will not rain."

"I see; can you control any other weather patterns?" That was probably rude to say, but in all honesty I was still smarting over his open bigotry. He missed my sarcasm entirely.

"Yes, I can, but today I will control the rain and make it stop."

"Oh, you're in luck; here's a Muslim brother who speaks Spanish."

My friend Achraf, who had randomly walked by, looked at me, startled. "Huh? What?"

"I gotta go, Achraf! Good luck!"

Ten minutes later it began raining. And almost as if to troll me specifically, it rained most of the day. "Worst-prophet-ever," was all I could think to myself.

And I still hadn't found my gem.

Day 3

By day three of the book fair I was getting desperate. I'd been proverbially hung up on enough times and I needed something to cling on to. I needed someone to talk to me and remind me that there are people willing to step out of their comfort zones without wanting to burn all books or spread hatred of an entire religious group.

The third day was much better, weather-wise. It didn't rain much and the temperature was quite comfortable. It was still morning when an older white gentlemen stopped and watched our booth on Islam from a short distance away. He was heavyset and looked like Archie Bunker from the sitcom *All in the Family*. In fact, let's just call him Archie.

I stood with Achraf—the same Achraf I left stranded with the terrible weatherman from yesterday. Achraf is a Moroccan Ahmadi Muslim and a convert to Islam. I mention that only because it soon became amazingly relevant.

As we saw Archie observe us, I noticed a bit of a scowl on his face. In the spirit of ongoing dialogue I called out to him.

"Good morning, sir, how are you?"

He wasn't as forthcoming. "Oh, you, you don't want to talk to me; you won't like what I have to say."

I shrugged. "Try me."

"You Islamics and your deception, I'm not gonna fall for it."

I smiled, partly because I wasn't sure if he was serious or not, but a smile is charity regardless. "All right, you figured us out, but what aren't you falling for?"

Now he raised his voice. "Everywhere you go you kill people! Why do you insist on killing people?"

Achraf remained silent for the moment. I stepped forward and responded calmly. "Tell me more. Where is everywhere?"

"Oh you know, everywhere in the world. You never hear of Christians killing people. Only you people kill everyone."

"I see. Well, if that's the measuring stick, it's not a very good one. But if you insist, there's the IRA and the KKK, and the Lord's Resistance Army is a so-called Christian terrorist group that has maimed, raped, and killed more than a hundred thousand in Uganda and—"

He cut me off and raised his voice again. "You see!! You see!! *Uganda*. Who the f*$% cares about Uganda! I'm talking about the two-thousand-by-three-thousand-mile country we live in called A-MER-IC-CA."

"But I thought you said everywh—OK, 9/11 aside, whom have 'we' killed in America?"

"Oh, there's so many; you're killing people in Africa, in Europe, in Asia."

"Wait, but, you just said in Amer—"

"The point is, I don't trust you people; you're evil. I told you that you wouldn't like what I tell you."

"Right, so I recall the Oklahoma City bombing, I recall the horrible Columbine shooting—I was in high school when that happened and—"

He cut me off again. "You were *not* in high school during Columbine. You're bald. You were not in high school in 1999. You are so bald."

"OK, look, first of all, yes I was in high school. Second of all, you're bald too and I don't have a comb-over. Third of all, thirty thousand

Americans die from gun violence every year; do we blame Christians? Of course not. That's stupidity."

Stumped, he defaulted to the safe haven of his comfort zone. "I don't trust any of you people."

"How many Muslims do you know?"

"I don't trust you people; why would I want to know any of you? Besides, I go to Morocco, so I know what Islam is."

Inside I sighed. Here was the chicken-and-egg dilemma. Do you get to know someone to trust them or do you trust someone before you get to know them? I believe in the former; Archie here believed in the latter and wasn't willing to budge. Meanwhile, as soon as Archie mentioned Morocco, Achraf jumped into action.

"Oh, I'm from Morocco."

"What? You are?"

"Yessir. And frankly, we don't have terrorism there. It's a very progressive nation."

Undeterred, Archie steamrolled on. "Good, then both of you should go back to Morocco but you, you go back to wherever the hell you came from."

I jumped in again, "Well I'm not Moroccan, but bigotry aside, what can we do to 'prove' to you we're 'good' people?"

"Nothing; there's nothing you can do; just give up already."

"We raised thirty thousand blood donations since 2011 to save up to ninety thousand lives. That doesn't convince you?"

"No; I know this is just lies so you can kill me easier. Just go back where you came from and give up."

"My brother's a US marine veteran. Did you serve in the military?"

"No; he can stay, but you need to give up and go. We don't need you here." By now Archie steamed with anger. His face was blood-red. Neither Achraf nor I reacted to his anger and insults. We continued to smile and maintained our effort to engage him. Archie turned to walk away and threw his hand back at us as if he was swatting a fly.

"Well, we love you anyway, and if you need blood, we'll donate ours."

Without turning around Archie yelled back, "I don't want it; just go home!"

Achraf looked at me and just shook his head. "What do you say to a guy like that?"

I shook my head. "It's not easy, is it? That's why these dialogues are so important. They don't happen enough. And if you react negatively to someone like Archie you only validate his ignorant beliefs that Muslims are somehow evil. It's all the more important you keep your cool, lead by example, and hope and pray for the best."

A few minutes passed as Achraf and I were discussing the sheer importance of continuing such interfaith dialogue. Suddenly Archie popped back by, as suddenly as the first time. This time he didn't wait for either of us to say hello.

"Hey you, the Moroccan one. What are you doing wasting your time with Izlam? I know plenty of Moroccans who are atheist and agnostic like me. Why don't you just be like your countrymen and stop with this religion-following bullshit?"

I smiled and stayed silent because I knew Achraf's backstory. Achraf smiled and spoke up. "Well, it's funny you mention that, because I was agnostic until I studied Islam. And after studying Islam and meeting Muslims I made the choice to become Muslim."

Archie's jaw dropped. Achraf continued speaking.

"So basically you're barking up the wrong tree."

"I can't believe it. They got to you too. What a shame."

"Not from my point of view."

Archie turned around and stormed off into the crowd. We thought he might come back once more but we were wrong. That was the last of Archie. I have to admit, getting made fun of by a bald guy with a comb-over was just uncalled for. But worse yet, it was another hang-up. Another reminder of just how much more work we need to do to maintain dialogue and communication across religious lines.

The day wasn't over yet, so Achraf and I and the rest of the booth volunteers continued our dialogues and interactions as best we could. It was almost time to close up shop when Achraf, Oswaldo (a Mexican convert to Islam), and I walked over to the food area to grab a quick bite. Oswaldo turned to me. "Hey, Qasim, I met some Muslims from another Muslim group. It's a Sunni Muslim tent down that row. One of the guys is from Chicago. Wanna go say salaam to them?"

"A fellow Chicagoan? Sure! Let's go." Oswaldo is from Chicago and I grew up in the Windy City.

Achraf, Oswaldo, and I made our way to a booth set up by a local Miami mosque. Oswaldo greeted the person he'd mentioned, an older black gentleman named Jamil. Another black gentleman, probably about the same age, sat on the other side of the booth. I greeted them both with the traditional Islamic greeting of *as-salaam alaikum*, "peace be upon you." They both returned the greeting, as is customary for all Muslims.

Jamil turned to me and Achraf. "So which one of you brothers are from Chi-town?"

I smiled and extended my hand. "I'm from Chicago but live in Virginia now." Jamil grabbed my hand and pulled me in for a bear hug.

I asked Jamil, "What part of Chicago are you from?"

"The South Side; you?"

"Well, I lived in the suburbs most of my time there," I said, "but one of the mosques I worshipped at is on the South Side, right over there on Forty-Fifth and State."

"I don't recall a mosque on Forty-Fifth and State."

"It's the oldest mosque in Chicago and the country. Masjid Al Sadiq."

Jamil's smile disappeared and his face turned stoic. Right then Achraf called out, "Hey Qasim, you gotta see this." I looked up to see him holding a book titled *Why Quadianis Are Not Muslim.*

"Quadiani" is a derogatory term extremists use for Muslims who join the Ahmadiyya Muslim Community. Jamil became stone-faced because he realized the mosque I referenced was a mosque built by that Community. Simultaneously, Achraf, Oswaldo, and I realized that the imam of the mosque who set up this booth was an extremist and vehemently bigoted against Ahmadi Muslims.

Inside I thought to myself, "Dang, zero for four."

Jamil took a step back and looked down. "Look, brother, I ain't looking to convert to your religion or nothing, so I hope that's not why you came here."

Oswaldo and Achraf were speechless. This was the first time they'd encountered open antagonism from other Muslims. Unfortunately, this was the umpteenth time for me. I maintained my composure. "Brother, I only came to say peace and greet a fellow Muslim; that's all," I said. "I heard you were from Chicago so I wanted to say hello; that's all."

Jamil seemed to loosen up, making eye contact once more. "You're not here to propagate your religion to me?"

"My religion is Islam. I interpret it differently than you. But I assure you, no, I'm not here to propagate anything. Just wanted to talk to you and hope you talk to me. That's all."

For a moment Jamil relaxed, but only for a moment. His expression turned cold again and he walked back inside the booth without saying another word. Achraf and Oswaldo were facing me and I saw them suddenly looking behind me as well. I turned to find myself facing the imam who'd set up the booth. The shirts we wore said *Ahmadiyya Muslim Community* on the back, so he knew our affiliation right away.

And by the angry scowl on his face, he was furious.

Trying desperately to salvage the situation I reached out to the imam and said, "As-salaam alaikum, Imam, how are you." He did not touch my hand. Hoping that perhaps he just hadn't seen me I walked up to him. He stepped aside to avoid contact and kept walking toward the booth. I paused, took a deep breath, then turned to walk toward the imam, again, to try one final time: "As-salaam alaikum, Imam. My name is Qasim, and my friends and I are from the Ahmadiyya Muslim—"

"I know where you're from!" He interrupted me. "You're from the place of infidels. And I do not touch the hands of infidels. Get your hand away from me!"

"But I'm offering you peace as the Qur'an teaches Muslims—to greet each other with peace."

"You are not a Muslim; you are an infidel and you have no place here."

"How much is that book?" I pointed to the anti-Ahmadi book Achraf was holding.

"Take it. It's free for you infidels. Perhaps you'll leave your infidel beliefs and come back to Islam."

"Brother, I am a Muslim. I recite the Islamic declaration of faith that there is no god but Allah and Muhammad is His messenger."

"You're a liar and an infidel. You can leave now. And don't return."

I turned to Jamil. "Jamil, brother, nice meeting you, as-salaam alaikum."

Jamil didn't look up. I felt pained to see his evident embarrassment at the actions of his imam. But something inside told me he was more embarrassed that he didn't stand up to his imam's intolerance. He whispered back to me, "Wa alaikum as-salaam" (may peace be upon you too). The imam gave him a look; Jamil didn't respond and didn't look up.

I was saddened; Achraf and Oswaldo, too, were mortified, stunned.

"Come on bros, let's head back," I said and, turning back to the Miami mosque's booth one last time, added loudly, "Peace be upon all of you. God bless." The imam gave me the same look he'd given Jamil but this time didn't speak. He didn't need to. His actions had already spoken much louder than any of his lacerating words.

We marched back to our booth, heads hung but spirits high. This is what we were up against. This was the ultimate hang-up, the ultimate insult, the ultimate letdown. Interfaith dialogue isn't easy. No one said it is. I knew that, but I was in desperate need of that gem.

Day 4

Day four of the Miami book fair was the final day for me. I was set to fly out that evening back to Virginia. The weather was beautiful; the sun shone brightly. It was close to high noon when I saw an elderly man observe us from a distance, check his watch, and then walk up to our booth.

I greeted him with a smile. "Morning sir, how are you today?

"Oh, I'm doing well young man; how are you?"

"I am doing phenomenal, beautiful day, great people, what's not to love?"

"Why does this bookmark say Love for All Hatred for None?"

"That's our Muslim community's motto; feel free to keep the bookmark."

"Well, that's good, I've always been bothered by the nonsense they spew in the media. Every religion has terrorists; my religion, Christianity, is no different."

"Well, I appreciate your compassionate viewpoint, sir."

Without missing a beat he continued, "You know, my son is the director of community services for a university here in Miami. And I can see how much he loves interacting with people of all different backgrounds."

"Well, that's great! You know we run a community service blood drive every September to honor 9/11 victims. I'm actually wearing a shirt from that event now."

"Really? Have you had any success?"

"Yes, for sure! We've collected over thirty thousand blood donations since 2011!"

"See, that's the Islam the media needs to report on! I commend you, young man."

"Let me ask you something, sir."

"Sure."

I stepped out from behind the booth to speak to him with more ease. "Do you think we could connect with your son to get his university involved next year?"

He lit up like the Fourth of July. "Yes! Yes. That's a great idea."

I smiled. "Wonderful."

"In fact, here's his private cell phone number. Call him and tell him I gave it to you, and I will be the first to donate blood next fall."

I didn't know what else to say, so I said the only thing that seemed right. "I...I love you sir."

That made him blush bright red. He chuckled and said, "Well, you're all right yourself, young man. I have to get going now, but you be sure to call him, and keep up the great work! We're proud to have neighbors like you."

I smiled ear to ear and fought the urge to hug him, thinking it might be super awkward. I suddenly found myself losing the urge to keep my arms down. Finally I gave in and hugged the old man like my son hugs his grandpa. He laughed loudly and hugged back. After a few seconds, he patted me on the back. "OK, son, I think that's probably good."

"Sorry, sorry, I got a little carried away."

We shook hands one last time and smiled and parted ways. I grinned. After multiple painful hang-ups, I'd finally found my gem. A gem so precious it opened the door to continued interfaith community service that would definitely save lives. I couldn't stop smiling.

He took the time to talk to me, and somewhere up there an angel just got its wings.

Chapter 40

Death of a Human, but Not of Humanity

"So you run and you run to catch up with the sun but it's sinking,
Racing around to come up behind you again.
The sun is the same in a relative way but you're older,
Shorter of breath and one day closer to death."

—PINK FLOYD

I spent the last week of Ramadan in the mosque, a common practice of many Muslims. It was the month of Ramadan in 2006, sometime in October. Muslims often spend the last ten days of Ramadan in the mosque as a means of self-reflection and prayer—not unlike how Moses spent forty days on the mountain and Jesus spent forty days in the desert. With me was my old friend Muhaimin. This was the last time I would see Muhaimin in a long time, because he was moving to Ghana.

I knew I would miss him, for obvious reasons. Not long after Ramadan ended I would head to Pakistan for another few months' tour. At that time, unbeknownst to me, I was collecting data and interviews for what eventually became *The Wrong Kind of Muslim*. As we began leaving the mosque, I went to say farewell to my friend.

"Muhaimin, it's been good, brother. When are you leaving for Ghana?"

"Why, you going somewhere?"

"Yeah, I'm heading to Pakistan for a few months. I should be back sometime in late January."

"I should still be here. Gotta wrap up a few things. Sell the barbershop. Take care of some family matters."

"Oh, great. So I'll see you in Chicago when I get back?"

"God willing, brother!"

"You promise!"

Muhaimin smiled. "I promise, God willing."

It's funny how unremarkable so many of our differences appear when we view them through the lens of death. Whatever our differences, when our hearts stop, all permanently closed eyes look the same. And this is the single biggest reason I include death as a conversation we need to have. I'll elaborate in a moment.

I gave Muhaimin a hug and wished him Eid Mubarak. (Eid is the name of the holiday at the end of the month of Ramadan.) I left the mosque with my head high that day. A few weeks later I left on a plane to Pakistan to pick up my work where I'd left off the year prior.

Muhaimin returned to his barbershop, Karim's Kuts. He continued his work to serve the poor and build interfaith and race relations. He would commonly pick up food from grocery stores—food that would've been thrown out—and deliver it to homeless shelters. In his barbershop rival gang members would make their peace, knowing he wouldn't so much as allow cursing on his premises. Everyone on the South Side who frequented his shop affectionately called him Uncle Mo.

The night of December 24, 2006, Muhaimin closed up late with two of his employees. It was after 11:00 p.m. when they both left the shop for the night. But soon Muhaimin heard yelling and sounds of struggle in a nearby alley. He immediately called 911.

"There's something wrong behind my shop. There's yelling and screaming; I think there's a fight happening."

"Sir, stay in the shop and wait for the police to arrive."

Muhaimin hung up and waited a moment. But that wasn't who he was. He wasn't willing to sit idle if someone was getting hurt. Intending to help, he ran toward the back door of his shop. He opened the door and saw a robber holding his employees hostage. The robber had waited in ambush for closing time; now he pointed his gun at an employee's head.

The robber hadn't seen Muhaimin yet; Muhaimin could have retreated and saved his own life. He could have waited for the police to arrive. He could have left his employees to their own fate. Muhaimin was a Muslim; his employees were Christian; and if you believe the Islamophobic rantings of some bigots you'll hear the lie that Islam doesn't command Muslims to protect Christians. Muhaimin was biracial—black and white. If you listen to the rantings of racist bigots they'll tell you the lie that African Americans are "thugs."

But Muhaimin was dedicated to the service of humanity. He was proud of his African heritage. He was proud of his Ahmadi Muslim identity. He would not run away from an opportunity to serve. Muhaimin had a choice to make, and choose he did. He used his element of surprise and ran toward the robber, grabbing him tight. The robber dropped his gun and the employee escaped the robber's grip. Muhaimin's employee next grabbed the gun and hit the robber on the head to try to knock him out. Meanwhile, Muhaimin pulled the mask off the robber's face to see who it was.

The robber was subdued, but sadly, he was not alone. A second thief lurked in the shadows. No one saw him coming. Like a hidden snake he raised his arm and fired his weapon multiple times. The bullets sliced through the air and hit Muhaimin through his chest and stomach.

Muhaimin died instantly.

The robbers scrambled like cockroaches. By the time police arrived, it was all over. They said Muhaimin didn't suffer any pain. But that didn't make anyone feel any better. Muhaimin lay there on that cold concrete behind his barbershop. He lay there with his eyes closed, his heart stopped, and his lungs silent. He lay there. It was the death of a human being loved by thousands. Left in Muhaimin's hand was the first robber's mask. Years later, DNA from that mask eventually helped in the apprehension and conviction of one of the perpetrators.

Meanwhile, in Pakistan, around 6:00 p.m., I'd just arrived at my cousin Danyal's home. As we sat talking about I don't know what, the phone rang. It was my brother Tayyib.

"Hey, bro, what's going on? What's it, like, 7:00 a.m. there?"

"Qasim, are you sitting down?"

"Yeah, what's wrong?"

"Muhaimin's been shot."

"What!? What the hell do you mean?"

"He was shot last night at his barbershop. I don't know all the details."

"Oh, man, that's terrible. Have you gone to see him yet? What hospital is he in?"

"Qasim. You're not understanding."

"What?"

"Muhaimin's not in the hospital."

"OK, where is he then?"

Even now as I remember that moment I don't understand why I was so oblivious to what Tayyib was telling me. Maybe I knew deep down inside but didn't want to believe it.

"Qasim. Muhaimin died."

Stunned, I dropped the phone. I sat speechless, furious, pained, and confused, all simultaneously. I thought back to the promise Muhaimin made to me, that he'd be there upon my return—God willing. I thought about the last look on his face as I said my salaam to him—it was a smile a mile wide. As I later learned what happened a million questions went through my mind, as they go through anyone's mind who has lost a loved one.

But in the end, nothing ever changes what's already been done. And I hung my head in pain. As Muslims we keep our faith that from God we are and to God must we return. Indeed, death is not the opposite of life—it is the result of life. It doesn't exist on its own. It exists because of life. And this is why I felt compelled to include conversations about death in this book. Muhaimin's death was the death of a human, but not of humanity.

Death is the great equalizer. Pauper or prince, black or white, male or female, parent or child, Muslim, Christian, Jew, Hindu, or atheist—we all are mortal beings and one day will all breathe our last. Death is an opportunity for us to focus on the people we know and love, who've given everything they have to make this world a better place. It's about recognizing those individuals in our lives here and now, not waiting until they're gone to appreciate them. It's about heroes who literally sacrifice themselves to create a better world for their children, for humanity of all colors, of all religions—and in doing so become legendary leaders.

Please don't let use of the word "legendary" register as cliché.

"Legendary" is a word that's often thrown around to glamorize celebrities, athletes, and politicians. But in reality you can find living legends in your own life, if you only look. Ask any child who casually used the word "hate," not realizing its destructive force, and then my legendary brother in faith Muhaimin pulled me aside and helped point me toward a wholly different trajectory. Ask any high school cross-country runner and think about my legendary coach Andy Preuss, who pulled me aside and told me, when no one else would, that I could be good if I put my mind to it. Ask any law student who knew he didn't have the grades to get into a top-tier law school, but his legendary admissions dean Michelle Rahman saw deeper, gave him admission anyway, and set him on a path of previously unimaginable scholarship. Ask any first-year lawyer about his legendary mentors like Carol, Mick, and Bert, who took the time to give him a shot because they valued his worth, even when he didn't.

I include these conversations about death because of beautiful individuals like Muhaimin, Sharon, Bert, Stephen Jaycox, Jan, Zachery, Sevi, Professor Carroll, and many, many more. These are all people I knew or whom the contributing authors in this book knew on some intimate level or another. These beautiful individuals left a legacy of pluralism and tolerance behind them, and it is imperative we carry that legacy forward. There's too much good happening in the world and too little awareness it is happening. Some of these human beings may have died, but their humanity lives on.

How do we ensure that happens?

Well, we have seen now how important it is to talk to our kids, to reach across racial lines, to reach across religious lines, and to become educated leaders in these important dialogues. We've experienced great joy in seeing how we can overcome the barriers that divide us. We've also experienced the pain in understanding what barriers still divide us. And hopefully, we recognize how important it is to use the time we have here and now to serve one another and leave this world better than we found it.

We ensure their humanity lives on by continuing their narrative for tolerance, pluralism, compassion, and love. It is my sincere hope that you continue this conversation in your own lives. Think about those who've inspired you to do better, be better. Talk about them, emulate them, and keep them living. Even if they've breathed their last, delay their second death as long as you have your breath.

I often reflect on how in the Islamic tradition Muslims pray five times a day. And before each prayer there's a call to prayer, known as the adhan, to remind everyone that the prayer is but moments away. Interestingly enough, when a child is born to Muslim parents, the first thing the parents do is issue the adhan softly in the child's ear. But there's no prayer afterward. When a Muslim dies, the last rite is his family and friends offering a funeral prayer for him—but there's no adhan for this funeral prayer.

Or is there?

As it turns out, the adhan called at a Muslim's birth is for the funeral prayer at that Muslim's death—thus completing the circle. And just as the adhan for regular prayer during the day indicates that prayer is ever near, the adhan called at birth is a reminder that death is ever near. Indeed, even a person who lives a hundred years attests that life flew by in an instant. This should set the tone for how we live our lives.

Death is not a subject we like to talk about because we see it as so final, so unknown, and so one-directional. But that is to look at death all wrong—and the aforementioned individuals prove what I mean. Mark Twain once wrote, "The fear of death follows from the fear of life. A man who lives fully is prepared to die at any time." And thus is how we should live our lives. Not in fear of death, nor in fear of life. But fully prepared, fully grateful, fully embracing of what we have, for we know it can go at any time. And in the time we have here, let's work to make it better for one another.

They say that every person dies twice. Once, when they stop breathing, and then when someone says their name for the last time. Perhaps it's my foolish hope, in writing about my inspirations, that they never die—though some may have already breathed their last.

And whether my reasoning is informed or naive, this is one reason I write. They say when a writer falls in love with you, you'll never die. Deep down inside I hope the many people we've talked to and talked about in this book—I hope they never die. Though some may already be gone from this world—indeed, eventually we all will be—I hope they live on forever in our hearts and minds. That is the transition we need to embrace. Theirs are the stories that should be dominating our headlines. Theirs are their stories that should be relayed to our children, building bridges of interfaith and interracial relations, and inspiring new leaders for tomorrow. Their stories are the transitions in this life from one great person who has passed on to another great person who can carry on. Nothing will bring back these amazing individuals, but we can continue to carry on their respective legacies with courage, compassion, and meaningful communication with one another.

Death awaits us all. That is a fact. But rather than live in fear, let us use the time we have here to serve humanity. It all begins by taking the time to talk to one another.

Conclusion

#TalkToMe about the Future

"Education is the passport to the future, for tomorrow belongs to those who prepare for it today."

—MALCOLM X

Every passing day I appreciate more and more the shift in trajectory Muhaimin gave me by making me "hate conscious." Stifling hate permits justice and compassion to grow. It reminds a child how to maintain that compassion even when the child is ridiculed, bullied, or worse. But when hatred grows, it becomes a cancer that slowly kills a society until there's nothing left to save. Hatred uses ignorance and fear as its fuel and advances the causes of racism, Islamophobia, misogyny, and anti-Semitism.

In 1938, more than 67 percent of Americans said America should *not* accept refugees from Europe. In 1939 Americans turned away the S.S. *St. Louis*, which carried nearly one thousand Jewish refugees escaping Nazi Germany.[13] Americans ignorantly feared that a secret Nazi might be in their midst, and that fear overcame their justice and compassion. As a result the S.S. *St. Louis* was forced to return to Europe, where nearly one-third of those Jewish refugees died in the Holocaust. In 1942 the US government illegally arrested and sent 110,000 Japanese Americans to concentration camps. Fear and ignorance won, and it is foolish to think that fear cannot, or has not, again reared its ugly head.

Since 2001 the US government has illegally held people at Guantanamo Bay—all without any charges filed or any due process of law. A significant number of Americans support this illegal detention, barbarically arguing that non-Americans are not entitled to basic human rights enshrined in the Universal Declaration of Human Rights or the United States Constitution. And in 2016, 74 percent of South Carolina Republicans demanded an end to Muslim immigration. Today, America comprises 5 percent of the world's population but 25 percent of the world's prison population—the disproportionate majority of whom are black and people of color. Police violence against civilians—disproportionately against black Americans and people of color—is higher in the United States than it is in any developed country on earth. In America, over a thousand women a year are murdered by their husbands and boyfriends, a woman is assaulted every nine seconds, and 98 percent of rapists will never see a day in prison. Violence against women is epidemic. Meanwhile, as politicians advocate special Muslim ID cards and concentration camps, will future generations write about how America repeated 1942 by swapping Japanese Americans for Muslim Americans?

What will 2017 and beyond bring?

#TalkToMe is a call to engage in meaningful communication to counter this growing polarization and antagonism we're seeing in our

---

[13] https://www.jewishvirtuallibrary.org/jsource/Holocaust/stlouis.html

country and world today. This polarization advances racism, Islamophobia, anti-Semitism, misogyny, and hatred. It holds our education opportunities hostage and stifles our growth. It destroys our society and our future.

I've seen what happens when that polarization and demonization goes unchecked, dialogue is stifled, and pens are replaced with weapons. My birth country, Pakistan, was once a promising nation focused on the ideals of secular governance, private faith, and universal freedom of conscience. But Pakistan let extremists write its narrative, and the nation as a whole now suffers. Over fifty thousand innocent civilians have died as a result of terrorism since 9/11 alone.

In America, we live at a time of increasing violence, discrimination, and intolerance of one another. We cannot let extremists in America write our future. We must raise our voices and write our narratives for tolerance, education, and compassion. At the end of *The Wrong Kind of Muslim* I asked you to #TalkToMe about your narrative for tolerance to overcome the intolerance around us. And you did, beyond my wildest expectations.

This book is the result of your choice to talk to me. It not only allowed me to connect with inspiring thought leaders to explore how the power of dialogue can overcome racism, xenophobia, intolerance, and violence, but it also allowed me to convey their inspiring stories to you. These real-life stories demonstrate ways ordinary Americans are rising beyond the forces that seek to drive us apart, instead finding paths to peace and understanding.

These are the stories you won't hear in the media because the fact is, good news just doesn't sell newspapers. They are stories that remain untold because bigotry sells more than unity. Terror more than tolerance. Fearmongering more than faithfulness. I wanted to give these powerful stories of pluralism the platform they deserve. I wrote *#TalkToMe* because I believe that our differences are a source of strength, not division. I believe things aren't hopeless and I believe we can repair the damage done. But for that to happen, we must work together. And it all begins with dialogue. We cannot sit idle and we cannot waste another day. This thinking isn't mere theory. Together, we can overcome the extraordinary intolerance around us.

It starts at home. And it starts with respecting your children. Respect their humanity, their mind, and their rights. This means swallowing your ego and having the humility, rather the courage, to admit when you are wrong. This means exposing them to new thoughts and ideas and empowering them to choose what they want to believe. This means respecting their beliefs—even if they choose differently than you. As my wife and I go through this process right now with our children, we find it frightening at times, but always rewarding.

That respect ensures communication remains ongoing, honest, and meaningful. Regardless of religion or race, respecting your children is the best way to teach them how to respect others. And as we look at America and the world's landscape, this is a matter especially crucial. The number of hate groups that have emerged since President Obama's election is at an all-time high. The number of racially and religiously motivated attacks continues to rise. The levels of intolerance toward minorities show no sign of slowing.

Children raised with respect infuse that respect into others. They become more confident, more courageous, and more compassionate when interacting with those different from them. The future our children will see will be vastly different from the one we saw. In 2014, more nonwhite children were born in America than white children. India and China now account for roughly one-third of the world population. How do we navigate this increasingly changing racial landscape that is our nation and our planet? Well, we have two quite obvious choices. We can dig in and stay lost in the previous century—stay in our bubble and pretend we exist in a vacuum to one another. Or, we can march on forward and embrace racial pluralism and diversity. The former path is deceptively easy, the latter deceptively scary.

But if we expect to give our children the peaceful world they deserve, it is imperative we look past the fear of what we don't understand and learn to understand. As America becomes increasingly diverse, with white Americans expected to become a minority by 2050, we need to talk to our children about race on a regular basis.

In connecting with people of different faiths it becomes even easier to improve race relations. And here many people (read: parents) often throw up another objection because they seem to confuse interfaith dialogue with evangelism. The two are distinctly different. Evangelism doesn't necessarily care what the other person believes. Or if it does, it cares to the extent to try to convert the other person to one's own belief.

Interfaith dialogue is not that. Interfaith dialogue necessarily and deeply cares about the other person. It wants to understand the other person's beliefs not to convert them, but as a vehicle for understanding and respecting the other person. Rather than the sword fight that evangelism can turn into, interfaith dialogue is a mutual effort to build a bridge across a chasm of uncertainty.

And while evangelism is usually a one-way conversation, interfaith dialogue is inherently two-way. It requires you to talk to me, and for me to talk to you, and for both of us to listen to each other. Most important, it doesn't ask you to compromise your faith or beliefs. Quite the contrary; it obliges you to recognize those different from you for the differences they bring to the relationship and to respect that difference.

With that forward-thinking attitude in mind, the question is simply this—who has the courage to step up and become that leader? Who has the courage to risk stepping out of a bubble, accepting the reality that sooner or later he will get burned by someone else launching assaults from inside his own respective bubble? Sometimes that assault comes from an anonymous troll on Twitter or Facebook. Sometimes it comes through a nasty e-mail, hate mail, or a death threat. And sometimes it is a public hate march like we see with the KKK or the anti-Muslim armed protests. Leaders recognize these cancers for what they are and step out of their bubbles to show the world we are better off working together against these cancers, rather than pretending they don't affect us.

And as we've seen, faith leaders wield immense power to help, or harm this process. Community activists can help mend race relations or aggravate them with more antagonism. Parents can raise children with a focus on self-reflection and public service to humanity, or they can build further barriers to solidify a comfort zone devoid of such obligations. Teachers and educators can use education as a vehicle of empowerment, but only if they act with justice and compassion.

Whether it is in parenting, education, race relations, or interfaith relations, success in each category boils down to one fact: leadership matters.

Humanity needs leaders willing to step out of their comfort zones and delve into what today appears a scary abyss of interfaith dialogue. It is these leaders who will also help mend race relations. It is these leaders who have the courage and compassion to respect their children, and raise them on pillars of pluralism. It is such leaders who convey and inspire their circle of influence with meaningful communication.

Regardless of our faith, race, or social differences, leadership is a human need. And considering the state of the world today, leadership is sorely lacking. Meaningful communication can remedy this.

Yet sometimes, despite everything we say and do, we make mistakes. Sometimes despite it all, we fail. It is natural. I know I've failed countless times, and I make mistakes to this day. I'm far from perfect. But I'm also far from quitting. Recognize that disagreement isn't failure, and failure isn't game over. Some extremists don't want us to work together. I've met antitheists (people who actively want to destroy religion) who have demanded the military destruction of Islam. Some of these antitheist

340